A CHECKLIST OF NARRATIVES OF

SHIPWRECKS AND DISASTERS

AT SEA TO 1860,

with Summaries, Notes, and Comments

"Remarkable Shipwrecks, Fires, Famines, Calamities, Providential Deliverances, and Lamentable Disasters on the Seas . . ."

A CHECKLIST OF NARRATIVES OF

SHIPWRECKS AND DISASTERS

AT SEA TO 1860,

with Summaries, Notes, and Comments

BY

Keith Huntress

THE IOWA STATE UNIVERSITY PRESS / *Ames*

1979

KEITH G. HUNTRESS, Professor of English and Distinguished Professor in Sciences and Humanities at Iowa State University, is a collector of books in three fields—Western Americana, early American fiction, and maritime history. He holds the B.A. and M.A. degrees from Wesleyan University and the Ph.D. degree from the University of Illinois. Professor Huntress has written published poetry and fiction; textbooks for freshman English, propaganda analysis, and American history; and also scholarly articles, chiefly on Melville. His lifelong fascination with maritime history led to the publication (and a subsequently revised edition) of *Narratives of Shipwrecks and Disasters: 1586–1860*. The *Checklist* is a natural outgrowth of his maritime researches.

© 1979 The Iowa State University Press
All rights reserved

Composed and printed by The Iowa State University Press, Ames, Iowa 50010

First edition, 1979

Library of Congress Cataloging in Publication Data

Huntress, Keith Gibson, 1913–
    A checklist of narratives of shipwrecks and disasters at sea to 1860.

    Includes index.
    1. Shipwrecks—Bibliography. I. Title.
II. Title.: Shipwrecks and disasters at sea to 1860.
Z6016.S55H86 [G525] 016.910′453 79–14648
ISBN 0-8138-0885-5

. . . the inscription [on a gravestone] of Captain Skinner says that, "Having served forty years in the Navy, he was not proficient in maritime knowledge."

JOHN BYNG, *The Torrington Diaries 1781–1794*

No man will be a sailor who has contrivance enough to get himself into a jail; for being in a ship is being in jail, with a chance of being drowned.

DR. SAMUEL JOHNSON

A shipwrecked sailor buried on this coast
    Bids thee take sail.
Full many a gallant ship, when we were lost,
    Weathered the gale.

FANNY DIXWELL HOLMES,
an epitaph translated from
The Greek Anthology

CONTENTS

INTRODUCTION

I

A FEW YEARS AGO I edited an anthology of narratives of shipwrecks and disasters at sea (Iowa State University Press, 1974), with a checklist of all such printed reports known to me. In making up this list I of course went through the only compilations in this field that I could find, which were William Vaughan's appendix to the *Narrative of Captain David Woodard* (1804), the *Catalogue of the Books, Manuscripts, and Prints and other Memorabilia in the John S. Barnes Memorial Library of the Naval History Society* (1915), and E. G. Cox's *A Reference Guide to the Literature of Travel* (1938). These three sources list only about fifty or sixty items, with duplications, and I had found the titles of many other narratives in the catalogues of antiquarian booksellers specializing in maritime history. When the anthology appeared it listed 189 such narratives, and when another printing was required in 1975 I was able to add fifty-three titles to the first list.

Perhaps I should have left well enough alone at that point. There is, after all, a limit to what the world wants to know about shipwrecks and other maritime disasters of the past. But I continued to find new narratives, and in the course of my searches I had turned up nuggets of information that seemed to me worth recording. Hardly anyone remembers the stories of Robert Adams, James Riley, Judah Paddock, and Archibald Robbins, for instance, and yet Adams was one of the first non-Africans to reach Timbuctoo, and the stories of the other three, slaves of the North African Arabs, may have influenced the course of slavery in the United States. People who were horrified to discover that cannibalism was involved in the crash of a plane in the Andes a few years ago should not have reacted so strongly; they simply did not know what happened on board the *Frances Mary* or the *Francis Spaight* or the *Mignonette*. A few weeks ago there was a discussion of *triage* in the New York *Times*. It is a fashionable French word for the process of picking out weaklings to sacrifice if the population pressures and the energy crunch create too great a strain on the resources of our world. No mention was made of the Portuguese *St. James,* the American *Arctic,* the French *Medusa,* the emigrant ship *William Brown,* though each of these wrecks provided a test case of considerable interest. In each one the powerful and the skilled saved themselves and left the weak to die; I fear that is what will happen in the future, no matter how much theorizing is devoted to the problem. I also discovered that some narratives that have been considered authentic are really fiction, and I have located a large number of anthologies of shipwreck narratives and have listed the disasters covered in most of them.

It seemed a pity that this knowledge should vanish with me, and that some future delver into maritime obscurities should have to repeat my work. Iowa State University most kindly awarded me a Faculty Leave to continue my research; I used my free time to explore collections of maritime books on the East Coast and in England. This annotated checklist is the result.

II

So far as I know, only a dozen or so people of the twentieth century have known anything about these books. Librarians have catalogued them, and antiquarian booksellers have listed and sold them, but there is almost no evidence that the books have been read. Ralph D. Paine, who wrote and edited many books on maritime history, based his *Lost Ships and Lonely Seas* (1922) on an unnamed anthology; J. G. Lockhart used some of these narratives for *Strange Adventures of the Sea* (1925) and his fine *Blenden Hall* (1930); C. Fox Smith, my favorite of modern essayists on naval history and a charming writer on London's docklands, levied on *The Mariner's Chronicle* and some other unnamed sources for *Adventures and Perils of the Sea* (ca. 1930); and Edward Rowe Snow, indefatigable recorder of Atlantic naval history, also used some of these narratives for his books.

Studies of single catastrophes have been quite common. Apparently there are always people interested in the mutiny on the *Bounty,* the raft of the *Medusa,* the sinking of the whaleship *Essex.* There have also been well-written studies of such obscure disasters as the loss of the *Grosvenor,* the wreck and mutiny of the *Batavia,* and the sinking of the *Arctic.* I should be gratified if clues in this compilation lead to other books.

III

Two other points should be made about these narratives. The first is the obvious fact that they record historical events and describe patterns of life that have been almost completely forgotten. Every generation, in my experience, thinks of its own beginnings, perhaps the fifteen years between ages ten and twenty-five, as a kind of norm, and judges all times that follow as better or worse by that standard. Most people, unfortunately, know almost no history, and are consequently ready to label as the best of times, and the worst of times, periods that any historian would place in the middle of a graph. Students in my classes have told me, with underlining, that the Viet Nam War was the worst in the history of the world, that pollution at the present time is the worst that can be imagined, that their generation is the most unfortunate that has ever lived. They have never heard of the Thirty Years' War, and do not know the dates of our own Civil War; they know nothing of epidemics of typhus and plague and polio, or of almost universal tuberculosis; and they recite their woes through orthodontist-straightened teeth, and from bodies that are bigger and healthier than any other group has ever lived in.

I think it is important to realize that there was a time when there was no Weather Service, nor any information on which to base one, nor any effective means of communication to pass on the information that did exist. People as intelligent as we are put to sea with hurricanes just over the horizons. And the same situation existed with navigational aids. Reefs were uncharted, or unmarked; ships wandered hundreds of miles off their courses; whole continents were misplaced on maps.

We should also be reminded that our social services in cases of disaster are only a couple of generations old. The Medical Department of the Union Army at the outbreak of the Civil War consisted of a half-dozen seventy-five-year-old doctors, and no nurses at all. When a ship went ashore a century or two ago there was a chance that the people who came to watch would help the poor castaways, but they were just about as likely to plunder them. Sir Cloudesly Shovell survived the wreck of the *Association* off the Scillies in 1707, only to be knocked on the head by a woman who coveted his emerald ring. This collection of narratives should underline the fact that it is terribly hard to persuade people to work together, to submit to even the most sensible regulations, to postpone the slightest momentary advantage for future gain. What little civilization we have has been hardly won.

Most people nowadays know nothing, or almost nothing, about social conditions of the past, the exploitation of the poor and the helpless that has been reality for almost all of human history. For most of the past there was so little energy available, so little wealth, that equality would have meant almost nothing in terms of improving the lot of most people. Only recently has it been *possible* for many people to be educated and well fed and healthy and long-lived. In 1976, in the course of our bicentennial celebration, millions of Americans thrilled to the sight of the "Tall Ships" in New York harbor, sailing ships from many countries brought together in a fleet to remind the people of the world what commerce was like two hundred years ago. I was moved to see them on TV, as others were, but I was also profoundly grateful that so few of these beautiful artifacts survive. They are like the great houses of England—Knole, Woburn Abbey, Hampton Court, Blenheim—in that both depended for their existence on cheap labor endlessly exploited. No reader of these narratives could think of a return to the days of sailing ships. C. S. Forester, author of the Hornblower stories, made a telling point in his introduction to *The Adventures of John Wetherell* (1953), a source for some of the incidents of his novels. Writing of flogging, which remained a standard punishment in the American and British navies until the 1850s, Forester guessed that it was kept not out of cruelty or simple inertia, but because some punishment *had* to be available that was worse than simply being on a ship. Imprisonment could not frighten a wooden-ship sailor, and his food could not be cut without starving him to death. Hence came the cat-o'-nine-tails, keelhauling, and flogging through the fleet.

My other point is a comment upon our present-day civilization, which can in some ways be thought of as an enormously complicated mechanism for lessening the need for physical and perhaps psychological courage. We are not really very far from times when individuals had to meet head on and in person all the crises of life—armed enemies, criminals, diseases, accidents, natural dangers. Now we hire armies, police, doctors and nurses, ambulance attendants, undertakers, and civil servants, to cope for us, to handle our births and diseases and insanities and deaths and dangers. The saintly Ralph Waldo Emerson wrote in 1840:

> Now for near five years I have been indulged by the gracious Heaven in my long holiday in this goodly house of mine, entertaining and entertained by so many and gifted friends, and all this time poor Nancy Barron, the mad-woman, has been screaming herself hoarse at the Poor-house across the brook and I still hear her whenever I open my window.

In the years since, we have decided to hire others to hear the Nancy Barrons of our society.

Though most of us remain uninvolved, our continued interest in stress and danger is obvious. We have professional soldiers, the police, jailers, football and basketball and hockey players, racing drivers, test pilots—*they* take chances and are paid for doing it, while most of us sit quietly at home in front of the TV set. And yet it seems to me almost certain that these evasions of dangers and stresses have brought with them no reliefs, have made us no happier than people were before. If we do not need to worry about things outside ourselves, then we will find things inside us to agonize over. We hire others to cope with external irritations and dangers; there are only the psychiatrists to help us deal with our dangerous selves. In many ways the external threats are easier. I remember reading that when the student protests at Berkeley were at their height, the number of students seeking help from the University psychiatric service dropped by two-thirds. I am a professor of English, and in my classes must deal with authors of the past and present. I have done my best to explain, during recent years, why Hemingway shot himself, why Sylvia Plath and Anne Sexton and John Berryman decided that whatever death offered to them was preferable to continued life. It is dreadful to think of the internal agony that forced these sensitive and intelligent people to want to end their existences, but long reading of these narratives of hurricanes and fires at sea and wrecks on unknown reefs has made me wonder if perhaps our relative safety and outward ease have forced an unhealthy concentration on ourselves. George

Orwell was writing about a different situation, the contrast between the attitude of the soldier and that of the civilian, but it may apply:

> Nearly all soldiers—and this applies even to professional soldiers in peace time—have a sane attitude towards war. They realize that it is disgusting, and that it may often be necessary. This is harder for a civilian, because the soldier's detached attitude is partly due to sheer exhaustion, to the sobering effects of danger, and to continuous friction with his own military machine. The safe and well-fed civilian has more surplus emotion, and he is apt to use it up in hating somebody or other—the enemy if he is a patriot, his own side if he is a pacifist.[1]

"The safe and well-fed civilian has more surplus emotion. . . ." I think that this statement is true, and that it explains a great deal of what happens in our lives, in these safe and well-fed days.

The other side of the coin is easy enough to find and look at. In January, 1955, the steam trawlers *Lorella* and *Roderigo* sailed from Hull for fishing grounds off Iceland. Both ships were quite new, powerful, well cared for, with about twenty men and boys in each crew. In late January a very severe storm struck Denmark Strait, between Iceland and Greenland, and for more than sixty hours the two ships headed up into the wind and fought to stay afloat. Little by little the ships iced over, little by little they grew less stable. Captain Blackshaw of the *Lorella* called his friend Captain Coverdale of the *Roderigo* on the radio:

> "*Lorella* calling *Roderigo*, *Lorella* calling *Roderigo*. Been dodging full speed and half-speed all night to keep her up. Getting serious now. It is getting serious now. Been trying to get her round but no go. I am going over and I cannot get back."

Not long after that, still in Skipper Blackshaw's quiet voice, the *Lorella* was heard to say:

> "I am going over now. Going over. Going over. Mayday! Mayday! Mayday!"

At seven P.M., four hours later, came the last message from the *Roderigo:*

> "I am going over," said Skipper Coverdale. "I am going over now. I cannot abandon ship. Mayday! Mayday! Mayday!"[2]

These two ships were lost, lost with all hands, only a little more than twenty years ago. Men faced with such dangers as were brought by the

---

1. George Orwell, *As I Please 1943-1945* (New York: Harcourt, Brace and World, Inc., 1968), p. 200.
2. Alan Villiers, *Posted Missing* (New York: Scribner's, 1956), pp. 115-16.

storms and the ice and the seas of Denmark Strait have little time or energy for the ills within themselves, I believe, and not very long ago all people were in very much those situations most of the time.

These narratives should serve to remind us of our vulnerability to forces outside ourselves. In past times mere survival was success for most.

I must express my gratitude to three groups of people without whose help this checklist could not have been put together. I owe a debt to-the librarians of the world, but particularly to those who labor so efficiently at the reference desk of the Iowa State University Library. I am grateful also to the staffs at the Library of the American Antiquarian Society, Worcester, Massachusetts; at the Peabody Museum, Salem, Massachusetts; at the Library of Congress; at the British Museum; and at the National Maritime Museum, Greenwich, England. I have had help from fifty other libraries, but regrettably I cannot list them all.

My debt to antiquarian booksellers dealing in maritime history is perhaps as great as my debt to librarians. "My heart leaps up when I behold" a catalogue of voyages and travels. Particularly valuable have been the catalogues of Francis Edwards, Ltd., London; Cavendish Rare Books, Ltd., London; James Thin, Edinburgh; Alfred W. Paine, Bethel, Connecticut; Caravan-Maritime Books, Jamaica, New York; and Edward Lefkowicz, Fairhaven, Massachusetts. And I recommend to anyone who loves books the *Bookman's Weekly / Antiquarian Bookman* of Clifton, New Jersey, with its weekly lists of the attainable and the unattainable.

With this annotated checklist I hope to make life a little easier for both librarians and booksellers.

My thanks should go also to the professional staff of the Iowa State University Press. And daughter Deborah Adams and granddaughter Kathy Adams will find their work enshrined—or entombed—within the pages of the index.

Finally, I wish to express my heartfelt gratitude to George Montgomery, M.D., to Allyn Mark, M.D., and to Creighton Wright, M.D., without whose timely skills this book would *not* have been finished, and *I* would have been.

KEITH HUNTRESS

Iowa State University

A CHECKLIST OF NARRATIVES OF

SHIPWRECKS AND DISASTERS

AT SEA TO 1860,

with Summaries, Notes, and Comments

CHECKLIST

INTRODUCTION

W<small>HEN</small> I FIRST planned this book I had in mind a formal bibliography like the beautiful *Voyages & Travel* volume of the catalogue of the National Maritime Museum Library, but I soon discovered why such compilations are almost always of specific collections. Only when one has the books at hand is it possible to include all of the minutiae required for a genuine bibliography. When one is partly dependent on entries in library catalogues and on descriptions of books for sale by dealers, the compiler must do the best he can with what he has.

In the following material I have given the names of authors or editors, short titles—in most cases—of books and pamphlets, dates, publishers, and editions if I could discover them. I have listed page numbers, illustrations, and any peculiarities of which I knew. Finally, I have told the story of each disaster I have been able to read about, since I feel that the facts are what most people will find interesting and worthwhile. I have pointed out examples of borrowing from these sources by established authors, and I have made comments and judgments about the value of some of the narratives. I have used numbers for the items followed by *C* for *checklist,* so that these listings will not be confused with those in my earlier books.

I am sure that there are a great many errors of omission and commission in this checklist, but I have done my best with material that has been hard to find and sometimes difficult to deal with. The items are arranged chronologically. Within the year's listings I have arranged the authors alphabetically, with a retreat to titles for the numerous *Anonymous* citations.

With books as old as these, there are many problems of regularization and correction. Should Deperthes be changed to De Perthes in every case? Should the names of all ships be italicized, whether or not they were in the originals? Should all misspellings be corrected? We have tried to follow a middle course in solving these problems, primarily by following the originals except where difficulties might be created for the reader or student.

I trust that the index, on which I have labored long, will ensure that the reader will find something of interest herein, even though it may not be what he started to look for.

1 5 5 0

1C. RAMUSIO, GIOVANNI BATTISTA (1485–1557)
Primo volume delle navigationi et viaggi, nel qual si descrittione del
Africa e del paese del Prete Ianni, con varii viaggi del mar rosso
a Calicut, etc.
Venice, 1550
Other editions, all "corrected and amplified," Venice, 1554–1559, 3
vols.; Venice, 1563–1574, 3 vols.; Venice, 1563, 3 vols.; Venice,
1606, 3 vols.; Venice, 1613, 3 vols.

This collection contains the narrative of Pietro Quirino, who, in 1431, sailed from
Candia for Flanders. A hurricane carried the ship out into the Atlantic and left
her completely unmanageable, so that the crew was forced to take refuge in a
longboat and a yawl. A few survivors finally reached the Lofoten Islands off
the coast of Norway, and were rescued. One source states that two accounts of
this voyage survive, one by Quirino, and another by his shipmates Cristoforo
Fioreventi and Nicolo di Michiel.

1 5 6 5

2C. DIAS, ENRIQUE
Viagem & naufragio da nao Sam Paulo que foy Pera a India o anno
de mil a quinhentos & sescuta . . .
[Lisbon], April, 1565. 44 pp., woodcut, small 4to

The Sam Paulo sailed from Lisbon for India April 15, 1560. She was wrecked on the
island of Sumatra, January 20, 1561.

1 5 8 9

3C. HAKLUYT, RICHARD
The principall navigations voiages and discoveries of the English na-
tion . . .
. . . imprinted at London, 1589
This collection has been reprinted many times. Probably the best
edition is that published in Glasgow by James MacLehose,
1903–1905, 12 vols.

Hakluyt printed the narrative of Sir Humphrey Gilbert's voyage to Newfoundland
in 1583, written by Edward Haies, Master and owner of *The Golden Hinde,*
one of the ships involved. In the course of the voyage, which seems to have
been badly managed or unlucky from beginning to end, the ship *Delight* was
lost two days' cruise south of Newfoundland. Fourteen men escaped in a small
boat, and twelve survived when she reached Newfoundland. Sir Humphrey
Gilbert himself refused to come aboard *The Golden Hinde,* a ship of forty
tons, and sailed back for England in the tiny ten-ton *Squirrell.* Both ships were
beset by a storm north of the Azores, and Gilbert shouted to the people on *The
Golden Hinde* his famous last words, "Wee are as neare to Heaven by sea as by
land." That night the lights of the *Squirrell* vanished, and she was never seen
again.
Hakluyt also told the story of the *Tobie* of London, which sailed from
Portsmouth October 6, 1593. The ship was lost October 19 on the coast of
Morocco, a few miles south of Cape Espartel. The ten men survived of fifty,

and were ransomed from the Moors by the generosity of English merchants. The ten men were ransomed for 700 ounces, or 1400 shillings, according to the narrator.

Another narrative, reprinted in both Hakluyt and Purchas, is that of Henry May, who set out with a small fleet for the East Indies in 1591. The ships reached the island of Nicobar, where they traded cloth for "reals of plate" which the natives had obtained from the wrecks of two Portuguese ships by diving. Putting back toward England, the fleet was driven all the way to the West Indies, and May was finally put aboard a French ship, captained by one Charles de la Barbotiere, to carry news of the English ships to the owners. The French ship sailed from Hispaniola, but was lost on one of the Bermudas, December 17, 1593. Twenty-six of about fifty men survived. They built a small bark of Bermuda cedar, set sail, and were finally rescued by a fishing ship of Falmouth off Newfoundland. May reached England in August, 1594.

1 5 9 4

4C. [FERNANDES, ALVARO]
  Navegacao e lastimoso sucesso da perdicam de Manoel de Sousa de Sepulveda
  Lisbon, 1594

The prologue in the translation of this narrative by Charles David Ley states that the unnamed writer of the narrative received the story from Fernandes, boatswain's mate in the *Sao Joao,* whom he met by chance in Mozambique in 1554. Probably the narrative was published in pamphlet form in 1594, and was later collected with other narratives by Gomes de Brito in his *Historia Tragicomaritima* of 1735.

The Portuguese galleon *Sao Joao,* Cochin for Lisbon, was left helpless by a series of violent storms, the last of which forced the officers to try to beach the ship on the coast of Natal, Africa, in 1552. Of approximately five hundred passengers, crew, and slaves on board only about twenty-five survived to reach Mozambique. Manoel de Sousa [frequently spelled Sosa] was a distinguished Portuguese nobleman. Part of the popularity of this narrative probably lay in a Paul-and-Virginia episode involving his wife. She fought against being stripped by natives, buried herself in sand, and died of thirst and starvation.

1 6 0 0

5C. [HEEMSKIRK, JAMES, AND BARENSZ, WILLIAM]
  Vraie description des trois voyages de mer, faits par le nord, vers les voyaumes de Catay et de China . . .
  Amsterdam, 1600. Folio

Contains, by Heemskirk and Barensz, "The loss of a Dutch vessel, and the wintering of its crew on the eastern coast of Nova Zembla, during the years, 1596, and 1597."

1 6 0 1

6C. [CARDOSO, MANOEL GODINHO]
  Relacao do naufragio da nao San-Tiago, e itinerario da gente, que nella se salvou
  Lisbon, 1601

Cardoso is named as the author of this account by Charles David Ley, the translator. Probably published as a pamphlet in 1601, it was collected in Gomes de Brito's *Historia Tragico-maritima* in 1735.

The Portuguese nao Santiago [St. James], Lisbon for India, struck on a reef south of Madagascar, perhaps the so-called Jew's Shoal, on the night of August 18, 1585. Some hundreds of people died, but fifty-seven survivors escaped in a boat and a few others reached the coast of Africa on rafts.

1 6 0 7

7C. NICHOLL, JOHN
     An houre glasse of Indian newes. Or a true and tragicall discourse, shewing the most lamentable miseries and distressed calamities endured by 67 Englishmen which were sent for a supply to the planting in Guiana in the yeare 1605. Written by John Nicholl, one of the aforesaid company
     London, printed for Nathaniel Butler, and are to be solde at his shop neere Saint Austens Gate, 1607. Reprinted, Boston, 1925

1 6 1 0

8C. ANONYMOUS
     A true declaration of the state of the colonie in Virginia
     London, 1610
Includes a description of the wreck of Sir George Somers in the *Sea Venture* on the Bermudas. This pamphlet and the next item are believed to have been used by Shakespeare as bases for *The Tempest.*

9C. JOURDAIN, SYLVESTER
     A discovery of the Bermudas, otherwise called the Ile of Devils . . .
     London, 1610
Another pamphlet telling the story of Somers's wreck.

1 6 1 2

10C. [COVERTE]
      Relation of an Englishman shipwrecked on the coast of Cam-
            boya . . .
      London, 1612
      Cox, II, 451
Deperthes, II, 96, states that this 1612 publication was by one Coverte, or Covertte. Another narrative of the voyage, by Jones, was published in Purchas. The *Ascension,* Captain Sharpey, sailed from England for the Indies in an attempt to establish English trade in opposition to that of the Dutch and Portuguese. The *Ascension* had trouble with the natives at the island of Pemba, and was wrecked on the coast of Camboya.

1 6 1 8

11C. PYRARD, FRANCOIS
[English title: The voyage of Francois Pyrard of Laval to the East Indies, the Maldives, the Moluccas and Brazil]
Third French edition, 1619. Translation published by the Hakluyt Society, 1887–1889

De Laval commanded the *Corbin,* which was sent on an exploring voyage to the East Indies. This was an attempt by the French to get a share of the trade and colonies developed by the Spanish, Portuguese, and Dutch in that part of the world. The *Corbin* sailed from St. Malo on May 18, 1601. She visited St. Helena, the Cape, and Madagascar, but then was wrecked on one of the Maldive Archipelago in the Indian Ocean. The French were well treated by the islanders, and the narrative is valuable for the material it gives on native life of the time. Raiders from Bengal attacked the islands and captured M. De Laval, who was carried to Goa and finally made his way back to Rochelle in 1611.

1 6 2 5

12C. PURCHAS, SAMUEL
Purchas his pilgrimes. In five bookes . . .
London, Henrie Fetherstone, 1625, 4 vols.

Contains the narratives of Gates and Somers of their voyage to Bermuda and Virginia, in 1610, probable sources for Shakespeare's *The Tempest;* and also the narrative of Henry Hudson's voyage towards the Pole, 1607–1609.

1 6 3 2

13C. LALEMANT, CHARLES (b. 1587)
"The shipwreck of Father Charles Lalemant, Philibert Noyrot, and others, off Cape Breton"
First printed in Champlain's *Voyages,* Paris, 1632

An English translation of Father Lalemant's letter, which was written at Bordeaux, November 22, 1629, was published by John Gilmary Shea in his *Perils of the Ocean and Wilderness* (401C), Boston, n.d. [1856?].

Father Lalemant, with three other Jesuit priests, was on board an unnamed ship in 1629, bringing supplies from France, when they encountered a violent southwest storm. The ship was driven on a reef off Cape Breton, and broke up. There were ten survivors of the twenty-four on board the ship. These survivors were taken off a small island by a Basque fishing boat, which was itself lost on the coast of Spain near San Sebastian after a forty-day voyage from the Canadian coast. Father Lalemant was saved in a small boat, and lived to be eighty-seven years old.

1 6 3 3

14C. WATTS, WILLIAM [and James, Captain Thomas?]
The strange and dangerous voyage of Captaine Thomas James; with an address concerning the philosophy of those late discoveries by W. W.

London, J. Liggatt for J. Partridge, 1633. Other editions, 1705,
    1740. French edition, 1787
This voyage was made in 1631–1632; it was a search for a North-West Passage.
    James wintered in the bay named for him, and explored much of the shores of
    Hudson's Bay.

1 6 3 7 •

15C. DUNTON, JOHN
    A true journal of the Sally fleet with the proceedings of the
        voyage. . . . Whereunto is annexed a list of Sally captives
        names and places where they dwell, and a description of the
        three townes in a card
    London, John Dawson for Thomas Nicholas, 1637. 4to, fldg. plate
Bookseller's note: "Moroccan pirates were plaguing the Channel coast, taking cap-
    tives and even causing Trinity House to object to the Lizard Light on the
    grounds that it attracted marauders. A fleet of six ships under the command of
    Rainborough were sent to blockade their base, Sallee. The King of Morocco
    did not resist and delivered 271 English captives; their names are listed at the
    end of the book."

1 6 4 1

16C. ANONYMOUS
    Sad news from the seas . . . loss of the good ship called the Mer-
        chant Royall . . . cast away ten leagues from the Lands end,
        on . . . 23 Septem. 1641
    London, 1641
    Cox, II, 451

1 6 4 6

17C. BONTEKOE, WILLEM YSBRANTZ
    Journal or memorable description of the East Indian voyage of
        Willem Ysbrantz Bontekoe of Hoorn, comprehending many
        wonderful and perilous happenings experienced therein; begun
        on the 18th of December, 1618, and completed on the 16th
        November, 1625
    At Hoorn, printed by Isaac Willemsz, for Jan Jansz Deutel, book-
        seller in the East Street, in Biestkins Testament; anno 1646.
        London, 1646, 1929
I have taken this translation of the Dutch title page from the Broadway Travellers
    edition, London, George Routledge & Sons, 1929. Bontekoe's ship, the *Nieuw-
    Hoorn,* caught fire and burned in the Straits of Sunda, 1619. About 70 sur-
    vivors, of 119 aboard the ship, reached Batavia.

1 6 4 7

18C. JANSZ, JAN
Ongeluckige voyagie van't schip Batavia
Amsterdam, 1647

The *Batavia,* a Dutch East Indiaman, sailed from Holland for the Dutch East Indies
and was wrecked on the Abrolhos Islands, off the coast of western Australia,
June 4, 1629. Part of the ship's company mutinied after the wreck, and theft,
rape, and murder occurred as a result. The mutineers were overcome by a
ship's company sent from Batavia, and a number were hanged. The wreck was
rediscovered in 1963, and cannons, coins, and other artifacts were lifted by
divers. The story of the wreck and rediscovery is fully if somewhat sensational-
ly told in Hugh Edwards's *Islands of Angry Ghosts,* New York, 1966.

The Dutch East India Company, like all far-traders of early years, suffered many losses at sea. I have found only three contemporary narratives—
this story of the *Batavia,* Camstrup's record of the loss of the *Blydorp* (46C),
and Janssen's *Schelling* (23C). Peter Marsden's *The Wreck of the Amsterdam,*
London, 1974, is an admirable account of the loss of that ship near Hastings,
England, in 1749. Marsden also lists other located wrecks of Dutch East In-
diamen, and his book is almost a text for marine archeology. The wrecks he
lists are those of the *Batavia,* 1629; *Lastdrager,* 1653, off the Shetlands;
Vergulde Draeck, 1656, on the Abrolhos Islands; *Kennemerland,* 1661, off the
Shetlands; *Princesse Maria,* 1685, off the Scillies; *'t Huijs t'Kraijensteijn,*
1698, also off the Scillies; *Merestijn,* 1702, off South Africa; *de Liefde,* 1711,
off the Shetlands; *Zuytdorp,* 1712, off western Australia; *Akerendam,* 1725,
off Norway; *Zeewyk,* 1727, off western Australia; *Adelaar,* 1728, off Barra;
Hollandia, 1743, off the Scillies; an unidentified ship ca. 1746, in Meob Bay,
South Africa; *Amsterdam,* 1749, near Hastings; and *Middelburg,* 1781, South
Africa. Dutch wrecks not yet located were those of the *Fortuyn,* Australia, in
1724; *Aagtekerke,* also Australia, in 1726; and the *Blydorp,* north African
coast, in 1733.

1 6 5 5

19C. SEVERIM DE FARIA (Manoel)
Noticias de Portugal
Lisbon, Officina Craesbeeckiana, 1655

Bookseller's note: ". . . devoted to the Guinea Coast, shipwrecks on the India
route, and exploration."

1 6 6 4

20C. JOHNSON, WILLIAM
Sermon and narrative of the dangers and deliverances at sea . . .
London, 1664; 3rd edition, titled *Deus Vobiscum,* 1672; 6th edition,
1769

Johnson sailed from Harwich on September 29, 1648, in the ship *William and John,*
Captain Morgan. The ship started a timber and foundered, but all on board got
into the longboat and were saved. The next day they were taken into a Danish
vessel, a "Howzoner" bound for Norway. That ship was driven on a reef off
the Norwegian coast; the captain and four sailors were drowned, but Johnson

was among those who reached shore at a small island. There they made a raft and with it got word to the mainland of their plight. Johnson was taken to Fredericstadt, in Norway, and put on a ship for England. He was landed at Yarmouth a few days later. Apparently Johnson recounted his adventures in a successful sermon, and then put them into a book.

1 6 7 1

21C. ANONYMOUS
A description of a great sea storm, that happened to some ships in the Gulph of Florida, in September last
London, Putlick and Simpson [1671?]
Cox, II, 452
This is a broadsheet in verse.

1 6 7 5

22C. JANEWAY, JAMES (1636–1674)
Mr. J. J.'s legacy to his friends, containing twenty-seven famous instances of God's providence in and about sea-dangers and deliverances; with the names of several that were eye-witnesses to them
London, printed for Dorman Newman, at the King's Arms in the Poultry, 1675
Introduction by John Ryther, Wapping, 14 April, 1674
1. Major Gibbons, Boston
2. Five Scottish ministers en route to America, 1636
3. Newfoundland a-fishing, 1636
4. Small vessel, Captain Philip Haugave
5. Captain Jonas Clark of New England
6. An Irish famine
7. Shallop *Bohemian* wrecked off the Bahamas, 1642
8. Gregory Crove of Maulden in Essex, boat sank
9. A Dutch ship at Novaya Zemblaya
10. A Flemming named Pickman, Trondheim to England
11. A ketch, Salem to Barbadoes, 1668, Captain Thomas Woodberry of Salem
12. Admiral Hauteen, 1606
13. English at Guyana, 1607
14. The *Phenix*-Frigot, Captain Whetston, Mr. May, Master, Rye to Dieppe
15. John Blackleach, New England to Barbadoes, attempted mutiny
16. Ship *Prosperous* of Bristol for Galloway in Ireland, wrecked Nov. 1669
17. Abraham Darby in a small ketch, James Janeway's own report
18. John Grafting wrecked among the Leeward Islands, 1671
19. Abandoned child found

20. A Bristol man fell into the river
21. Mr. Savage, master of the *Sociate* ketch, saved the men of the *George,* 1671
22. Captain Trankmore, near Exeter, was washed overboard but was picked up by another ship
23. *Bristol* frigot, Captain Fenn, incident of battle
24. Two ships bound home from Newfoundland
25. Adventure of the *Salutation* of London, voyage to Greenland
26.‘ Short comment on Greenland
27. The *Peach-tree* of London, bound for Guinny for slaves, June 1668

This book seems to have been the first anthology of shipwrecks and disasters at sea. It is also remarkable because Janeway seems to have done his own research and not to have depended on narratives in collections of voyages or on individual printed narratives in books. A later edition was *A Token for Mariners,* 1708 (33C).

23C. JANSSEN, FRANS
Vervarelyke schip-breuk van t'Oost-Indisch jacht ter Schelling, onder het landt van Bengale; . . .
Amsterdam, Johannes van Someren, 1675. Quarto, engraved frontis., 9 plates

The Dutch ship *Schelling* was wrecked on the coast of Bengal, 1661. See 143C, Vol. V.

1 6 8 2

24C. SMITH, WILLIAM, AND HARSHFIELD, JOHN
A full account of the late shipwreck of the ship called the President, which was cast away in Montz-Bay in Cornwall on the 4th of February, . . . 1682
London, 1682. 8 pp.
Cox, II, 453

1 6 8 3

25C. STRUYS, JOHN
The perillous and most unhappy voyages of John Struys, through Italy, Greece, Lifeland, Moscovia, Tartary, Media, Persia, East-India, Japan, and other places in Europe, Africa, and Asia. Containing, I. Most accurate remarks and observations of the distinct qualities, religion, politie, customs, laws and properties of the inhabitants: II. A due description of the several cities, towns, forts and places of trust, as to their site and strength, fortifications by nature, or art, &c. . . . and, III. An exact memorial of the most disastrous calamities which befell the author in those parts (viz) by ship-wrack, robberies, slavery, hunger, tortures, . . . To which are added 2 narratives

sent from Capt. D. Butler, relating to the taking in of
Astrachan by the Cosacs. Illustrated with divers curious plates,
first designed and taken from the life by the author himself.
Rendered out of Nether-Dutch by John Morrison
[London], printed for Samuel Smith, 1683. Quarto, pp.
(xxiv) + 378 + (ix). Twenty folding engraved plates, mostly
views of cities, including the first view of Moschate [Muscat].

1 6 8 4

26C. ANONYMOUS
Strange news from Plymouth; or, a wonderful and tragical relation
of a voyage from the Indies, whereby extraordinary hardships
and the extremities of the late great frost, several of the seamen
and others miserably perish'd, and for the want of provisions
cast lots for their lives. and were forced to eat one another;
etc., in a letter to Mr. D. B. of London
[London], printed for J. Conyers at the Black Raven in Duck Lane,
1684

This is the first narrative I have discovered that refers to casting lots to determine a
victim, and then killing and eating him to preserve the others. Two other such
incidents occurred after the dismasting of the ship *Peggy,* in 1765, and in the
captain's boat after the sinking of the *Essex,* 1820. Probably there were many
other examples which were never admitted by survivors. Edgar Allan Poe's
Narrative of Arthur Gordon Pym, which is based on narratives of shipwrecks
and disasters at sea, is a fictional use of casting lots, murder, and cannibalism.
It is interesting to note that apparently there was no attempt made to arrest and
charge those individuals who, on board the *Peggy* and in the *Essex*'s boat,
committed murder. In the 1880s, a yacht, the *Mignonette,* foundered on a
voyage to Australia. Three men and a seventeen-year-old boy put off in a small
boat and survived for three weeks before the three men decided to sacrifice the
unconscious and dying boy. The three survivors were picked up and landed at
Falmouth, where they were charged with murder. Convicted and given nominal
sentences, all were released almost at once. This was believed to be the first case
in which seamen in this position were found guilty of murder.

1 6 9 4

27C. NARBOROUGH, TASMAN, WOOD, AND MARTEN
An account of several late voyages and discoveries to the south and
north, towards the Straits of Magellan, the South Seas, the vast
tracts of land beyond Hollandia Nova, &c. Also towards Nova
Zembla, Greenland, or Spitsberg, Groynland, or Engrondland,
&c. by Sir John Narborough, Captain Jasmen Tasman, Captain John Wood, and Frederick Marten of Hamburg . . .
London, Smith and Walford, 1694

Contains Captain John Wood's "Shipwreck of the English frigate, the Speedwell,
on the western coast of Nova Zembla, at Point Speedill, in 1676."
The book is dedicated to Samuel Pepys.

1 6 9 9

28C. DICKINSON, JONATHAN

God's protecting providence man's surest help and defence in the
times of the greatest difficulty and most imminent danger;
evidenced in the remarkable deliverance of divers persons,
from the devouring waves of the sea, amongst which they suffered shipwrack, and also from the more cruelly devouring
jawes of the inhumane canibals of Florida, faithfully related by
one of the persons concerned therein, Jonathan Dickenson
Printed in Philadelphia by Reinier Jansen, 1699; London, T. Sowle,
1700; London, printed and sold by J. Phillips, 1787; 7th edition, J. Phillips, 1790. Nineteen printings have been made.

The barkentine *Reformation,* Captain Kirle, sailed from Port Royal, Jamaica, for
Philadelphia on August 23, 1696. On board were nine sailors and a small group
of Quakers including Robert Barrow, a well-known missionary, and the author
of this account, Jonathan Dickinson. The ship lost the convoy in which it had
sailed, and was struck by a violent storm on September 22. Either that night or
the next the *Reformation* struck on the Florida coast, about five miles north of
Jupiter Inlet, and was lost. All on board reached shore safely. There they were
captured by Indians, who treated them somewhat roughly but finally consented
to their making their way northward to Charleston, which they reached the day
after Christmas.

1 7 0 4

29C. ANONYMOUS

Exact relation of the late dreadful tempest: or, a faithful account of
the most remarkable disasters which hap'ned . . . in the city
and country; the number of ships, men and guns, that were
lost, etc.
[London], A. Baldwin, 1704. 24 pp.

30C. ANONYMOUS [Defoe, Daniel?]

The storm: or, a collection of the most remarkable casualties and
disasters which happened in the late dreadful tempest, both by
sea and land
London, G. Sawbridge, 1704, 8 + 272 pp., 8vo

31C. [DEFOE, DANIEL?]

A collection of the most remarkable casualties and disasters which
happened in the late dreadful tempest, both by sea and land
London, George Sawbridge, J. Nutt [1704?]. Second edition

Probably the second edition of the preceding item, which may also have been written by Defoe.

1 7 0 8

32C. GEARE, ALLEN
Eben-Ezer; or, a monument of thankfulness; being a true account
of a late miraculous preservation of nine men in a small boat
which was enclosed within islands of ice . . .
London, 1708
Cox, II, 454

Geare was the chief mate of an unnamed ship which sailed from Plymouth for Newfoundland in March, 1706. At the end of that month the ship was surrounded
by ice, and so buffeted that she became waterlogged and was obviously sinking. Twenty-one of the ninety-six men of the crew got into a small boat and left
their companions, who were never heard of again. The boat was in turn caught
in the ice a number of times, but finally escaped to open water and reached
Newfoundland. Nine men survived.

33C. JANEWAY, JAMES
A token for mariners
London, printed for H. N. and sold by the booksellers, 1708.
Another edition, London; printed for T. Norris at the Looking
Glass on London Bridge, and A. Bettesworth at the Red Lyon
in Pater-noster Row, 1721

The material in this book is the same as that in James Janeway's *Legacy* (22C), except that item 26 in the *Legacy,* a short comment on Greenland, is combined in
this book with item 25, and item 27, about the *Peach-tree* of London, becomes
item 26. New items are:

27. The relation of Dr. William Johnson concerning a most
remarkable sea-deliverance; in his own words. He was a
passenger on the *William and John* of Ipswich, on a voyage
from Harwich, Daniel Morgan, Master. September 29, 1648.
See 20C, 1664.

[28.] The great dangers and merciful deliverances of William Okel
and his company from slavery in a canvas boat, &c.

[29.] The Mary of London, for Providence in the West Indies, 1639

[30.] Captain Blese [Blose?] and his ship's company, cast away on
an island of ice near Russia, on a voyage to Archangel in the
Riga merchant, 1697

This volume ends with prayers for sailors, to be said in time of danger. These
probably served as a model for other books, such as 145C, 1805.

1 7 1 0

34C. GADBURY, (John)
Nauticum astrologicum: or, the astrological seaman: directing mer-
chants, mariners, captains of ships, ensurers, &c. how (by
God's blessing) they may escape divers dangers which com-
monly happen in the ocean &c.
[London], George Sawbridge, 1710. Diagrams, small 8vo

Bookseller's note: "Inserted before and after the book is a closely but clearly written manuscript, c. 1825, on approx. 140 pages, concerned with the same subject. This gives examples of ships lost c. 1822 in diagrammatic form with astrological symbols similar to the original work."

1 7 1 1

35C. DEAN, JOHN; DEAN, JASPER; AND WHITWORTH, MILES

A sad and deplorable, but true account of the dreadful hardships, and sufferings of Captain John Dean, and his company, etc. . . .

[London?], 1711. 36 pp., 8vo. Other editions: A narrative of the sufferings, preservation and deliverance of Captain John Dean and company; in the *Nottingham* galley of London, etc., pp. IV, 23, S. Popping, London, 1711; London, revised and reprinted, 1726, 1727; Boston, 1727; London, 1730, 1738, 1762

The *Nottingham* galley, 120 tons, fourteen men, sailed from England and Ireland for Boston in September, 1710. On December 11, in a severe snowstorm, she struck on Boon Island, north of the Isles of Shoals on the Maine coast. The ship broke up, but all the crew reached the tiny, rocky island. They were unable to make a fire, and suffered terribly from cold and starvation. Two men were lost in trying to reach the mainland on a raft, and two others died of exposure; one of these last was eaten by the survivors. They were finally rescued by a shallop from Portsmouth. Kenneth Roberts based his *Boon Island,* 1956, on the narratives of John Dean and Christopher Langman.

36C. LANGMAN, CHRISTOPHER; MELLEN, N.; and WHITE, G.

A true account of the voyage of the Nottingham-Galley of London, John Dean Commander, from the river Thames to New England. Near which place she was cast away . . . by the captain's obstinacy, who endeavored to betray her to the French, or run her ashore; with an account of the falsehoods in the captain's narrative, etc.

London, 1711. 8vo

As the title indicates, there was bad feeling aboard the *Nottingham* galley. Dean had a subsequent career of some distinction, and there is not the slightest reason to believe that his narrative of the wreck was not correct. It is hard to imagine a captain insane enough to deliberately wreck a ship on the Maine coast in midwinter. Langman's narrative provided the conflict in Kenneth Roberts's treatment of the story. See 35C.

1 7 1 2

37C. ROGERS, WOODES

A cruising voyage round the world . . . begun in 1708, and finished in 1811 . . .

London: A. Bell and B. Lintot, 1712, pp. xxi, 428, 56; London, 1718, 1766, 1774, 1806, 1928

On this cruise Rogers picked up Alexander Selkirk from Juan Fernandez Island,
where he had been left, at his own request, by Captain Stradling of Dampier's
privateering expedition. Selkirk had been alone on the island from 1704 till
1709. Selkirk's story was, of course, the basis for Daniel Defoe's *Robinson
Crusoe.*

1 7 1 9

38C. DEFOE, DANIEL
   The life and strange surprising adventures of Robinson Crusoe, of
   York, mariner: who lived eight and twenty years, all alone in an
   uninhabited island on the coast of America, near the mouth of
   the great river Oroonoque; having been cast on shore by ship-
   wreck . . .
   London: W. Taylor, 1719. Pp. 364. There have been hundreds of
   editions.
See Woodes Rogers's *Voyage,* (37C). Alexander Selkirk, the original of Robinson
Crusoe, was alone on Juan Fernandez for four years, not twenty-eight, and
had chosen to be put ashore after a quarrel. Juan Fernandez is off the coast of
Chile, a long way from the Orinoco.

1 7 2 0

39C. BURCHETT, JOSIAH
   A complete history of the most remarkable transactions at sea, from
   the earliest accounts of time to the conclusion of the last war
   with France
   London, 1720. Engr. port., 9 maps, title in black and red
Burchett was Secretary of the Admiralty, and this book is chiefly valuable for the
period of which he had personal knowledge. He was an administrator, not an
historian, and the early material, according to the DNB, is worthless.

40C. FALCONER, RICHARD (Captain) [Chetwood, William R.?]
   The voyages, dangerous adventures and imminent escapes of Captain Richard Falconer . . . in his shipwreck . . . intermixed
   with the voyages and adventures of Thomas Randal, his shipwreck in the Baltic . . .
   London, 1720; 5th edition, 1764.
   Cox, II, 455
According to Halkett and Laing, the author was William Rufus Chetwood, who
also wrote other picaresque books of adventure on the sea. One authority says
that the book was considered to have been based on a true life at sea, but to
have been intermixed with fiction. The narrative reads very much like Chetwood's *Voyages and Adventures of Captain Robert Boyle . . . ,* 1726.
Falconer's narrative is a somewhat confusing account of piracies and shipwrecks and desert islands in the Caribbean and the Gulf of Mexico. Randal's
narrative was a yarn told on an island to use up time and point a moral, and the
teller's body was later eaten by his starving shipmates. My own guess is that the
book is almost completely fiction.

1 7 2 6

41C. ROBERTS, CAPTAIN GEORGE [?] [Defoe, Daniel?]
The four voyages of Captain George Roberts: being a series of un-
common events which befell him in his voyages to the Canaries,
Cape of Verde and Barbadoes . . . shipwrecked on the Isle of
St. John . . .
London, 1726. Four plates and fldg. map of the Cape Verde Islands

May be fictional, or may be factual and ghosted by Defoe, or may really be by
Roberts. According to the narrative, Roberts set out on a slaving expedition,
but his ship was captured and plundered by pirates off the African coast. After
a number of adventures the ship struck on one of the Cape Verde Islands, and
was lost. Roberts joined another ship and eventually reached Barbados in
December, 1725.

42C. SHELVOCKE, CAPTAIN GEORGE
A voyage round the world by way of the Great South Sea, per-
form'd in the years 1719, 20, 21, 22, in the Speedwell of London, of 24 guns and 100 men, till she was cast away on the
Island of Juan Fernandes, in May 1720; and afterwards continued in the Recovery, the Jesus Maria and Sacra Familia, &c.
London, J. Senex, W. & J. Innys, J. Osborn & T. Longman, 1726

After the *Speedwell* was wrecked on Juan Fernandez, Shelvocke continued his
voyage in captured Spanish vessels. The incident of killing the albatross in Col-
eridge's "Rime of the Ancient Mariner" is believed to have been derived from
this narrative.

43C. URING, NATHANIEL
A history of the voyages and travels of Captain Nathaniel Uring; a
relation of the late intended settlements of the islands of St.
Lucia and St. Vincent, in right of the Duke of Montagu . . .
London, W. Wilkins, 1726, 1727, 1745, 1749. Four folding charts.
Reprinted 1928

This narrative covers almost a lifetime of voyaging to most parts of the North
Atlantic and the seas connecting. Uring was twice shipwrecked in the Caribbean, and narrowly escaped losing vessels elsewhere. This is a very important
book for the life of a merchant captain in the early eighteenth century.

1 7 2 9

44C. DRURY, ROBERT [Defoe, Daniel?]
Madagascar: or, Robert Drury's journal, during fifteen years captivity on that island . . .
Printed and sold by W. Meadows, &c., London, 1729. Ill. with map
of Madagascar and cuts. xvi, 464 pp. London, W. Meadows,
1743; London, Stodart and Craggs, 1807; Hull, Stodart and
Craggs, 1807; London, Hunt and Clarke, 1826; London, 1890,
1897; Paris, 1906. *The Universal Spy* printed *Robert Drury's
History of Madagascar* in a series of numbers in 1739; they

could apparently be collected into a volume, a pattern followed
later by J. Cundee and Thomas Tegg in London
The British Museum Catalogue cards list Daniel Defoe as the author of this book.

The *Degrave,* Captain Young, left Bengal for the Cape of Good Hope late
in 1701. The ship grounded just after leaving port, and was probably leaky as a
result. She reached Mauritius, however, and sailed for the Cape a month later.
The pumps could not cope with the leaks and she foundered just off
Madagascar. The survivors suffered great tribulations ashore, being enslaved
and involved in native wars. Robert Drury and John Benbow were apparently
the only two from the *Degrave* ever to reach England again.

The chief importance of this narrative is its picturing of the native life of
Madagascar, an almost unknown island when the book appeared. Sir J. G.
Dalyell in his collection (167C), stated that there were doubts about the truth of
this narrative, but that comparison with "another history of the same disaster"
showed that it was probably genuine. I have not been able to locate "another
history."

1 7 3 2

45C. MAY, CHARLES
An account of the wonderful preservation of the ship Terra Nova of
London
[London?], 1732
Cox, II, 457

1 7 3 5

46C. CAMSTRUP, NICOLAAS JANSZ
Rampspoedige reys-beschriving ofte journaal van's ed: Oosten-
dische compagnies schip Blydorp, zynde gestrand en
verongelukt op de Guineese ofte Moorse kust in Afrika, 's
nagts tusschen den 7 en 8 augustua, anno 1733 . . .
Amsterdam, 1735

47C. GOMES DE BRITO, BERNARDO
Historia tragico-maritima em que se escrevem cronologicamente os
naufragios qui tiverao as naos de Portugal, depois que se poz
exercicio a navegacao da India
Lisbon, 1735
Published in English as *The Tragic History of the Sea, 1589–1622,* London,
Hakluyt Society, II, 112, and II, 132. There are twelve narratives in the Por-
tuguese original, twenty-four in the two Hakluyt volumes. *Portuguese Voyages
1498–1663,* London, Dent, 1947, gives on pages 237–287 translations by C. D.
Ley of narratives of the losses of the *Sao Joao,* 1552, and the *Santiago,* 1585.
These narratives are also the bases for James Duffy's *Shipwreck and Empire,*
Harvard University Press, Cambridge, 1955. According to Maggs Bros.
Catalogue, 1933, de Brito published two volumes of these narratives, and then
eleven other volumes with the same dates and imprints as the original two.

1 7 4 0

48C. DEAN, JOHN

> A true and genuine narrative of the whole affair relating to the ship Sussex . . . wrecked on the Bassas de India . . . by John Dean, the only surviving person of them all . . .
>
> London, T. Cooper, 1740. Another edition, London, C. Corbett, Fleet-street, 1750

The *Sussex* sprang a leak and was deserted by the captain and most of the crew. Fifteen men repaired her, but she was later lost on the Bassas de India, near Madagascar. Five men reached Madagascar, where three of them died. If Dean's title is correct, the other survivor must have died also before the book appeared.

1 7 4 2

49C. CRESPEL, EMMANUEL

> Voyages de . . . Emmanuel Crespel dans le Canada et son naufrage en revenant en France. Mis au jour par le Sr. Louis Crespel, son frere
>
> Francfort sur le Meyne, 1742. 16mo, (8) 135
>
> Second edition, same press and place, 1752; London, S. Low, 1797 [Cox II, 174]. An English translation is printed in John Gilmary Shea, *Perils of the Ocean and Wilderness . . . ,* Boston, Patrick Donahoe, n.d. [Preface dated 1856.]

Father Crespel left France for the Canadian missions in 1724. He accompanied expeditions to Michilimackinac, Green Bay, and the Wisconsin River, to Detroit, and to Crown Point on Lake Champlain. He was ordered to return to France in 1736, and set sail from Quebec in the *Renommée,* a ship of 300 tons and 14 guns. On November 14, 1736, the *Renommée* struck on a reef south of Anticosti Island, and broke up. Crespel with one group of survivors set out in the ship's longboat for the mainland, while another group stayed near the wreck of the ship. Crespel was one of three survivors of the first group, and three sailors also survived near the wreck. Starvation, freezing, and scurvy killed all the others.

1 7 4 3

50C. BULKELEY, JOHN, AND CUMMINS, JOHN

> A voyage to the South Seas, in the years 1740–1. Containing a faithful narrative of the loss of His Majesty's ship the Wager on a desolate island in the latitude 47 South, longitude 81: 40 West: with the proceedings and conduct of the officers and crew . . .
>
> London, Jacob Robinson, 1743, 1752, 1810; Lyons, *Voyage à la Mere du Sud . . . Wager . . . ,* 1756; Philadelphia (enlarged), reprinted by James Chattin, for the author, 1757; New York, McBride, 1927

This is one of the most interesting of all narratives of shipwrecks, primarily because of what happened after the loss of the *Wager.* Bulkeley was a quarter-gunner and Cummins the carpenter on that ship, which was a store-ship for Anson's squadron on his voyage of circumnavigation and attack on the Spaniards, 1740–1744. The squadron of seven ships sailed from England on September 18, 1740, and left Madeira on November 3. The crews were already suffering from scurvy, indicating bad diet and bad management so early in the cruise, when the fleet touched at Brazil and Patagonia. The fleet had a very hard time getting to the west of Cape Horn, and when the *Wager* started north up the coast of Chile she was in bad shape and many of the crew were helpless in their hammocks. Anson had set the island of Socorro as a first rendezvous, and Juan Fernandez as a second. Captain Cheap of the *Wager* was a competent seaman and brave man, but inflexible and no leader of men. In attempting to reach Socorro, with dreadfully defective charts, he let the *Wager* become embayed in the Gulf of Peñas and the ship struck a reef May 14, 1741. Most of the crew reached an island, but the Navy rules of the time provided that the pay of the crew ceased when a ship was wrecked, and therefore the crew took the quite reasonable position that the officers no longer had authority over them. Drunkenness, theft, and a kind of half-anarchy ensued. Cheap was determined to try to reach Socorro; most of the crew, led by Bulkeley, wanted to try to backtrack through the Straits of Magellan and reach the friendly Portuguese settlements of Brazil. Cheap, in a fit of anger and fear, shot and killed a drunken midshipman named Cozens on June 10. By that time 45 men were dead and 7 had deserted the group, leaving 100 men on the island. After a great deal of squabbling and fighting and suffering, the group led by Bulkeley and Cummins placed Captain Cheap under arrest for the murder of Cozens. They lengthened the longboat and sailed for the Straits of Magellan on October 13. The group that remained with Cheap eventually got in contact with Indians who led them to the Spanish settlements on the island of Chiloe, where they were made prisoners. Bulkeley and Cummins led the survivors of their group to Brazil in a masterpiece of endurance and suffering, and finally reached England in February, 1743. The few survivors with Cheap were freed by the Spaniards, and they reached England April 10, 1746. Of the approximately 152 men who sailed in the *Wager,* 35 seem to have survived.

This narrative by Bulkeley and Cummins was published in an attempt to justify their conduct after the wreck, since they fully expected to be charged with mutiny. In the end no such charge was ever made, primarily because so much time had elapsed and because at that particular time the leading officers of the Navy were very unpopular with the British public. Byron, Campbell, and Morris, all midshipmen on the *Wager,* wrote accounts of their experiences, and so did John Young, the cooper on board. Walter's account of Anson's voyage also tells of the loss of the *Wager.*

S. W. C. Pack's *The Wager Mutiny,* London, 1964, summarizes the material in these several accounts.

1 7 4 4

51C. ANONYMOUS

A voyage to the South-Seas, and to many other parts of the world, performed from the month of September in the year 1740, to June 1744, by Commodore Anson, in His Majesty's ship the Centurion, having under his command the Gloucester, Pearl, Severn, Wager, Trial, and two storeships. By an officer of the squadron

London, R. Walker, 1744. 12mo, portrait of Anson, five folding
plates, pp. 408, 54, 1
This book cannot be the same as 53C since it is so much the longer. This listing is
taken from Maggs Catalogue.

52C. ANONYMOUS [Wright?]
A woeful voyage . . . account of the voyage, adventures,
distresses . . . of "Nimble Nancy" commanded by Captain
Wr——t . . .
London, 1744

53C. ANONYMOUS
An authentic account of Commodore Anson's expedition: containing all that was remarkable, curious and entertaining, during
that long and dangerous voyage. . . . Taken from a private
journal
London, M. Cooper, 1744. 60 pp., 12mo
Probably a pirated condensation of the work by John Philips (54C).

54C. PHILIPS, JOHN
An authentic journal of the late expedition under the command of
Commodore Anson, containing a regular and exact account of
the whole proceedings . . . to which is added a narrative of the
extraordinary hardships suffered by the adventurers in this
voyage
London, J. Robinson, 1744. i–ii, 516 pp., 8vo
Philips was a midshipman on the *Centurion*. This is another of the narratives of the
loss of the storeship *Wager* on the coast of Chile.

1 7 4 5

55C. THOMAS, PASCOE
A true and impartial journal of a voyage to the South-Seas and
round the globe in H.M.S. the "Centurion" . . . Commodore
George Anson . . . 1740–1744
London, 1745. 8vo
This account is an unofficial and unauthorized history of the Anson expedition. The
loss of the *Wager* is mentioned. See 50C.

1 7 4 7

56C. CAMPBELL, ALEXANDER
Sequel to a voyage to the South Seas, or the adventures of Captain
Cheap, the Hon. Mr. Byron, Lieut. Hamilton, Alexander
Campbell, and others, late of H.M.S. Wager
London, 1747

This sequel to the Bulkeley and Cummins *Voyage* (50C) of 1743 was written primarily to justify Campbell in his conduct long after the wreck of the *Wager*. He had married a girl of Spanish descent in South America, had become a Roman Catholic, and was accused of offering his services to the Spanish Navy.

1 7 4 8

57C. ANSON, ADMIRAL OF THE FLEET GEORGE, FIRST BARON [Walter, Richard, MA, Chaplain of His Majesty's ship the *Centurion*]
A voyage round the world in the years MDCCXL, I, II, III, IV. Compiled from papers and other materials of the Right Honorable George Lord Anson, and published under his direction, by Richard Walter . . .
London, J. & P. Knapton, 1748. 16 pl., 417 pp., 42 copper plates, 4to. Other editions: 4th, 1748, London; 6th, 1749, London; 12th, 1767, London, T. Osborne &c.; 15th, 1776, London, W. Bowyer, &c.; Amsterdam and Leipzig, 1751, Arkstee & Merkus; Ayr, 1790, printed by John Wilson, 2 vols.; London, 1928.

Refers to the loss of the *Wager*. See 50C, 1743.

1 7 5 0

58C. ANONYMOUS
A narrative of the journal of the Duke of Cumberland, Indiaman, cast away near Cape Verde . . .
[London?], 1750

59C. BAILEY, JOSEPH
God's wonders in the great deep: or, a narrative of the shipwreck of the brigantine Alida and Catherine, Joseph Bailey, Master, on the 27th of December, 1749. Bound from New York for Antigua . . . written by the master himself
New York. Printed and sold by James Parker . . . , 1750

60C. MORRIS, ISAAC
A narrative of the dangers and distresses which befel Isaac Morris, and seven more of the crew belonging to the Wager store-ship, which attended Commodore Anson, in his voyage to the South Seas, . . .
London, S. Birt [1750?]. 8vo

See 50C.

61C. WILLS, WILLIAM
Narrative of the very extraordinary adventures and sufferings of William Wills, late surgeon on board the Durrington, East Indiaman, in her late voyage to the East Indies, under the con-

voy of Admiral Boscawen; with account of his banishment to
Goa, voyage to Brazil, etc.
[London?], 1750–1751 [?]. 8vo

1 7 5 1

62C. YOUNG, JOHN
An affecting narrative of the unfortunate voyage and catastrophe of
H.M.S. *Wager,* one of Commodore Anson's squadron in the
South Sea expedition
London, 1751
This narrative is called by S. W. C. Pack, in *The Wager Mutiny,* 1964, the best of all
the narratives of the loss of the *Wager.* Young had no axe to grind, as Bulkeley,
Cummins, and Campbell did, and gives a relatively unbiased narrative of
events as they occurred.

1 7 5 2

63C. ANONYMOUS
Account of the shipwreck of a Dutch vessel on the coast of the Isle
of Quelpaert. Together with the description of the Kingdom of
Corea . . .
London, 1752. 26 pp., folio. Excerpt from Churchill's *Voyages*
Henry Hamel, the purser, wrote the narrative. The *Sparrowhawk,* Captain Eybertz,
a Dutch East Indiaman, sailed from the Texel for Batavia on January 10, 1653.
She sailed north from Batavia, and on August 15th was caught in a bad storm
and struck on Quelpaert. Thirty-six of the crew of sixty-four reached shore.
Over many years of captivity twenty of these thirty-six died, and at last the
others stole a small ship and reached Japan in 1687. They were brought back to
Amsterdam the next year. This narrative is important for its picture of life on a
Korean island in the seventeenth century.

1 7 5 3

64C. PELLOW, THOMAS
The history and long captivity and adventures of Thomas Pellow in
South Barbary . . . for 23 years . . . the bloody wars of Fez
and Morocco, 1720–1736
Dublin, 1753. Fldg. map

1 7 5 4

65C. BATHER, JAMES
A full and faithful account of the life of James Bather, boatswain of
the brig Nightingale, by himself, containing a narrative of all
the steps taken by the Master and others to burn and sink the
vessel
[London?], 1754. 8vo, 30 pp.

1 7 5 5

66C. MORRIS, DRAKE

The travels of Mr. Drake Morris, merchant in London. Containing
his sufferings and distresses in several voyages at sea. Written
by himself

London, 1755. Printed for the author, sold by R. Baldwin. Pp. xix,
328. Second edition, London, R. Baldwin, 1755; another edition, *An interesting narrative of the voyage, shipwreck and extraordinary adventures of Drake Morris.* New edition. London, 1797. 12mo

1 7 5 6

67C. ANONYMOUS

A journal from Calcutta in Bengal . . . by Mr. Bartholomew
Plaisted . . . to which are added . . . a journal of the proceedings of the Doddington East-Indiaman, till she was unfortunately wrecked on the east coast of Africa . . .

London, T. Kinnersley, 1756. 289 pp., 2 maps, 12mo. 2nd edition,
London, T. Kinnersley, 1758

The *Doddington* sailed from England for India April 23, 1755. All went well till the
captain tried a new course from the Cape of Good Hope and struck on an
uninhabited rock about 750 miles east of the Cape. Twenty-three out of 270
people reached the rock. The survivors showed great ingenuity in making a
forge and tools, and the carpenter eventually built a 30-foot boat in which they
left the rock. Eighteen survivors finally reached Delagoa Bay on the African
coast, where they were fortunate enough to find the *Rose,* Captain Chandler.
The shipwreck occurred July 17, 1755.

68C. BROSSES, CHARLES DE [editor?]

Histoire des navigations aux terres australes

Paris, 1756, 2 vols., 7 folding maps

Bookseller's note: "Includes accounts of voyages of Magellan, Drake, Cavendish,
Quiros, Narborough, Dampier, Pelsart, Tasman, Roggewin, Frezier [?], and
Anson." Pelsart was wrecked on the Abrolhos Islands in the *Batavia* (1629),
and Anson's expedition lost the *Wager* on the coast of Chile (1740). See 18C
and 50C.

69C. PEIRCE, NATHANAEL

The remarkable deliverance of Captain Nathanael Peirce. An account of the great dangers and remarkable deliverance of Capt.
Nathanael Peirce, who sailed from Portsmouth, in New-
Hampshire, bound for Louisbourg; and being taken up at sea
was carried to Oporto. Written by himself

Boston, Edes and Gill, Queen Street, 1756

This narrative was reprinted in its entirety as Chapter VI in William G. Saltonstall's
Ports of Piscataqua, Cambridge, Mass., 1941. A note to that reprinting states
that only three copies of the original are known to have survived.

Captain Peirce, of the brigantine *Portsmouth,* sailed out of the Piscataqua for Louisbourg on November 22, 1752, with a cargo of lumber. There was a crew of eight. The ship ran into storms and cold, and the crew persuaded the captain to reverse his course and make for the West Indies. On December 5 the ship sprang a leak and filled, but was kept afloat by the cargo. She drifted a derelict until December 24, when the wreck was sighted by the snow *Elizabeth,* of Halifax. By that time every member of the crew had died of thirst and exposure, and Captain Peirce was alone. At Oporto the American Consul and a Captain Morris took care of Peirce, who was almost helpless still, and made sure that he was given passage back to New England.

1 7 5 8

70C. ANONYMOUS
Loss of the Doddington
Annual Register for 1758, Vol. I, p. 297
Woodard's list of shipwrecks and disasters
See 67C.

71C. ANONYMOUS
Loss of the Prince George, Admiral Broderick's ship, off the coast of Portugal, April 13, 1758
Annual Register for 1758, Vol. I, p. 300
Woodard, 244
The *Prince George,* England for Gibraltar, caught fire while in convoy. The fire could not be contained, but the magazines were flooded and most of the ship's company might have been saved had not the accompanying merchantmen feared an explosion. One of the ship's boats was overloaded and foundered, and another capsized in being hoisted out. In all, 260 were saved of about 745 on board, a very bad record in view of the fact that there were many ships close by, and that the *Prince George* did not explode.

1 7 6 0

72C. ANONYMOUS
Loss of the Ann and Mary, of Galway, from Drontheim in Norway . . .
Annual Register for 1760, Vol. III, p. 75
Woodard
This ship sailed from Drontheim for Galway September 1, 1750. She was close to her destination when she was overset in a storm on October 10. The nine men on board were entirely without provisions, and in the course of the next month four of them were killed and eaten after lots were drawn. The first of these sacrifices asked to be partly butchered while alive, and wanted to eat his own flesh, but that was refused and he was soon killed. On December 1, 1750, the ship with two survivors drifted on shore at County Kerry. The captain died soon after reaching shore, and only Michael M'Daniel remained to tell of the tragedy.

1 7 6 1

73C. SUTHERLAND, JAMES [Lieutenant]
A narrative of the loss of His Majesty's ship, the Litchfield, Captain
Barton, on the coast of Africa . . .
London, 1761, 1768; 7th edition, for T. Cadell, London, 1790
Cox, II, 461

The *Litchfield* sailed from Ireland for Goree in November, 1758. She ran into a
storm on November 28 and struck on the African coast the next day. The ship
broke up and those who reached shore were harassed by the desert Arabs.
About 130 died of 350 on board. Two other small ships also struck and were
lost. A Dane and an Irishman at Saffy, 30 miles away, intervened for them
with the Arabs. The survivors were marched to Morocco where the sailors were
forced to work. In April, 1759, Captain Milbank paid $170,000 ransom for all
the English prisoners. They arrived in England in August, 1760.

1 7 6 2

74C. BY A SAILOR [Falconer, William]
The shipwreck: a poem in three cantos
London, 1762; London, T. Cadell, 1790 (7th), 1811; Phila-
delphia, 1788; New Bedford, 1802. Many other editions

This has been called the most popular English poem of the eighteenth century, a
precursor of the Romantic Movement, and an influence on Byron's *Don Juan.*
Falconer was a genuine sailor, and was the first to use correct nautical terms in
telling of a disaster at sea in poetry. The London, 1811, edition contains a
biography of Falconer by James Stanier Clarke.

This poem is based on Falconer's experiences on board a ship in the
Levant trade, which was lost on the coast of Greece; Falconer was one of only
three survivors. After the successful publication of this poem, Falconer worked
on a dictionary of naval terms, which was published in 1769. In spite of having
written two successful books, Falconer was a victim of poverty, and was
therefore glad when friends obtained for him the position of purser on board
the *Aurora,* sailing for India. She left England, September 30, 1769, touched at
the Cape, and was never heard of again.

1 7 6 4

75C. OKELEY, WILLIAM
William Okeley's narrative of himself and four others, and their
recovery from slavery at Algiers, in 1764 [1644]; or Ebenezer,
or a small monument of great mercy in their delivery
[London?], printed for Buckland, Keith, and Dilly, 1764 [1644?
1664?]
Woodard, 248

The ship *Mary,* London for the West Indies, was captured by Turkish men-of-war,
and the crew sold as slaves in Algiers. These five men built a boat in sections,
launched it, and succeeded in reaching Mayork—Majorca—after suffering
from hunger and thirst. They reached London in 1644 after five years of
slavery. They must have been extraordinarily resolute and able—and
fortunate—men.

Woodard's date for Okeley's return to England is wrong by 120 years. Probably the book was published in 1664, but I did not find it in the British Museum Catalogue. The story is told in *The Mariner's Chronicle,* Vol. V, pp. 23–28.

1 7 6 6

76C. HARRISON, DAVID [Captain]

The melancholy narrative of the distressful voyage and miraculous deliverance of Captain David Harrison of the sloop Peggy, of New York . . . until relieved by Captain Evers of the Virginian trade. Written by himself

London, 1766

Cox, II, 461

The brigantine *Peggy* sailed from Fayal, in the Azores, for New York on October 24, 1765. Toward the end of that month the ship encountered a series of storms which left her dismasted and helpless. The *Peggy,* a leaking hulk, drifted for over two months in the North Atlantic, speaking three ships but unable to obtain help. Her cargo of wine kept the crew alive, but they were starving. In the middle of January the crew proposed to draw lots and kill one of their number for food; they settled on a black slave of the captain. On January 29, 1766, the crew decided to sacrifice another of their number, and David Flat drew "the fatal billet." Flat requested an hour to prepare himself for death, and was given till eleven the next morning. At 10 A.M. on January 30, after a fire to cook Flat had been kindled, the *Susan,* Virginia to London, was sighted, and the ship was saved. Captain Evers of the *Susan* provided stores and rigging, and the *Peggy* finally reached England. This narrative was one of those used by Poe in writing *The Narrative of Arthur Gordon Pym.*

77C. PURNELL, THOMAS

The following is a true and faithful account of the loss of the brigantine Tyrrell, Arthur Coghlan, Commander . . . by Thomas Purnell, Chief Mate thereof

Hoxton, 1766; London, 1776. 8 pp.

The *Tyrrell* [sometimes *Tyrrel*] sailed from New York for Antigua June 28, 1759. The ship was very crank and the crew persuaded the captain to put in to North Carolina for more ballast; just as the ship settled on her new course, a sudden gust of wind laid her over on her beam-ends and she never rose. All seventeen on board got into the small boat, which broke loose, but they had neither food nor water. One by one all of these unfortunates died except Purnell. He was finally discovered by a Marblehead schooner, carried aboard, and taken into port. Purnell was without fresh water for twenty-three days; he had drunk some salt water and urine. The men tried cannibalism but were unable to swallow anything. Purnell recovered completely.

1 7 6 8

78C. BYRON, JOHN

The narrative of . . . the Honourable John Byron . . . containing an account of the great distresses suffered by himself and his companions on the coast of Patagonia from the year 1740, till their arrival in England, 1746. With a description of St. Jago de Chile . . . also a relation of the loss of the Wager man of war, etc.

London, S. Baker and G. Leigh, T. Davies, 1768. Pp. viii, 257. Other editions: 2nd, 1768; 3rd, 1778; 4th, 1780; W. Bancks, Wigan, 1784; London, 1785; S. Wilkinson, Morpeth, 1812; Oliver and Boyd, Edinburgh, 1814; James Johnston, Aberdeen, 1822; W. Folds & Son, Dublin, 1822; Society for the Promotion of the United and Scriptural Education of the Poor, Dublin [1825?]; C. J. G. and F. Rivington, London, 1831; Society for the Promotion of Christian Knowledge, London, 1842; *Foul Weather Jack: being the narrative of the Hon. John Byron, etc.,* John Neale, London, 1844; reissued with Isaac Morris's narrative of the loss of the *Wager,* Blackie's School and Home Library, London, 1925; Spanish edition, Santiago de Chile, pp. xiii, 155, 1901

See 50C, 1743. Admiral Byron, known as "Foul-weather Jack" because his commands seemed to attract storms, was a midshipman on the *Wager* when the ship was wrecked on the coast of Chile. His grandson, the poet, may have used this book in his treatment of a shipwreck in *Don Juan.*

79C. DRAKE, EDWARD C.

A new universal collection of authentic and entertaining voyages and travels . . . discoveries, conquests, . . . shipwrecks . . . with list of subscribers

London, 1768. 50 plates and 9 maps

80C. DUBOIS-FONTANELLE, JEAN GASPARD (1737–1812) [editor?]

The shipwreck and adventures of Monsieur Pierre Viaud . . .

Bordeaux and Paris, 1768. Other editions: Bordeaux, 1770, 1772, pp. 144; translation from the French by Mrs. Griffith, Davies, London, 1771; Bell, Philadelphia, 1774; with Falconer's *The Shipwreck,* Bell, Philadelphia, 1774; S. Fisher, London, 1798, pp. 112; Dover, N.H., 1799; London, not Mrs. Griffith's translation, 1814; *Captain Viaud and Madame La Couture: their true and surprising adventure, shipwreck and distresses* . . . I. Nicholson & Watson, London, 1935

This narrative is listed in at least one collection as being fiction. Viaud claimed that he was a sea captain and merchant of France. Finding himself at a small island, St. Louis, near Santo Domingo, he joined with another Frenchman in making up a cargo for Louisiana. Sixteen people embarked in the *Tyger,* but the ship was caught in a bad storm and struck on a reef off the Gulf coast of what is now Florida. All on board reached an island and hoped that natives would ferry them to the mainland, but they were robbed and deserted, and finally separated into two groups. Viaud, his black slave, and the captain's wife and son moved from island to island in a confused and miserable journey. Viaud, his slave, and Madame la Couture at last reached the mainland. They suffered greatly from hunger, and at last Viaud killed his slave. The two survived by eating the body. They were finally rescued by a ship from Fort St. Mark, and Mme. la Couture's son was found alive on an island; those three were the only survivors of sixteen.

The story tells of lions and tigers in the mainland jungle; there were, of course, panthers and perhaps jaguars, and poor Viaud was in no position to be a careful observer. Probably the story of cannibalism accounted for the popularity of this narrative.

1 7 6 9

81C. KENNEDY, CAPTAIN
       Annual Register for 1769, Vol. XII, pp. 190–191
       Woodard, 211–215, 238

Contains the story of the loss of Kennedy's ship in the Caribbean. The captain and crew reached the Bay of Honduras after eight days without food.

1 7 7 0

82C. WHITWELL, WILLIAM
       A discourse . . . Marblehead, Dec. 17, 1769. By William Whitwell, Salem
       Printed and sold by Samuel Hall, 1770. 21 pp.

1 7 7 3

83C. ANONYMOUS
       Verses on the sudden and awful death of Mrs. Rebecca Giles, Mr. Paul Kimball and wife, Mrs. Desire Holman, and six others, all of Salem, who were drowned June 17, 1773
       Salem, 1773. Broadside

1 7 7 4

84C. STAEHLIN-STORCKSBURG, J., VON
       An account of the new northern archipelago. . . .
       London, 1774. 8vo
       Contains, pp. 41–118, Pierre L. LeRoy's "Narrative of the singular adventures of four Russian sailors, cast away on the desert island of East Spitzbergen . . ."

A small Russian ship, carrying only fourteen men, set sail from Archangel for Spitzbergen in 1743. Contrary winds drove the ship to East Spitzbergen, an island not much visited by whalers and sealers, where the ship was caught in an ice flow. The mate remembered that some men of Mesen, in Russia, had built a hut on the island, and, fearing that the ship would be crushed, led a group of four men to find the shelter. While they were gone the ship was apparently caught in the ice, since she disappeared and was never heard of again. The four men killed reindeer while their powder and shot lasted, and then made spears and a bow and arrows, with which they killed 250 reindeer, many foxes, and 10 polar bears during the more than six years they were on the island. They burned the fat of the deer for fuel. One man died during their stay. They were finally rescued by a Russian ship that, like their own, was driven off the shore of that island by contrary winds.

Interestingly enough, these men seem to have done by necessity what Steffansson describes in his *The Friendly Arctic,* living comfortably and in good health on fresh meat alone for a long period of time.

1 7 7 9

85C. LEONARD, T.
Memorable accidents and remarkable transactions; containing an account of several strange events . . . translated from the French by . . . R. B.
Philadelphia, William Mentz, 1779; Worcester, Mass. [by Isaiah Thomas, Jr.], 1795

1 7 8 0

86C. DUNN, SAMUEL
A new directory for the East Indies . . . methodised, corrected, and . . . enlarged by S. D.
[London], 1780
This was a new edition of *Navigator's Guide to the Oriental or Indian Seas . . . ,* London, 1755. This 1780 edition is said by Percival R. Kirby in his *The True Story of the Grosvenor East Indiaman,* Capetown, 1960, p. 147, to contain a detailed analysis of the wreck of the *Doddington* East Indiaman, which occurred near Algoa Bay, South Africa, in 1755. This analysis was by a shipmaster named William Nichelsen, who believed that the loss of the *Doddington* was caused by reliance on outdated and faulty charts. Kirby believed that the loss of the *Grosvenor* was partly the result of this same reliance.

1 7 8 1

87C. ANONYMOUS
Pamphlet No. 2, "Dreadful hurricane in the West Indies, with losses of ships of the Royal Navy"
Extracts from the *Westminster Magazine,* 1781
Barnes Catalogue

88C. DEPERTHES, JEAN LOUIS HERBERT SIMON
Histoire des naufrages, ou recueil des relations le plus intéressantes des naufrages . . .
Rheims, 1781; Paris, 1788–1789, 1794–5, 3 tom. English translation, London, 1833. New edition, with "les aventures de Drury à Madagascar; celles de Quirini . . . les naufrages du Grosvenor, du brig Américain le Commerce, du vaisseau l'Alceste, de la frégate le Meduse, etc." Par J. B. B. Eyries, Paris, 1821, 3 vols.

I. Shipwreck of a Dutch vessel on Nova Zembla, 1596 & 1597
II. English sailors on the coast of Greenland, 1630
III. Captain Thomas James in Hudson's Bay, 1631 & 1632
IV. Seven Dutch sailors left on Greenland, 1634
V. Seven Dutch sailors left on Spitzbergen, 1635
VI. Wreck of the *Speedwell,* 1676
VII. Four Russian sailors on East Spitzbergen, 1743
VIII. Wreck of the Russian ship *St. Peter* off Kamtschatka in 1741
IX. Wreck of an English brigantine on Isle Royale in 1780
X. Shipwreck of Emmanuel Soza
XI. Sufferings aboard the French *Le Jacques* in 1558
XII. Wreck of the Portuguese *St. Jacques* in 1605
XIII. Wrecks of the English *Ascension* off Camboya in 1609, and the *Union* off Brittany in 1611
XIV. Burning of the *New Hoorn* in 1619
XV. Wreck of the *Batavia* in 1630
XVI. Wreck of the Dutch *Sparrowhawk* off Korea in 1635
XVII. Shipwreck of a Portuguese vessel off Cape Comorin, in 1645
XVIII. Wreck of the Dutch *Dragon* off Australia in 1658.
XIX. Wreck of the Dutch *Coromandel* off Bengal in 1660
XX. Wreck of the French *Taureau*'s shallop on the coast of Africa in 1665
XXI. Shipwreck of the Dutch *Lausden* off the Ganges, and the adventures of de Lestra, a French traveller
XXII. Shipwreck of a Portuguese frigate on the American coast in 1678
XXIII. Shipwreck of Occum Chamnan in 1686
XXIV. Wreck of a Portuguese ship in the Indian Ocean in 1688
XXV. Shipwrecks of two British vessels in the Mozambique Channel in 1700
XXVI. Story of Alexander Selkirk
XXVII. Shipwreck of the Countess de Bourke in 1719
XXVIII. Shipwreck of the British *Pembroke* on the Coromandel Coast in 1749
XXIX. Shipwreck and fire of the *Prince,* French East India Company, in 1752
XXX. Wreck of the British *Doddington,* off the Cape in 1755
XXXI. Loss of the *Betsey* off Guiana in 1766
XXXII. Shipwreck of the British *Fatty Salem* on the Coromandel Coast in 1701
XXXIII. Famine on board the *Peggy,* Azores to New York, in 1765
XXXIV. Tragic adventures of Mme. Denoyer, near Cuba in 1766
XXXV. Shipwreck and adventures of Mme. Godin on the Amazon in 1769

XXXVI. Wreck of the English ship *Union* off the Isle de Rhé in
1775

XXXVII. Shipwreck of the French *Le Duras* near the Maldives in
1777

XXXVIII. Shipwreck of a French vessel near Dieppe in 1777, and
the heroism of Pilot Boussard

It is obvious that all of the later anthologies of shipwrecks and disasters at sea levied
on Deperthes, either directly or by stealing from each other. There are very few
of the shipwrecks in the above list which have not been reprinted again and
again.

1 7 8 2

89C. ANONYMOUS

Dreadful wreck of the brig "St. Lawrence" from Quebec to New
York, 1780, which struck on an island of ice near the Gulph
of St. Lawrence . . .

London, n.d. [1782?]. Wrappers

Perhaps a pirated version of Prentice's narrative (90C).

90C. PRENTICE, S. W. [Prenties in some accounts]

Narrative of a shipwreck on the Island of Cape Breton in a voyage
from Quebec, 1780. By S. W. Prentice, Ensign of the 84th
Regiment of Foot . . .

London, T. Egerton, 1782; 2nd and 3rd editions, 1783

Prentice was entrusted with despatches for General Clinton in New York, and sailed
from Quebec November 17, 1780, in the brigantine *St. Lawrence*. Duplicate
despatches were put on board an accompanying schooner. The two ships
dropped down the river together. There were nineteen passengers and crew on
board the *St. Lawrence*, and sixteen on board the schooner. The two ships soon
encountered ice and heavy weather, and the brigantine sprang a leak. Prentice
complained that the sailors were incompetent, and that the captain was usually
drunk. The weather grew worse, and the schooner was lost with all on board,
about December 3, on the Isle des Coudres. The *St. Lawrence*, leaking and en-
cumbered with ice, was struck by an enormous wave which broke in the stern-
post. She then drifted helpless, and was finally beached on the shore of Cape
Breton Island, where she broke up, December 4, 1780. All on board reached
shore, and some supplies were saved from the wreck, but three men soon died
from exposure. The survivors patched the ship's boat and six of the strongest,
including Prentice, set out to find help. They had a very bad time coasting the
island, but finally happened upon a group of Indian hunters about February
20, 1781. Prentice sent some Indians back to the scene of the wreck, where only
three of eight survived; they had resorted to cannibalism. The Indians carried
Prentice and his companions to Halifax, which they reached about April 27,
1781, and Prentice got passage on a ship to New York about two months later.
He "delivered . . . despatches to General Clinton in a very tattered condition." Nine men survived of the thirty-five who had set out from Quebec in the
two ships.

1 7 8 3

91C. ANONYMOUS
>A narrative of two sailors, lately arrived in England . . .
>London, n.d. [1783]

Kirby calls this account of the wreck of the *Grosvenor* "unreliable." See 95C.

92C. ANONYMOUS
>The British navigator containing Captain Cooke's three voyages round the world . . . Commodore Byron . . . Captain Wallis . . . Captain Carteret . . . to which is prefixed an account of the loss of His Majesty's ship the Centaur, commanded by Captain Inglefield . . .
>London, John Fielding, n.d. [1783], 2 vols.

See 97C.

93C. ANONYMOUS
>The Gentleman's Magazine and Historical Chronicle, July and September, London, 1783

These two issues contain articles on the loss of the *Grosvenor*. See 95C.

94C. CROZET, J. M.
>Neue reise durch die südsee, 1771–72, angefangen von dem Herrn von Marion, und geendiget durch den Ritter Duclesmeur . . .
>Leipzig, 1783. Engraved frontispiece, wrappers

In June 1772 Marion and twenty-six of his crew were massacred at the Bay of Islands, New Zealand. The voyage was continued under the command of Crozet.

95C. DALRYMPLE, ALEXANDER
>An account of the loss of the Grosvenor Indiaman, commanded by Captain John Coxon, on the 4th of August, 1782 . . . on the coast of Africa, inferred from the Portuguese description of the coast of Africa to have happened between 20 and 29 South—with a relation of the events which befel those survivors who have reached England, viz. Robert Price, Thomas Lewis, . . . being the report given in to the East India Company by Alexander Dalrymple
>P. Elmsly and C. Nourse, J. Sewell and J. Law, London, 1783, pp. 39, 8vo. Second printing, 1783. New edition, J. Sewell, J. Debrett, London, 1785, pp. 58

Dalrymple had not himself made the voyage; he was the examiner who interrogated the survivors for the East India Company. The *Grosvenor,* an East Indiaman of 729 tons, sailed from Trincomalee for England June 13, 1782, with 139 crew and passengers. The voyage was uneventful until August, when there were two days of overcast so that the captain could not make an observation. He was sure that he was safely clear of the African coast, but on the morning of August

4, 1782, the *Grosvenor* struck on a reef close to the shore of Pondoland, near the mouth of the Tezani River. One hundred twenty-three of the passengers and crew reached shore. These survivors suffered a good deal from harassment by natives, and soon decided to set out for the Dutch settlements to the south. The number was too large to find food or be fed by the natives, there were many rivers to cross, and some native tribes were very hostile. The group soon scattered, and most died of starvation, thirst, and exposure. Nine Europeans and 9 East Indians survived.

The Dutch of the nearest settlements and the Cape sent two expeditions to search for survivors, one in 1783 and one in 1790–91. There was a great deal of popular interest in the loss of the *Grosvenor,* chiefly because there were three European women and three girl children among those who got ashore, and there was much speculation about their fate. Popular writers assumed that any surviving females would have been taken as wives by native chiefs, and this titillating prospect certainly was a major factor in arousing interest. One of the Dutch expeditions did actually find a white woman who had apparently reached shore from a wrecked ship in the same area in about 1740; she was reasonably happy as a wife and mother with one of the native tribes.

The story of the *Grosvenor* has been a source for many writers. Among books relying on this narrative have been the following:

Dibdin, Charles, *Hannah Hewitt; or the Female Crusoe,* London, 1792, 2nd edition, 1796

[Meadows, Mary Jane?] *The Life, Voyages and Surprising Adventures of Mary Jane Meadows,* London, 1802. Bookseller's note: "Voyage of the Grosvenor, wreck on African coast at Caffraria, and nine years' imprisonment."

Marryat, Captain Frederick, *The Mission, or Scenes in Africa,* London, 1845

Lee, Jonathan [Adele Lezard], *The Wreck of the Grosvenor,* London, 1937; *The Fate of the Grosvenor,* New York, 1938
Mama the Tiger, London, 1942. A sequel to the above

Hendriks, R., *Ek is Antoinette Duke,* Johannesburg, 1946

Du Plessis, I. D. and Cooper, H. R., *Die Wrak,* Johannesburg, 1951

Percival R. Kirby, Professor Emeritus at the University of Witwatersrand, has made himself the chief authority on the loss of the *Grosvenor.* Anyone interested in shipwrecks should know his *A Source Book on the Wreck of the Grosvenor East Indiaman,* Cape Town, 1953, and his *The True Story of the Grosvenor East Indiaman,* Cape Town, London, New York, 1960. W. Clark Russell's *The Wreck of the Grosvenor,* 1874, has nothing to do with the actual wreck of the East Indiaman. Russell borrowed the name of the ship and also the name of the captain, Coxon, but his book is about a mutiny and wreck in the Atlantic and is entirely fictitious.

96C. HUBBERLY [Habberly], WILLIAM
Appendix to the account of the loss of the Grosvenor Indiaman, containing the report of William Hubberly, one of the survivors . . .
London, n.d. [probably 1783]. Another edition, London, 1786

97C. INGLEFIELD, JOHN NICHOLSON
Narrative concerning the loss of His Majesty's ship the Centaur, of 74 guns . . .

London. Printed for J. Murray and A. Donaldson, 1783, 36 pp; ". . . a new edition, corrected . . . , " J. Murray and A. Donaldson, 1783, 36 pp.; ". . . with a report of the Court Martial . . . ," J. Murray and A. Donaldson, London, 1783, 36 + 2 pp.

The *Centaur* was one of a large fleet sailing from the West Indies for England in 1782; many of the ships, including the *Centaur,* were in bad condition because they had taken part in the Battle of the Saints the year before, in which Rodney had defeated the combined French and Spanish fleets. On September 16, the fleet ran into one of the worst hurricanes in the history of the Atlantic, and the *Centaur* soon became a sinking hulk. A few men got into the pinnace, and Inglefield, ignoring the hazy theory that a captain should go down with his ship, joined them and cast loose. None of those left on the *Centaur* was ever heard of again; she must have sunk soon after the pinnace left. The people in the pinnace had a bad time of it and one man died before they reached Fayal in the Azores. A dozen other ships of the fleet were lost in the same storm, including the *Ramillies* and the captured *Ville de Paris.* It was one of the most destructive storms ever recorded.

98C. STEEL, D[AVID?]
Steel's original and correct list of the Royal Navy, improved . . . and a list of the ships lost or destroyed since the commencement of the war . . . corrected to October 31, 1783, and to be continued monthly
London, for D. Steel [1783]. 12mo, wraps., 31 [2] pp.

1 7 8 5

99C. ANONYMOUS
Annual Register for the year 1783, London
Contains an account of the wreck of the *Grosvenor.*

1 7 8 6

100C. DOWNS, BARNABAS
A brief and remarkable narrative of the life and extreme sufferings of Barnabas Downs, Jr., who was among a number of those who escaped death on board the privateer brig *Arnold,* James Magee, Commander, which was cast away near Plymouth Harbor, Dec. 26, 1778
n.p., 1786. Another edition, Yarmouthport, Mass., 1972

101C. MERITON, HENRY, AND ROGERS, JOHN
A circumstantial narrative of the loss of the Halsewell East-Indiaman, Captain Richard Pierce, which was unfortunately wrecked at Seacombe in the Isle of Purbeck . . .
London, Lane, 1786
Cox, II, 463

Meriton was Chief Officer, and Rogers the Third Mate, of the *Halsewell.* They were among 74 who survived out of about 240 passengers and crew. The *Halsewell,* 758 tons, sailed from the Hope for "Coast and Bay" on January 1, 1786. She was caught in the narrow confines of the Channel by a violent storm which began on the morning of January 3. The ship beat back and forth in the storm, but sprang a leak and became almost helpless. The masts were cut away and the anchors dropped, but the ship drove and could not be kept off the shore. She struck at the foot of a cliff near Seacombe, between Peverel Point and St. Alban's Head, at a point where a cave had been cut into the rocks by the waves. Among the passengers were 7 young ladies, including 2 daughters of Captain Pierce, and they, with some other passengers and wives of soldiers, took refuge in the roundhouse. The ship broke up completely, drowning all on board except a few men who reached the rocky sides of the cavern. Two men, a cook and a quartermaster, climbed the rocks to the top and carried word of the wreck to a nearby house. The quarrymen of the Isle of Purbeck were mustered and put down ropes over the cliff, by which they drew up all who survived. "The benevolence and generosity of the master of the Crown inn, at Blanford, deserves the highest praise. When the distressed seamen arrived at that town, he sent for them all to his house, and having given them the refreshment of a comfortable dinner, he presented each man with half a crown to help him on his journey."

1 7 8 7

102C. BOYS, WILLIAM [Boyce and Boyes in some sources]
   An account of the loss of the Luxborough galley, by fire on her
     voyage from Jamaica to London . . . in the year
     1727. . . . Edited by William Boys, F.S.A. . . .
   London, J. Johnson, 1787. 4to
   Cited in Woodard as the *Luxemburg* galley

This account was edited by William Boys, but came originally from Captain Boyce, who had been second mate of the *Luxborough* and died in 1774 the Lieutenant Governor of Greenwich Hospital. The *Luxborough,* a South Sea Company ship, sailed from Jamaica May 23, 1727, probably for England. On June 25 two black boys wondered whether some spilled liquid was water or liquor, and settled the matter by setting fire to it. The fire travelled to the barrel and the whole ship burst into flame. Twenty-three men and boys leaped into the yawl; sixteen others tried to hoist out the longboat, but the ship blew up and they were killed. The people in the yawl had neither food nor water as they headed for the coast of Newfoundland. By July 7, when they sighted land near Old Saint Lawrence Harbor, Newfoundland, only seven of them were alive. In the course of their suffering they had eaten a little of the flesh of the dead men, and drunk their blood. The captain died after they reached shore, so that of thirty-nine on board the *Luxborough,* thirty-three died. Boyce annually kept a fast day on July 7 in commemoration of their arrival in Newfoundland.

103C. HAWKINS, JAMES, CAPTAIN, R. N.
   An account of the loss of His Majesty's ship Deal Castle, com-
     manded by Captain James Hawkins, off the island of Porto
     Rico, during the hurricane in the West Indies, in the year 1780
   London, J. Murray, 1787. Pp. ii, 48, 2

1 7 8 8

104C. ANONYMOUS
   The habitable world described
   London, 1788[?]
Cox (II, 463) states that three narratives are printed in this book:
   Anonymous: An account of the loss of H.M.S. Deal Castle off the island
      of Porto Rico, 1787
   Inglefield: Captain Inglefield's narrative concerning the loss of H.M.S.
      the Centaur, 1783
   C. Smith: A narrative of the loss of the Catherine, Venus, and Piedmont
      [transports] and the Thomas, Golden Grove, and Aeolus [merchant-
      ships] near Weymouth, 1796
Since the Smith narrative is dated 1796, the 1788 date for *The Habitable
World Described* is obviously wrong. I could not find this title in the British
Museum Catalogue.

105C. ANONYMOUS [Wilson, Henry]
   Narrative of the shipwreck of the Antelope East-India Pacquet, on
      the Pelew Islands, situated in the western part of the Pacific
      Ocean; in August, 1783
   Perth, printed by R. Morison, Junr. For R. Morison and Son,
      Perth; and sold by C. Elliot, T. Kay and Co. near Sommerset-
      House, Strand, London. MDCCLXXXVIII [1788]. 8 + 268
      pp.
This is an abridgment of 108C.

106C. CLARK, JONAS [author, or publisher?]
   A short and brief account of the shipwreck of Capt. Joshua
      Winslow . . . July, 1788
   [Boston, 1788] by Jonas Clark. [Reprint 1795?]

107C. KEATE, GEORGE, ESQ., F.R.S., AND S.A.
   An account of the Pelew Islands, situated in the western part of the
      Pacific Ocean. Composed from the journals and communica-
      tions of Captain Henry Wilson, and some of his officers, who,
      in August 1783, were there shipwrecked, in the Antelope, a
      packet belonging to the honourable East India Company, by
      George Keate, Esq. F.R.S. and S.A.
   London: printed for G. Nicol, bookseller to His Majesty, Pall-Mall,
      MDCCLXXXVIII [1788]; London, 1788, 1789; Dublin, 1788,
      1793; Perth, 1788
This was one of the most popular of all shipwreck narratives, partly because of the
   happy ending of the adventure and partly because of the detailed descriptions
   of the Pelew Islands' natural features and society. The *Antelope*, about 300
   tons, Captain Wilson, sailed from Macao for England July 29, 1783, with a
   crew of fifty including sixteen Chinese. Nothing of importance occurred until
   the night of August 9–10, when the ship struck on an unknown reef in weather
   that was fortunately good. The boats were hoisted out and the masts cut away,

but the ship filled and was obviously lost. An island was seen about 3 leagues away, and with some difficulty all reached shore except for one seaman drowned. The natives, who had never seen Europeans, were friendly. Wilson exercised excellent control over his men, dealt smoothly with the natives, and must have been an extraordinary man. The crew set to work to build a schooner from native lumber, while some of their members fought for their hosts in native wars. When all sailed away in the schooner on November 12, 1783, one man, Madan Blanchard, chose to stay behind on the island, and Prince Lee Boo, a son of the local king, sailed off for England. The schooner arrived safely at Macao; the *Antelope*'s people reached Canton and took passage for England. Blanchard was killed a few years later in native wars, and Lee Boo died of smallpox in London. He was buried in the church at Rotherhithe.

108C. WILSON, HENRY
    Shipwreck of the Antelope, East India Company packet, H. Wilson, Commander, on the Pelew Islands, August, 1783, the adventures of the crew with a singular race of people hitherto unknown to Europeans, with interesting particulars of Prince Lee Boo, etc.
    [London?], 1788; Perth, 1788; Wilmington, 1794; New York, 1796

This narrative seems to have been less popular than Keate's story of the same shipwreck. See 107C.

1 7 8 9

109C. BRISSON, PIERRE RAYMOND DE
    Histoire du naufrage et de la captivité de M. de Brisson . . .
    Genève, 1789; Robert Baker, London, 1790, 112 pp.; Constable, Constable's Miscellany, Vol. 11, London, 1826; German edition, 1799; abridged edition, London, 1807

M. Brisson sailed from France for the island of St. Louis, in Senegal, in June, 1785. His ship, the *St. Catherine*, struck on the coast of Africa in July, and all on board became slaves of the Arabs of the desert. Brisson fared very badly for a year, but he was finally bought by an Arab who hoped to receive a ransom for him, and was taken to Mogadore where he was freed. He reached France in 1787, and courageously sailed again for Senegal, which he succeeded in reaching without trouble. His narrative is frequently found reprinted with that of M. Saugnier (114C).

110C. EQUIANO, OLAUDAH [Claudah in one source]
    The interesting narrative of the life of Olaudah Equiano or Gustavas Vassa the African, written by himself
    London, 1789. 2 vols., printed for and sold by the author

There were other editions, including the United States, 1837. The autobiography is chiefly an antislavery narrative, but it includes an account of the wreck of the slaver *Nancy* in the Bahamas, 1767, and a cut of the wreck.

1 7 9 0

111C. BLIGH, WILLIAM

A narrative of the mutiny on board His Majesty's ship Bounty, and the subsequent voyage of part of the crew, in the ship's boat, from Tofoa . . . to Timor . . .

London, George Nicol, 1790. Illus. with charts, iv, 88 pp.; W. Smith, London, 1838; The dangerous voyage performed by Capt. Bligh . . . , R. Napper, Dublin, 1824, pp. 175; P. D. Hardy, Dublin [1825?]; Révolte arrivée a bord du Bounty, n.p., 1791; Narrative . . . subsequent fate of the mutineers, Nathaniel Cooke, London, 1853

As almost everyone knows, the *Bounty* sailed from England for Tahiti in 1787 in order to pick up small breadfruit trees and other tropical trees and plants so that they could be introduced into the West Indies. The voyage was prosperous, apparently, until April 28, 1789, when a mutiny broke out on board and Bligh, with fifteen crewmen, was sent off in the launch. Fletcher Christian, master's mate, was the leader of the mutiny; twenty-two men remained with him in the ship. Bligh, who was a difficult and demanding leader but an excellent seaman, managed to navigate the launch through one of the longest voyages on record for a boat of this size; she reached Timor on June 12, 1789.

The *Pandora* (119C) captured some of the mutineers at Tahiti, but for many years nothing was known of the fate of the *Bounty* and of Fletcher Christian, who had sailed the ship, with some Tahitians, to Pitcairn's Island. The whole story is told, and well told, in *Mutiny on the Bounty, Men Against the Sea,* and *Pitcairn Island,* by Nordhoff and Hall.

112C. [RIOU, LIEUTENANT?]

Miraculous escape of the Guardian man of war, Lt. Riou, striking on an island of ice, the 23rd December, 1789

[London?], printed for J. Forbes, 1790

Woodard, 245

Lt. Riou was in command of the *Guardian* sloop, England for Botany Bay with convicts and stores. After touching at the Cape of Good Hope, the ship sailed for New South Wales. A large iceberg was seen, and the Captain sent boats to collect fragments of ice for water. While the ship was attempting to clear the berg she struck on a submerged portion and was badly damaged. She was despaired of, and about a third of the crew left in three boats, only one of which was picked up. Those remaining with the ship kept her afloat until she was discovered and saved by a Dutch ship which provided men and stores and accompanied the *Guardian* 400 leagues back to the Cape. Lt. Riou, then Captain, was killed at the Battle of Copenhagen.

1 7 9 1

113C. CARTER, GEORGE

A narrative of the loss of the Grosvenor, East Indiaman, wrecked upon the coast of Caffraria . . . compiled from the examination of J. Hynes . . .

London, J. Murray and W. Lane, 1791. Copper plates, 174 pp.

See 95C.

114C. SAUGNIER AND BRISSON
      Relations de plusieurs voyages a la côte d'Afrique, a Maroc, au
      Senegal, à Goree, à Galam . . .
      Paris, 1791; London, G. G. J. and J. Robinson, 1792

M. Saugnier sailed from Bordeaux in the *Deux Amis,* Captain Carsin, on December
29, 1783, for Senegal. After encountering storms in the Bay of Biscay the ship
was caught in treacherous currents off the coast of Morocco and struck on a
sandbank near Cape Non. Most of those on board eventually reached the
shore, where they were captured by Arabs, who enslaved them. Saugnier was
passed from owner to owner, and finally reached Mogadore, where French and
English merchants aided him. He was freed, and returned to France in the fall
of 1784. Saugnier seems not to have been badly used by his captors, as com-
pared with Adams, Riley, and Paddock, for instance, who were captured under
similar circumstances. He even tells in his narrative of eating truffles while his
owner drank camel's milk.

1 7 9 2

115C. BLIGH, WILLIAM
      A voyage to the South Sea . . . including an account of the
      mutiny . . .
      London, George Nicol, 1792, 264 pp.; Paris, 1792

116C. DIBDIN, CHARLES
      Hannah Hewit: or the female Crusoe. Being the history of a woman
      of uncommon mental and personal accomplishments; who, in
      about every station of life, from splendid prosperity to abject
      adversity, was cast away in the Grosvenor East Indiaman: and
      became for three years the sole inhabitant of an island, in the
      South Seas. Supposed to be written by herself. There is an
      especial providence in the fall of a sparrow
      London, 1792. No author given. Second edition, London, 1796,
      Charles Dibdin listed as author

This novel is a fictional account of the loss of the *Grosvenor,* based on the Carter
narrative (113C).

117C. RIOU, CAPTAIN EDWARD [Reenen, Jacob van]
      A journal of a journey from the Cape of Good Hope, etc., by Jacob
      van Reenen. . . .
      London, 1792

The journal is an account of the second Dutch expedition to search for survivors of
the *Grosvenor* wreck. See 95C.

118C. THUNBERG, KARL PETER
      Travels in Europe, Africa and Asia, made between the years 1770
      and 1779
      Berlin, 1792–1794; 3rd edition, London, F. & C. Rivington,
      1795–1796, 4 vols.

J. S. Clarke, in his *Naufragia,* cites Vol. I, pp. 270–275, for an account of a ship-wreck on the coast of South Africa, and says that the narrative was published in Vol. III of the *Naval Chronicle.*

1 7 9 3

119C. HAMILTON, G.

A voyage around the world in H.M.'s frigate "Pandora" per-formed under the direction of Captain Edwards, 1790–92, with the discoveries made in the South-Sea and the many distresses experienced by the crew from shipwreck and famine in a voyage of 1100 miles in open boats between Endeavor Straits and the island of Timor

Pharson of Berwick, Law of London, 1793

The *Pandora* sailed from England for Tahiti to capture, if possible, the mutineers of the *Bounty.* Ten men were arrested on the island, but they were not able to give any information about the eventual fate of the ship and those who had sailed in her with Fletcher Christian. On the way back to England the *Pandora* struck on a reef off New Guinea, and was lost. All on board were able to get away in four boats. They made a voyage of 1100 miles to Timor, the same island that Bligh finally reached after the mutiny on the *Bounty.*

1 7 9 4

120C. SAUNDERS, DANIEL, JR.

A journal of the travels and sufferings of Daniel Saunders, Jr., a mariner on board the ship "Commerce" of Boston, Samuel Johnson, Commander, which was cast away near Cape Morebet, on the coast of Arabia, July 20, 1792

Salem, Thomas C. Cushing, 1794, Joshua and John D. Cushing, 1824; Leominster, Prentiss, 1797; New Haven, 1802; Hudson, N.Y., 1805; Exeter, A. Brown, 1830.

The *Commerce* was caught in a typhoon in the Indian Ocean while trying to reach the Malabar Coast of India. When she struck in the storm her people were sure that they were on the Indian coast, and could hardly believe that the ship had been driven to Arabia. There were various difficulties with the Arabs, and great trouble in getting passage back to India, but Saunders finally succeeded in returning to the United States.

1 7 9 5

121C. ANONYMOUS

An account of the escape of Messrs. Carter, Shaw, and Haskett, taken from a manuscript diary

The Bengal Hircarrah, Vol. 1, No. 9, March 17, 1795. Reprinted in *Oriental Repertory,* p. 521

Woodard, 181–200

The ship *Shah Hormazier* was attacked by natives of an island near New Guinea. These three men reached Timor after much suffering.

122C. ANONYMOUS
Authentic narratives of affecting incidents at sea, in a series of letters, interspersed with poetry and moral observations
. . . published by subscription for the benefit of a poor lame
boy . . .
Scarborough, printed by B. & W. Wilson, 1795. 32 pp.
Though this book was published by subscription, it may have been the first of the
"mendicant" books of such narratives, like those sold by Samuel Patterson
(191C) and Israel Potter (221C).

1 7 9 6

123C. CAMPBELL, DONALD
A journey overland to India, partly by a route never gone before by
any European, by D. Campbell . . . in a series of letters to his
son. Comprehending his shipwreck and imprisonment with
Hyder Alli and his subsequent . . . transactions in the East
London, Cullen & Co., 1795; J. Owen, V. Griffiths, London, 1796
[A condensation of this book was published in the next year:] A narrative of the
extraordinary adventures, and sufferings by shipwreck & imprisonment, of Donald Campbell, Esq. of Barbreck: with the
singular humors of his Tartar Guide, Hassan Artaz; comprising the occurrences of four years and five days, in an overland
journey to India. Faithfully abstracted from Capt. Campbell's
"Letters to his Son"
London, printed for Vernor and Hood, Birchin Lane, Cornhill,
1796, 1797, 1798; 6th ed., Vernor, Hood & Sharpe, London,
1808
Campbell set out for India across Europe in 1781, planning to sail only across the
Indian Ocean. He had many adventures before he finally reached Goa, and
sailed from that port May 18, 1782. On the next day the ship ran into a very
bad storm, became leaky and then waterlogged, and finally struck on the
Indian coast within the dominions of Hyder Ali. Captain Campbell and one
other Englishman reached shore, out of eleven European passengers, along
with fourteen of fifty-six lascars. Campbell was imprisoned by the Indians for
a term of years, but was released after Hyder Ali's death. He joined the British
Army in India, and then returned to England after being absent for four years
and five days. The shipwreck in the narrative is given considerable space, but
the major interest of the book lies in Campbell's other experiences.

124C. [SMITH, MRS. CHARLOTTE]
A narrative of the loss of the Catharine, Venus, and Piedmont
transports; and the Thomas, Golden Grove, and Aeolus
merchantships, near Weymouth, the 18th of November, 1796.
Taken by Mrs. Charlotte Smith
London, printed for Law, 1796
These ships were in a convoy bound for the West Indies. They sailed from St.
Helen's on November 15, 1795, and encountered a severe gale in the Channel
only three days later. These six ships were driven ashore on and near the Chesil
Bank, with great loss of life; 234 bodies were found along the beach, and were

buried nearby. A number of the survivors noted that the people of the area would do almost nothing for those who reached the beach; they were in general far more interested in the wreckage that came ashore, and in plundering the bodies. Only 1 woman and 1 boy survived of 40 on board the *Catherine*. It is not clear from the narrative whether the woman, who was quoted, was Mrs. Charlotte Smith referred to in the title.

1 7 9 7

125C. ANONYMOUS
"The Three Sisters, Nazby . . ."
Morning Chronicle, July 8, 1797
Woodard, 216

The ship was crushed by ice, but the crew reached the Shetlands in a boat.

126C. HUNTER, JOHN
Resa til nya sodra Wallis
Stockholm, 1797. 8vo

Bookseller's note: "Contains . . . Hamilton's Narrative of Captain Edwards' Voyage in the *Pandora* to arrest the *Bounty* mutineers, 79 pages." For the voyage of the *Pandora,* see 119C.

1 7 9 8

127C. ANONYMOUS [Stout, Benjamin]
A narrative of the loss of the ship Hercules, commanded by Captain Benjamin Stout on the coast of Caffraria, the 16th of June, 1796
Hudson, N.Y., 1798; London, 1798

Stout, after a voyage to India, chartered his ship to the East India Company, and sailed from Bengal for London with a cargo of rice March 17, 1796. She carried a crew of sixty-four, mostly lascars. All went well till June 1, when the ship encountered a terrible gale which strained her so that she became un-manageable. It was decided that the only hope was to run the ship ashore, and sail was set for the African coast. The ship struck on June 16, 1796. Stout believed they were near the scene of the sinking of the *Grosvenor* (95C) but actually the *Hercules* struck far south of that point. Practically the whole crew reached shore safely, and against all expectations the natives, Caffres, were friendly. They guided Stout and about half the crew to the Dutch settlements, from which wagons were sent back for the others. All who reached the shore were finally safe at the Cape.

Stout's narrative has been one of the popular accounts of shipwreck, reprinted again and again. Recently a source book on the wreck of the *Hercules,* like that on the wreck of the *Grosvenor,* has been published in South Africa. In it there are criticisms of the accuracy of Stout's account, which may have been published primarily to help the campaign against slavery. Apparently it is impossible to make sense of Stout's story of his journey to the Dutch settlements, and of the native tribes. Stout himself may have been almost illiterate, and not really responsible for the account.

128C. MACKAY, WILLIAM
        A narrative of the shipwreck of the Juno, on the coast of
        Aracan . . .
        London, Debrett, 1798; German translation, 1800, 1831
Mackay left a ship at Rangoon and signed on as second mate of the *Juno,* which
    was loaded with teakwood for Madras. She had a crew of fifty-three, chiefly
    lascars, and nineteen passengers including the captain's wife and a maid. She
    sailed from Rangoon May 29, 1795. Mackay said that the ship was in bad
    shape when she sailed. Just off Rangoon the *Juno* grounded on a sandbank but
    got off at high tide. On June 1 the ship encountered a gale and developed a bad
    leak at the sternpost, perhaps a result of grounding. The leak was located when
    the weather moderated, and the crew fothered the leak with a sail and oakum,
    secured with a lead plate. On June 12 she encountered a very severe storm and
    took in a great deal of water. On June 20 she broached to and foundered, drift-
    ing with the whole upper deck under water; the teakwood cargo probably
    prevented her sinking. The crew and passengers got into the mizzen-top and
    fore-top, without food or water, and continued there until the ship grounded
    on the coast of Aracan, a part of Burma, on July 11. There were fourteen sur-
    vivors who reached shore on spars and wreckage, including the captain's wife
    and her maid, four passengers, Mackay's boy, and six lascars. When they
    reached shore they had some difficulties with the natives, but eventually got
    word of the wreck to British authorities and were rescued. Mackay stated that
    he drank salt water while in the mizzen-top, and benefited from it.
        Byron read this narrative at school and used it in writing his account of a
    shipwreck in Canto II of *Don Juan.*

1 7 9 9

129C. ANONYMOUS
        The Naval Chronicle containing the current history of the Royal
            Navy, with original papers, biographies, lists of ships, &c. with
            numerous portraits and views
        [London], 1799–1818. Complete in 40 vols. Royal 8vo
Barnes Catalogue: ". . . the other contents include narratives . . . of shipwrecks
    and disasters of former periods." This periodical may well have been the
    primary source for many later narratives and anthologies.

130C. WRIGHT, JOHN (Lieutenant)
        Narrative of the loss of HMS the Prosperine [Proserpine], James
            Wallace, Captain
        [London?], 1799. 8vo

1 8 0 0

131C. ANONYMOUS
        Tales of the ship or the British seaman's wonderful museum and
            chearful companion, containing droll jests, shipwrecks . . .
        London, n.d. [1800?]

132C. AYME, JEAN JACQUES
 Déportation et naufrage de [J. J. A.] suivi de tableau de vie et de
 mort des déportés à son départ de la Guyane avec quelques
 observations sur cette colonie et sur les nègres
 Paris, Chez Maradan [1800]. 8 vo, 269, [26] pp. Sabin 2521

133C. PARDOE, MICHAEL
 The shipwreck and sea-fight of the Amazon frigate, Capt.
 Reynolds, and the Indefatigable, Sir Edward Pellew, Commander
 [London? 1800?] Wrappers, 36 pp.
This action took place in 1797; these two frigates were involved in a running fight
with the French *Droits de l'Homme.* The French ship was part of a fleet trying
to land troops in Ireland, but had to put back because of a storm. She was full
of troops and English prisoners. The *Amazon* and *Indefatigable* pursued her to
the French coast, where both the *Droits de l'Homme* and the *Amazon* struck
and were lost. There was very heavy loss of life, especially on the French ship.

134C. SOREN, JOHN
 John Soren's narrative
 Printed at the Oriental Press, Wilson and Co., Lincoln's-inn-fields
 [London], 1800, Woodard, 243. London, Cox and Bayliss,
 July, 1813, Barnes Catalogue
An American ship, the *Enterprize,* Captain St. Barbe, discovered a ship in distress
in the Atlantic. She bore down to offer aid, and was captured by the British
ship *Isabella,* Captain Porter, which was bound for the West Indies with three-
hundred troops aboard. The *Isabella* had 8 feet of water in the hold. Since the
United States and Britain were not at war in 1797, Soren seems to have had just
grounds for complaint. Apparently the British government eventually admitted
liability and paid the owners of the *Enterprize* some part of their losses.

1 8 0 2

135C. ANONYMOUS
 Asiatic Register, Vol. I, p. 17, for 1802
 Woodard, 241
Contains a narrative of the loss of the *Fazy Allum,* near Cape Orfoy, in 1801.

136C. ANONYMOUS
 Supplement to the *Calcutta Gazette,* July 8, 1802
 Woodard, 164–169
This issue of the *Calcutta Gazette* contains the narrative of the sufferings of six
deserters from the army at St. Helena in 1799. Six men stole a boat and three of
them survived to reach Brazil, after cannibalism and one suicide.

137C. [MEADOWS, MARY JANE?]
    The life, voyages and surprising adventures of Mary Jane Meadows
    London, 1802. 16mo

Bookseller's note: "Voyage of the *Grosvenor,* wreck on African coast at Caffraria,
    and nine years' imprisonment. A shipwreck and castaway narrative." As noted
    in the materials under 95C, there was a great deal of public interest in the wreck
    of the *Grosvenor* in 1782, and particularly in the fate of the women who
    vanished after the survivors reached shore. This novel, like Charles Dibdin's
    Hannah Hewit; or the Female Crusoe (1792), is a completely fictional narrative
    based on the genuine stories of the *Grosvenor.* This novel is not listed by
    Percival Kirby in *The True Story of the Grosvenor East Indiaman.*

1 8 0 3

138C. ANONYMOUS
    Narrative of the loss of the Hindostan East Indiaman, Capt. Edw.
        Balston, which was wrecked on the Wedge-Sand in the Queen's
        Channel, off Margate, on January 11, 1803. Compiled from
        the united testimony of many of the survivors
    London, published by John Fairburn, 146 Minories [price six-
        pence], printed by J. H. Hart, 23 Warwick-Square, n.d. [1803]
        26 pp., wrappers

The *Hindostan,* 1,248 tons, sailed from Gravesend January 2, 1803. She anchored
    near Margate in the Queen's Channel, off the Wedge Sand, on Sunday,
    January 9. A very bad storm struck and the anchor cable parted. Another an-
    chor was dropped, but the ship drove on the sandbank and foundered. For-
    tunately the wreck held together, and a small craft from Margate and a small
    yacht belonging to the Company eventually took off 129 of the 143 people on
    board. The *Active,* a West Indiaman of Greenock, was driven ashore near
    Margate by the same gale. Nine men were lost in that wreck.

139C. FELLOWES, WILLIAM DORSET
    A narrative of the loss of His Majesty's packet the Lady Hobart, on
        an island of ice in the Atlantic Ocean, 28th of June, 1803: with
        a particular account of the providential escape of the crew in
        two open boats . . .
    London, printed for John Stockdale, 1803. 8vo, 46 pp., wraps. 2nd
        edition, 1803. Another edition of this narrative is bound with
        three other accounts of shipwrecks—*Cabalva,* 1818; *Litchfield,*
        1758; *Centaur,* 1782. London, printed for C. & J. Rivington,
        1824

The *Lady Hobart* packet, Commander Fellowes, sailed June 22, 1803, from Halifax
    for England. On June 26 she captured a French schooner, *L'Aimiable Julie,*
    put aboard a prize crew, and sent all of the French except the captain and two
    others to St. John's on two English ships. On June 26, about 350 miles off
    Newfoundland, the *Lady Hobart* struck against an iceberg in the fog and was
    so badly damaged that she sank in about an hour. Eighteen people, including
    three women, were put into the twenty-foot cutter, and eleven into the
    fourteen-foot jolly boat. All of them suffered terribly from hunger, thirst, ex-
    posure, and fatigue, but by good discipline and great good fortune both boats

reached the Newfoundland shore and made harbor there. The only casualty was the French captain, who became insane and leaped overboard.

140C. GRANGER, WILLIAM, AND OTHERS
New Wonderful Museum and Extraordinary Magazine, being a complete repository of all the wonders, curiosities and rarities of nature and art . . .
[London], Alex. Hogg & Company, Paternoster Row, 1803–1808, 6 vols.

This magazine contains two or three accounts of contemporary shipwrecks, though it is primarily directed to readers interested in remarkable misers, murderers, horned ladies, and monstrosities of every kind.

[1 8 0 4]

141C. ANONYMOUS
An affecting history of the captivity and sufferings of Mrs. Mary Velnet, an Italian lady, who was seven years a slave in Tripoli. . . . Written by herself
Boston: William Crary [1804?]. The first American edition. 96 pp., 16mo, woodcut frontis.

This book is listed in Wright (I, 7a), where it is identified as *not* the first American edition, but as the first edition anywhere. Crary claimed that he was reprinting from a European edition, but no such edition has been discovered. Probably this was the first, and the prototype, of a number of spurious narratives of shipwrecks and disasters, like Crary's *Narrative of . . . Maria Martin* (156C), and the *Narrative of Eliza Bradley* (202C).

142C. ANONYMOUS
Loss of the Investigator, the Porpoise, and the Cato
Morning Herald, May or June, 1804
Woodard, 240–241

The *Porpoise* and *Cato,* sent out to explore the Australian Coast, were wrecked 800 miles from Port Jackson.

143C. DUNCAN, ARCHIBALD [editor]
The mariner's chronicle; or, authentic and complete history of popular shipwrecks: recording the most remarkable disasters which have happened on the ocean to people of all nations. Particularly the adventures and sufferings of British seamen, by wreck, fire, famine, and other calamities incident to a life of maritime enterprizes, by Archibald Duncan, Esq. late of the Royal Navy. In six volumes. Vol. I
London, printed and published by J. & J. Cundee, Ivy-Lane, Paternoster-Row

The dating of this set is a puzzle. My own set, uniformly bound and numbered on the spine 1–6, has the following information on the title pages. I have listed also the numbering of the similar set in the National Maritime Museum Library at Greenwich.

	My set		National Martime Museum Library
Vol. I	n.d. "In six volumes."	Vol. I	n.d.
Vol. II	1812 "In two volumes."	Vol. II	n.d.
Vol. III	n.d. "In four volumes."	Vol. III	1810
Vol. IV	1811 "In six volumes."	Vol. IV	1805
Vol. V	n.d. "In six volumes." Pref. 1808	Vol. V	n.d. Pref. 1818
Vol. VI	n.d. "In six volumes."	Vol. VI	n.d.

The British Museum Catalogue lists the first edition as 1804–[1808], in six volumes, and the second edition, four volumes, as 1804–1805. There is supposed to be another London edition in six volumes dated 1810. There are two Philadelphia editions listed, in 1806 and 1810, both in four volumes. I suspect that the early London editions were published in parts and bound up on demand, though I can see no certain evidence for that possibility. In the first volume Cundee advertised an edition of Joshua White's *Life of Nelson* in parts, and in Volume VI the same book is advertised, complete, in two formats.

Duncan's *Mariner's Chronicle* was probably the most popular source for other compilers of later years. Many American editors stole material from this set, and even the title was used three or four times. Probably the popularity of this collection influenced Tegg's collection of 1807–1810 and Sir J. G. Dalyell's collection of 1812.

Since this compilation was the basis for so many others, I am listing the wrecks and disasters in some detail.

Volume I

Narratives of shipwrecks, &c &c. The loss of the Doddington East-
Indiaman. Wrecked upon a rock in the open sea, the 17th of
July, 1755
See 67C, 1756.

Shipwreck of the Countess De Bourk on the coast of Algiers, and
adventures of her daughter, Mademoiselle de Bourk, in 1719
The Countess de Bourk, wife of an Irish officer in the Spanish service, sailed from Cette for Barcelona in a Genoese tartan, October 22, 1719. The tartan was captured by an Algerine corsair and was then wrecked on the North African coast. The countess and her son were drowned, but Mademoiselle de Bourk, ten years old, and four others were rescued from the wreck. All were held as prisoners for a time by savage tribesmen, but they were eventually ransomed and the young girl lived to become a marquise in Provence. An incident or two in *Candide*, by Voltaire, may come from this narrative.

The distress and providential escape of the Guardian Sloop, bound
to Botany Bay with stores, in the month of December, 1789
See 112C, 1790.

The shipwreck of Occum Chamnan, a Siamese Mandarin, at the
Cape of the Needles, in the southern extremity of Africa, in the
year 1683

This narrative is stated to be taken from Father Tachard's history of his second voyage to Siam. Occum Chamnan told Father Tachard that he had sailed from Batavia for Portugal in a Portuguese ship in 1673. The ship struck at the Cape of Needles, Africa, but most of the crew and passengers reached shore. The Portuguese deserted the group of Siamese, and all of them suffered greatly in their journey to the Dutch settlements of the Cape. Occum Chamnan finally reached Batavia and Siam in a Dutch vessel.

The sufferings of part of the crew of the ship Thomas, of Liverpool, bound from the coast of Africa to the Island of Barbadoes, in 1797

The *Thomas,* of Liverpool, was a slaver. Captain M'Quay had armed his male slaves to defend the ship against the French, but on September 2, 1797, the slaves revolted and took the ship. Twelve men escaped in a boat, without provisions or water. After a few days of suffering, they drew lots and killed and ate one of their number, but according to the narrative all who ate of him died. Two survivors finally reached Barbadoes on October 10, 1797. Nothing apparently was known of what happened to the *Thomas* and the slaves after their *Amistad*-like success.

The shipwreck of a Portuguese Sloop. Near the Calamian islands. Forming part of the Phillipines, in the year 1688

One Carreri of Naples reported this narrative, which he had from a Jesuit priest in Macao in 1696. This priest had sailed with sixty people in a Portuguese sloop, *Caromandel,* for the Philippines, and the ship was wrecked on the Calamian Islands. The few survivors of the wreck lived on one of the islands for seven years, living on turtles and boobies, but finally put together a small boat from wreckage. Sixteen of them reached the island of Haynan, off the coast of China, and were finally taken back to Macao.

The shipwreck of two English vessels, on the rocks near the island of Mayote. In the Channel of Mozambique, in the year 1700

This narrative, like the story of Occum Chamnan, is from Father Tachard. He had touched at the Comorro Islands in 1701, and discovered there two Englishmen, one the survivor of a wrecked East Indiaman and the other a buccaneer, originally from Boston. These two were the only survivors of many conflicts with the natives, and were finally taken to Surat.

The shipwreck of the Sloop Betsy. Philip Aubin, Commander. On the coast of Dutch Guiana, the 5th of August, 1756

This narrative is by Philip Aubin, captain of the *Betsy.* That ship, a small trader, sailed from Barbadoes for Surinam, August 1, 1756. The *Betsy* foundered four days later, apparently in good weather. Four men, including Aubin, righted a small boat and got into it, but had neither provisions nor water. Aubin and one other man reached Tobago, and were carefully treated by the "Caraibs," the native Indians. Aubin finally reached Barbadoes, but was so feeble that he sailed to London, where a diet of asses' milk and chicken wings restored him to reasonable health.

The loss of the Lady Hobart Packet, on an island of ice, in the Atlantic Ocean, June 28, 1803. And the providential escape of the crew in two open boats. Written by the Commander, William Dorset Fellowes, Esq.

See 139C, 1803.

Shipwreck of the Portuguese vessel the St. James, off the east coast of Africa, in 1586

See 6C, 1601.

The loss of an English Sloop, on the coast of the island of Cape Breton, in 1780

This was the ship *St. Lawrence,* called a brigantine in some sources. See 90C, 1782.

The loss of His Majesty's Ship Centaur, of seventy-four guns the 23d of September, 1782. And the miraculous preservation of the pinnace, with the Captain, Master, and ten of the crew. By Captain Inglefield

See 97C, 1783

The shipwreck of the Vryheid, a Dutch East Indiaman. Off Dymchurch Wall, near Dover, Nov. 23, 1802

The *Vryheid* was originally an English East Indiaman, the *Melville Castle.* She was bought by the Dutch government and fitted for a troop transport. On November 21, 1782, she sailed from Amsterdam for the Cape and Batavia with 454 on board, including 22 women and 7 children. Only one day out of port the *Vryheid* was struck by a very bad storm, and was driven ashore near Hythe at Dymchurch Wall. She broke up completely, and there were just 18 survivors. This narrative claims that Captain Scherman refused a pilot soon after the storm began, and that the ship might have reached a safe anchorage if he had accepted help.

The loss of His Majesty's Ship Sceptre, of sixty-four guns, in Table Bay, Cape of Good Hope, November the 6th, 1799

On November 4, 1799, the *Sceptre* was lying in Table Bay with about a dozen other ships, when a very severe storm struck from the only quarter for which this bay provides no protection. The anchor cables parted in succession, and the ship drove on a reef just off shore. The *Sceptre* broke up completely, and only 51 reached shore of the approximately 450 people on board. Nine of the ships in the bay drove on the shore in the same storm, and were lost. Many of the trophies taken at Seringapatam were lost in the *Sceptre.*

The loss of the Hector Frigate, in the Atlantic Ocean, October the 5th, 1782

The *Hector,* Jamaica to England in convoy, separated from the other ships on August 25, and was engaged with two French frigates, *L'Aigle* and *La Gloire,* on September 5. The two enemy ships sheered off after a severe action in which about fifty men of the *Hector,* including Captain Bourchin, were killed. The ship then encountered a gale in which she lost her masts and leaked very badly. Discipline broke down, and the very sentinels drank themselves to death. After drifting 200 leagues the crew sighted a snow from London, for Newfoundland, which took off the survivors. The *Hector* was burned.

An extraordinary famine in the American ship Peggy, on her return from the Azores to New York, in 1765

See 76C, 1766.

The loss of the Royal George, at Spithead, August the 19th, 1782

The *Royal George,* 108 guns, the oldest first-rate in the Navy, was anchored at Spithead August 19, 1782. She was hove down to repair a water pipe, heeled more than was expected, took in a little water, heeled still more, and filled and sank. Some accounts blame the heeling on taking in casks of rum on the low side. About 1200 people were on board, including 250 women and children; nearly 900 of them were drowned, including Admiral Kempenfeldt. The *Royal George* was launched in 1751, and had served as the flagship for Anson, Boscawen, Hawke, Rodney, and Howe. Her hull was finally broken up by exploding gunpowder in 1839–1841.

The loss of the Grosvenor Indiaman, on the coast of Caffraria, August 4, 1782; with particulars relative to the unfortunate survivors of the wreck

See 95C, 1783.

The loss of the ship Fazy Allum, near Cape Orfoy, June 7th, 1801. And the subsequent proceedings of the crew

This narrative is attributed to William Kinsey, first officer of the *Fazy Allum.* That ship, with about 130 passengers and crew, struck near Cape Orfoy on the coast of Africa, and broke up. Most of those on board reached shore, but the survivors suffered greatly from hunger, thirst, and harassment by natives. Kinsey and a few others reached Bunder Allulah on July 7, and they got in touch with the *Jehangeer* and the *Hercules* there. There were, apparently, 15 or 20 survivors of the *Fazy Allum.*

Shipwreck of the Degrave East Indiaman, on the coast of Madagascar, in the year 1701

See 44C, 1729.

The loss of the Minerva, September the 16th, 1782, by Mr. John Scott, Second Mate, the only person on board who was saved

The *Minerva,* West Indies for Glasgow, Captain Holmes, foundered in a severe storm on September 16, 1782. One Scott, the helmsman, caught hold of the crossjack-yard as the ship sank. He floated on it till about noon of the 17th, when he was picked up by the *Betsy* of Whitehaven, Captain Stooey.

The loss by fire of the French East India Company's vessel the Prince bound from L'Orient to Pondicherry, on the 26th of July 1752. By M. De La Fond, one of the Lieutenants of that ship

The *Prince,* with almost three hundred people, left L'Orient for Pondicherry. On July 26, 1752, fire was discovered in the hold which rapidly spread over the ship. Only the yawl was got overboard, and the *Prince* finally blew up. Lieutenant De La Fond was taken into the yawl to help with navigation, and the ten men in the small boat were the only survivors of the *Prince.* The yawl reached the coast of Brazil August 3, 1752, where the survivors were well treated and sent back to Europe.

The shipwreck of a Portuguese vessel, with Emmanuel Sosa and his wife Eleonoro Garcia Sala, on the east coast of Africa, in 1553

See 4C, 1594.

Volume II

Narratives of shipwrecks, &c. &c. The loss of the Halsewell East
    Indiaman, wrecked off Seacombe, in the Isle of Purbeck, on
    the coast of Dorsetshire, January 6th, 1786
See 101C, 1786.

The sufferings of six deserters, during their passage in a whale boat
    from the island of St. Helena to Brazil
See 135C, 1802.

The loss of the Winterton East Indiaman, off the island of
    Madagascar, August 20th, 1792. By the Third Mate
The *Winterton* sailed from Gravesend for India with about 300 passengers and crew
    on March 10, 1792. All went well until Captain Dundas tried the Mozambique
    Channel; his navigation failed and the ship struck a reef off the coast of
    Madagascar on August 20, 1792. The ship broke up, and about 50 of those
    aboard were drowned. The survivors repaired the yawl and the Third Mate
    sailed her to Sofala on the mainland of Africa. There he hired a ship and
    eventually rescued about 130 people; the others had died of disease or hunger.

The loss of His Majesty's Ship Resistance, Captain E. Pakenham,
    Commander, which was blown up in the Straits of Banca, July
    24, 1798; and the subsequent escape and deliverance of four of
    her crew, the only survivors of the catastrophe
The *Resistance* was cruising among the East Indian islands, primarily concerned
    with keeping down native piracy. The ship blew up early on the morning of
    July 24, 1798; none of the four survivors had any idea of the cause of the explo-
    sion. About three hundred people lost their lives in the *Resistance*. The four
    survivors were captured by Malays and were eventually ransomed.

The loss of the Nottingham Galley, of London, wrecked on Boon
    Island, near New England, Dec. 11th, 1710; and the sufferings,
    preservation, and deliverance of the crew. By Captain John
    Dean
See 35C, 1711.

The providential deliverance of Charles Sturt, Esq. written by
    himself
Sturt, a wealthy gentleman and yacht—*yatch* in the narrative—owner, foolishly
    decided to leave his yacht in Weymouth harbor and sail his small boat home.
    He got into a race called the Shambles and capsized. After some hours of strug-
    gling in and out of the water-filled boat, he was rescued by the last ship to come
    near him. He did distribute fifty guineas to the crew of the ship that saved him,
    including five guineas each to the four sailors who manned the rescuing boat.

The loss of the Proserpine Frigate. In a letter addressed by Capt.
    Wallis to Vice-Admiral Dickson
The *Proserpine* was bound up the Elbe to Cuxhaven when she ran into ice so thick
    that it was impossible to proceed. Going down the river under a pilot, the ship
    struck on a sandbank off Newark Island and eventually broke up. Fourteen
    people, including a woman and child, were drowned or frozen in reaching
    shore over the ice. See 130C, 1799.

The loss of the Hindostan East Indiaman off Margate, January 11th, 1803

The *Hindostan* sailed from Gravesend for India January 2, 1803, passed the Nore, and anchored in the Queen's Channel off the Wedge Sand. There a terrible storm struck her, and she drove on the sandbank and broke up. A small boat of Margate rescued 129 out of 143 on the *Hindostan;* the dead were drowned or frozen. The ship was carrying a good deal of specie, much of which was saved from the wreck.

Deplorable situation of the crew of the French ship Le Jacques, on her return from Brazil to Europe, occasioned by an extraordinary famine, and the bad state of the vessel, in 1558

This narrative tells the story of some French Calvinists who attempted to set up a colony in Brazil. After great troubles with a Roman Catholic leader, about forty-five of the colonists set sail for France in a badly provisioned ship, the *Le Jacques.* The ship leaked and the people would have died had they not brought with them many parrots, which they had designed as gifts and used as food. After great troubles the ship reached the harbor of Blavet. Lery, the author, described an island off the coast of Brazil in quite unlikely terms, and I have some doubts about the authenticity of this story.

The adventures of Madame Denoyer, who was turned adrift in a boat, in the open sea, between the Bahama Islands and Cuba, in 1766

Mme. Denoyer, her husband, two children, and a female slave set sail from Samana for Cape Francois, both in St. Domingo, with two shipwecked English sailors for crew. On the second night the two Englishmen killed M. Denoyer and put his wife, the children, and the slave into a dugout canoe, which they set adrift. After seven days all were rescued by a ship which took them to New Orleans, where a subscription was raised for them. The two pirates were never captured.

The distresses of the unfortunate crew of the ship Anne and Mary, on her passage from Norway to Ireland, in the year 1759

See 72C, 1760.

Destruction by fire of the Dutch East Indiaman, the New Hoorn, near the Streights of Sunda, in the East Indies, 1619

See 17C, 1646.

Shipwreck of the Dutch East Indiaman the Batavia. On the rocks of Frederic Houtman, near the coast of Concordia, in New Holland, in 1630

See 18C, 1647.

Narrative of the shipwreck of M. De Brisson, on the coast of Barbary, and of his captivity among the Moors, written by himself

See 109C, 1789.

Narrative of the loss of the Wager Man of War, one of Commodore Anson's Squadron, and the subsequent distresses suffered by the crew, during a period of more than five years. By the Honourable John Byron

See 50C, 1743; 78C, 1768.

Extraordinary deliverance of four shipwrecked English seamen, found upon a shoal of ice near Spitzbergen, in the year 1646

A Dutch whaler, at Spitzbergen in June, 1646, discovered four English sailors alive in an ice cave on a berg floating near the island. They were apparently the last survivors of forty-two men who had lost their ship some time earlier. Three of the four died after being taken into the Dutch ship, so that only a single survivor reached England.

Shipwreck of the Jonge Thomas, a Dutch East Indiaman. At the Cape of Good Hope, June the 2d, 1773

The *Jonge Thomas* was caught by a violent hurricane while anchored in "the road" off the Cape. She dragged her anchors and struck on the sands at the mouth of the Zoul River, where she broke up. Sixty-three of the passengers and crew survived of 212. This narrative makes much of the local officials and soldiers doing nothing to save those on the vessel, even driving away those who came to help; they cared only that as much of the cargo should be saved as possible.

Narrative of the loss of the Apollo Frigate, and twenty-nine Sail of West Indiamen, near Figueras, on the coast of Portugal, April the 2d, 1804. By an officer of the Apollo

The *Apollo* and *Carysfort* were warships convoying sixty-nine merchantmen from Cork for the West Indies, March 26, 1804. A gale was encountered, but an observation was taken April 1, and there seemed to be plenty of sea room. On the next day, however, the *Apollo* and 29 merchantmen struck near Figueras and were lost. The *Apollo* broke in two and 61 men were drowned out of the 240 aboard. Forty or 50 people reached the shore on wreckage, and the others were at last taken off by a boat from shore. The commodore was blamed for the bad navigation.

Account of the loss of His Majesty's Ship Phoenix off Cuba, in the year 1780, by Lieutenant Archer

The *Phoenix* was one of thirteen ships of the Royal Navy lost in a terrible hurricane about October 1, 1780. The ship was helpless in the storm, and just as it was feared that she would founder she struck on the coast of Cuba. Most of the crew, about 250, were rescued by small ships from Jamaica after Archer had sailed a ship's boat to Montego Bay. Most of the other ships lost had no survivors. Archer's lively letter to his mother gives many details of the cruise and wreck.

Narrative of the dreadful shipwreck of the French ship Droits De L'Homme, of 74 guns, driven on shore the 14th of January, 1797. By Elias Pipon, Lieutenant of the 63rd Regiment

The *Droits de l'Homme,* named for Paine's book, and probably the source for the *Rights of Man* in Melville's *Billy Budd,* accompanied a military force attempting to invade Ireland. On the return voyage to France she was engaged by the British *Indefatigable* and *Amazon.* After a severe engagement the *Droits de l'Homme* and the *Amazon* both struck on the rocks at Hodierne Bay on the French coast. About half the men on the French ship, including many English prisoners, died before they were taken off the wreck by a cutter. This narrative also includes a letter from Captain Pellew, of the *Indefatigable.*

The loss of the Ramillies, of seventy-four guns, in the Atlantic Ocean, September the 21st, 1782: with particulars relative to other vessels which suffered in the same dreadful hurricane

The *Ramillies* was the flagship of a large convoy which sailed from Jamaica for England July 25, 1782. In the fleet were three other English warships and six French warships captured by Rodney in the Battle of the Saints. On September 16, in the North Atlantic, the fleet encountered one of the worst hurricanes ever experienced. The *Ramillies* was so buffeted that she had to be abandoned and burned; the crew was taken off by a merchant ship. For another narrative of a ship lost in this same storm, see 97C, 1783.

Explosion of His Majesty's Ship Amphion, of thirty-two guns, in Hamoaze, September 22, 1796

The *Amphion,* lying quietly in Plymouth Sound, blew up and was completely destroyed. There were apparently nine survivors of the three hundred or more on board. The cause of the explosion was never discovered, though a drunken gunner's selling powder was blamed by some.

The loss of the Prince George by fire, April 13, 1758. Described in letters from the survivors of that dreadful event

See 71C, 1758.

The loss of His Majesty's Ship Invincible, of seventy-four guns, on the sands called the Hamondsburg, off Winterton, March 16th, 1801

The *Invincible* set sail from Yarmouth for the Baltic fleet, and struck the same day on a sandbank. Two boats were hoisted out and carried some crew members and the admiral to a fishing smack, but could not reach the *Invincible* again. That ship, the next day, slid off the bank into deeper water and sank, drowning almost everyone on board. One hundred ninety-six people survived of about six hundred on board. Captain Rennie was lost with his first command.

The loss of His Majesty's Ship La Tribune, off Halifax, Nova Scotia, November 1797

The *La Tribune,* captured from the French and taken into the Royal Navy, sailed September 22, 1797, from Torbay with a convoy for Canada. Late in October they came in sight of the harbor of Halifax, and the master tried to enter the harbor without waiting for a pilot. The ship struck near Herring Cove, and soon sank. About 100 people survived in the tops and rigging, but the night was cold and most of them lost their holds and drowned. Twelve were saved out of about 240. A thirteen-year-old boy in a small boat was the first to save anyone out of the tops, though the people on shore were close enough to talk to those on the wreck.

Narrative of the loss of the Luxborough, and the providential escape and sufferings of Captain Boyce, in the year 1727. Written by himself

See 102C, 1787.

The loss of the Generous Friends, in the Chinese Sea, in November,
1801,from the account of Joseph Pinto, supposed to be the
only European belonging to the ship that was saved

The *Generous Friends,* Captain Porter, sailed from Macao in November, 1801.
Two days later, after steering SW by S, she struck on a reef among high
breakers. Part of the crew reached a sandbank, while most of the men, Manilla
"seconnies," stayed on the ship and tried to loot it. Many of the crew, with the
captain, set off on rafts and were never after heard of. A Chinese boat arrived
at the bank and looted the ship, in the process killing twelve lascars who tried
to seize their boat. The eighteen men remaining on the bank were finally taken
off by the Chinese and eventually reached Hainan. Joseph Pinto, the narrator
and only European survivor, reached Macao where he told his story.

Volume III

Narratives of shipwrecks, &c. &c. Loss of the Hindostan Storeship,
commanded by Captain F. Le Gros. Which was burned in the
Bay of Roses, April 2, 1804. Extracted, por favour, from the
Log-Book

On March 29, 1804, the *Hindostan* was caught in a storm off Cape St. Sebastian. A
few days later, on April 2, smoke was seen coming from the hold. The
magazine was flooded, and the ship run aground in the Bay of Roses, Spain.
All but three people were saved, and the whole crew was taken off by the *Juno.*
Captain Le Gros was acquitted of responsibility for losing his ship at a subsequent court martial.

Narrative of the adventures, sufferings, and deliverance, of eight
English seamen, left by accident in Greenland, in the year 1630

This narrative was written by Edward Pelham, gunner's mate of the ship *Salutation.* The ship left London for Greenland May 1, 1630, and arrived off the
coast of Greenland June 11, in search of whales and seals. Eight men went
ashore with a small boat to kill deer [reindeer?] and were left when a storm
blew up. They built a small house and lived off walruses and polar bears. On
May 25, 1631, two ships from Hull appeared and took them off. Pelham
reported that when he ate polar bear's liver, his skin sloughed off.

Shipwreck of the Sparrow-Hawk, a Dutch East Indiaman, on the
coast of the island of Quelpaert, in the Sea of Corea, the fif-
teenth of September, 1653

See 63C, 1752.

Narrative of the loss of the Russian ship St. Peter, on the coast of
Beering's Island, in the Sea of Kamtschatka, in 1741, and
subsequent distresses of the crew

The *St. Peter* and the *St. Paul* were exploring ships sent out by the Russian government. Bering captained the *St. Peter.* Both the ships were in bad shape when
the *St. Paul,* Captain Tschirikoff, parted. The crew got scurvy, Bering was
sick, and they landed on an island, and went ashore. The survivors began to
build a small vessel, and reached Petropawlowski August 27, 1742.

Narrative of the loss of His Majesty's Ship the Repulse, of sixty
four guns, on the coast of France, March 10, 1800. In a letter
from one of the officers

The *Repulse,* 64 guns, struck on the Mace Rock 25 leagues SE of Ushant March 10, 1800. The ship pulled off, but filled and struck again. Eleven of the crew died, but most reached the Glenen Islands and were taken prisoner. Thirteen men in the cutter reached Guernsey.

Narrative of the loss of His Majesty's Ship Namur, of seventy-four guns, near Fort St. David's in the East Indies, April 13, 1749. By Lieutenant James Alms

The *Namur,* of Admiral Boscawen's fleet, was anchored off Fort St. David's on April 12, 1749. A terrible hurricane struck the fleet and the *Namur* struck and broke up. Only twenty-three of five hundred aboard were saved. The *Pembroke, Lincoln,* and *Winchelsea* were also lost.

Narrative of the loss of His Majesty's Ship Pembroke, of sixty guns, on Colderoon Point, near Fort St. David, in the East Indies, April 13, 1749. By Mr. Cambridge, the Master

The *Pembroke,* caught in the same hurricane as the *Namur,* was dismasted, struck, and broke up. Only 12 of her crew survived of 342, and they were captured by Mahrattas and kept for about two months as prisoners before they escaped.

Narrative of the loss of His Majesty's Ship Litchfield, of 50 guns, on the coast of Barbary, November 30, 1758. By Lieutenant Sutherland

See 73C, 1761.

Shipwreck of a Spanish Frigate, on the coast of Mexico, in 1678; related by the Captain

This unnamed Spanish frigate left Panama for Caldera in Mexico in the spring of 1678. The ship tacked and veered, was caught by storms and calms, her people starved and thirsted, the captain complained, and the pilot wept and got drunk. The ship at last struck and was lost. It is hard to see how a short voyage could have been worse managed.

Narrative of the sufferings and extraordinary adventures of four Russian sailors. Who were cast away on the desert island of East Spitsbergen, in 1743

See 84C, 1774.

Narrative of the loss of the Cumberland Packet, on the coast of Antigua, in the hurricane of the 4th of September, 1804. By one of the officers

The *Cumberland,* anchored off Antigua September 3, 1804, was caught in a very severe storm and dragged her anchors. When she struck the next day all thirty-one people on board were saved on ropes strung from the ship to rocks on the shore. A number of other ships were also lost.

Narrative of the shipwreck of the English East Indiaman, the Fattysalam. On the coast of Coromandel, the 28th of August, 1761

This narrative is from a letter by M. de Kearney, a French officer captured by the British. About 500 British soldiers and some French prisoners set sail in the *Fattysalam* [Fattysalem], Ponticherry for Bengal, August 26, 1761. The ship leaked badly, and Captain de Kearney, the ship's captain, the pilot, two women, and about 20 others left the ship in a longboat. The *Fattysalam* and the 575 aboard her were never heard of again. Those in the boat reached the mouth of the Ganges after a week, and landed. After a short time as prisoners, and the deaths of 13, they reached Calcutta.

Narrative of the proceedings on board His Majesty's Ship the Theseus, Captain Edward Hawker, from the 4th to the 15th of September, 1804, in the hurricane which that ship encountered in the West-Indies

The *Theseus* and the *L'Hercule* were caught in a terrible hurricane in the West Indies on September 6, 1804. Both ships suffered a great deal, and the *Theseus* was dismasted and barely afloat when the storm ended. Both ships reached Port Royal safely but in bad condition.

The loss of His Majesty's Ship Venerable, of seventy four guns, Captain Hunter. Belonging to the Channel Fleet, under the command of the Hon. Admiral Cornwallis, in Torbay. Communicated by Lieutenant Nicholson, of His Majesty's Cutter, the Frisk Plymouth-Dock

The *Venerable,* caught in a bad storm in Torbay, November 24, 1804, went ashore near Rounden-Head, near Paignton. The *Frisk* cutter ran close to the wrecked ship and took off almost the whole crew by ropes from the stern. Only about fifteen men were lost.

The loss of His Majesty's Frigate the Ethalion, of thirty eight guns, which was wrecked on the coast of France, in the night, December 24, 1799

The *Ethalion* was keeping track of the French naval forces near Brest when she struck on rocks near the French coast. Her consort, the *Sylph,* helped to get all her crew off safely, and the *Ethalion* was burned as she lay.

The disaster attending the Margate Hoy. Near the village of Reculver, February 7, 1802

The *Margate* hoy, a small vessel owned at Reculver, took goods and passengers from Margate to London. On February 7, with four crew and twenty-eight passengers, she set out on a routine voyage. Caught in a slight storm, she struck on the Reculver sands and all but ten of her passengers were washed overboard and drowned. The whole affair seems to have been very badly managed, since the ship was later floated off the bank and repaired.

An account of the escape of Messrs. Carter, Shaw, and Haskett, of the Chesterfield Whaler, from the coast of New Guinea to Timor Island, in an open boat, in 1793

The *Chesterfield,* Norfolk Island for Batavia, discovered Tate Island and sent a boat's crew on shore. The natives attacked them, and the ship, thinking the men were killed, sailed away. These three men, with Carter very badly wounded, finally reached Timor with the help of natives met along the way.

Loss of the Brig Sally, Captain Tabry, bound from Philadelphia to Hispaniola, and the extraordinary distresses which the surviving part of the crew endured

The *Sally,* caught in a gale October 8, 1767, was hove on her beam-ends by a violent gust of wind, and then turned keel up. Five of the crew were drowned, six survived. After six days of work with a knife and nails they cut through the bottom and reached some beer which kept all but one alive until they were rescued by the brig *Norwich,* Captain Noyes, on November 1.

The distress of M. de St. Germain and his companions, in the deserts of Egypt, after a perilous navigation to Sues, March 24, 1799

This is not a shipwreck narrative. M. de St. Germaine, on parole after being captured in Egypt, sailed up the Red Sea and then set off in a caravan for the Mediterranean. They were attacked by Arabs, and only St. Germaine survived to reach Cairo.

Narrative of the loss of the American ship Hercules, Captain Benjamin Stout; on the coast of Caffraria, the 16th of June, 1796; together with a circumstantial detail of the disasters attending the crew in their long and painful journey over the southern regions of Africa to the Cape of Good Hope

See 127C, 1798.

Loss of His Majesty's Sloop, the Brazen, commanded by Captain J. Hanson, wrecked under a cliff near Newhaven, Sussex, January 25, 1800

The *Brazen,* caught in a bad storm, struck amid dangerous rocks near Newhaven. Though people on shore did their best, 105 men died and there was a single survivor. This man, a sailor who could not even swim, could not tell how the ship happened to be wrecked.

Loss of a Jamaica Sloop, commanded by Captain Nathaniel Uring, in 1711

See 43C, 1726.

The destruction of His Majesty's Ship Queen Charlotte, of 110 guns, Captain Todd, bearing the flag of Vice-Admiral Lord Keith; which took fire off the harbour of Leghorn, on the 17th of March, 1800

The *Queen Charlotte,* one of the largest ships of the Royal Navy, caught fire and blew up off Leghorn. Boats from nearby ships feared her shotted guns and probably also an explosion. When she blew up, only 164 escaped of the 900 aboard.

Loss of the ship Cornelia, Captain Bliss; wrecked in her passage to New York, July 11, 1804

The *Cornelia* probably struck a derelict. She was sinking when two other ships fortunately appeared and took off the fourteen men on board.

The loss of the ship Anne, Captain Knight, on a reef of rocks, five leagues to the northward of the southernmost Souhelepar Island, on the 19th of April, 1804. By an officer

The *Anne* struck on rocks off the coast of India. The crew threatened mutiny, and the officers and some men, fourteen in all, made the Malabar Coast in the long-boat. The rebellious crew left the wreck in the pinnace and apparently escaped.

Loss of His Majesty's Ship Romney, Hon. Captain Colville; which was unfortunately wrecked on the South Haak, off the Texel, November 19, 1804

Captain Colville blamed the loss of his ship on the pilot. The *Romney* struck on a sandbank and then broke up. Nine men were lost, and the rest all became prisoners of the Dutch on shore.

Narrative of the loss of the Brig Tyrrel, Captain Arthur Coghlan; which was overset in a gale of wind in her passage from New York to Antigua, July 18, 1759. Communicated by T. Purnell, the Chief Mate

See 77C, 1766.

Volume IV

Narratives of shipwrecks, &c. &c. Narrative of the wreck of the Bangalore, Captain Lynch. Which was wrecked on a coral bank, in the Indian Sea, April 12, 1802

The *Bangalore,* Amboyna for Batavia, struck on a coral bank on April 12. The ship broke up and those on board left her in the pinnace, jolly boat, and longboat, and towing a raft with sixty men. They landed on a number of islands, including Bali, and reached Batavia on May 18, 1802.

Narrative of the loss of the Bounty, through a conspiracy, and the sufferings &c. of those who were cast adrift in the boat, 1789. Commanded by Lieutenant W. Bligh

See 111C, 1790.

The sufferings and providential escape of some of the crew belonging to the Guardian Sloop, who quitted her in the launch, December 25, 1785

See 112C, 1790.

Narrative of the total loss of His Majesty's Ship the Bounty; including the transactions of the Mutineers, after they gained possession of the vessel. Extracted from the letters of Lieutenant Christian

This item is fiction, based on spurious letters of Fletcher Christian, who, according to this account, took the *Bounty* to South America. There he was supposed to have left her and settled down in the Spanish settlements. Obviously, there was much interest in what had happened to the mutineers.

The loss of the Yacht Ingebord, commanded by Capt. Anders, which was pitched upon a sand bank, December, 1802

This yacht struck a sandbank in the Baltic and was lost. Fishermen rescued four of the six people on board.

Narrative of the loss of the Peggy, of London, Capt. Knight, which foundered in the western ocean, October 26, 1785, communicated by one of the crew

The *Peggy* sailed in ballast from Waterford September 28, 1785. Three weeks later she was struck by a bad gale, developed leaks, and started to break up. The crew left her in a small boat as she foundered. All were picked up by a Philadelphia schooner which later transferred them to a brig sailing for Antigua.

A narrative of the losses and distresses experienced by the Squadron sent out by the Court of Spain, commanded by Don Joseph Pizarro, to intercept the expedition under Commodore Anson, in 1741. By Richard Walters, Chaplain of His Majesty's Ship the Centurion

Six Spanish ships set out to meet Anson's expedition to the Pacific. They suffered from storms and disease as did Anson's ships, and two ships were lost trying to round the Horn.

The shipwreck of Captain George Roberts, in his passage from Virginia to the coast of Guinea, in the year 1721

See 41C, 1726.

Narrative of the loss of the Earl of Abergavenny, East Indiaman, Captain John Wordsworth, which drove on the Shambles, off the Bill of Portland, and sank in twelve fathoms' water, February 5, 1805

See 146C, 1805.

The loss of the Corbin, commanded by Francis Pirard De Laval, on the Maldivia Islands

See 11C, 1618.

Narrative of the loss of the Antelope Packet, Captain Wilson. Which struck on breakers off Pelew Island, August 10, 1783

See 107C, 1788.

Dreadful catastrophe on board the John and Elizabeth, bound from Jersey to England, December, 1795

The *John and Elizabeth,* a small 35-ton ship, was hired to transport soldiers from Jersey to Portsmouth. One hundred twenty men and women were taken aboard. The ship encountered heavy weather and sprang a leak, and the passengers had to be sent below decks and the hatches battened down. When the ship reached Cowes Roads forty-eight men and three women were found to have died, probably from asphyxiation.

Sufferings of Robert Scotney, Second Mate of the Brig Thomas, Capt. Gardner, who survived by himself seventy-five days in a perfect wreck, 1803

Scotney was sent out from the *Thomas* in a shallop with three other men near Staten Island. His three companions were swept overboard in a gale and Scotney survived seventy-five days alone. He sailed for the Cape of Good Hope, but was picked up by the ship *Europe* when he was at the point of death.

Loss of the Charles Baring West Indiaman, Captain Aris, in 1799

This narrative is based on a letter from two passengers. The *Charles Baring* sailed from Port Royal, Jamaica, September 6, 1799. The ship sprang a bad leak and was barely kept afloat until September 23, when she sank in a gale. Of those on board, twenty-seven were lost, and the others escaped in the ship's boat. The narrative does not tell how they were rescued.

Sufferings of Ephraim How, of New-Haven, who set sail for New England in a small ketch, which was wrecked near Cape Sable, 1676

How left New Haven for Boston in a small ketch, made his voyage, and started back September 10, 1676. He ran into bad weather, was driven out to sea, and finally ran on rocks near Cape Sable. Three of his crew had died before the ship struck, and two others died on the island they took refuge on. How was alone for seven months before he was rescued. He reached New Haven in August of 1677.

Sufferings of Alexander Selkirk, who was left on Juan Fernandez, a desolate island, 1704

Selkirk was left on the island of Juan Fernandez September 1704, and lived alone there until he was taken off February 13, 1709. As everyone knows, his story was the basis for Defoe's *Robinson Crusoe.*

Loss of the Hartwell East Indiaman, Captain Fiott, near the island of Bona Vista, May 24, 1787

The *Hartwell* had sailed from England for China. The crew mutinied near the Cape Verde Islands, and the ship struck a reef northeast of Bona Vista. Apparently there was no loss of life. A court martial dismissed the captain and chief mate from the East India Company's service, so perhaps the crew was not entirely to blame.

Loss of the ship Nabby, Philip Chandell, Master. Which was wrecked near Bantry Bay, Dec. 25, 1804

The *Nabby* sailed from Liverpool for Boston, December 19, 1804. She sprang a bad leak and ran for Bantry Bay where she was run ashore. All on board were saved, but the country people stole the whole cargo.

Loss of the Doris, Capt. Campbell, which was wrecked between a reef of rocks near the mouth of the Loire, January, 1804

The *Doris* was cruising off the mouth of the Loire, struck a rock, and became waterlogged. The crew set fire to her and went on board two accompanying ships. The *Doris* exploded January 13, 1804.

Loss of the Industry Schooner, Captain Dwyer, which was wrecked near Portland, December 20, 1804

The *Industry,* of Saco, Portland to Monserrat with lumber, was caught in a storm and capsized December 20, 1804. Borne up by her cargo she floated for fifty-four days with her starving crew. They were rescued by the *New Century* of Boston, and taken to Dublin.

Loss of His Majesty's Ship the Tartarus. Captain Withers, on the sands in Margate Roads, December 20, 1804

The *Tartarus* was anchored in Margate Roads in a storm when her cable parted. The ship drove on the sands, but the men on board were rescued by two luggers from Margate. Only one man died.

Loss of His Majesty's Ship the Severn, commanded by Commodore d'Auvergne, Prince of Bouillon. Which was wrecked on the points of a rock near Grouville, December 21, 1804

The *Severn*, in bad shape from an earlier grounding, drove on a reef near Grouville Bay, and was lost. Everyone on board, more than five hundred, was saved by ropes passed to the shore.

Narrative of the loss of His Majesty's Ship La Determinée, of 24 guns, Captain A. Becher, which struck on a sunken rock, in working into Jersey Roads. March 26, 1803

Captain Becher made several attempts to find a pilot for his cruise to Jersey, but could not get one. He tried to follow the *Aurora* but struck a rock and lost his ship. Nineteen of the crew were drowned.

Account of an Indian woman, found on the south side of Athapuscow-Lake, west of Hudson's Bay, in January, 1772 [related in Hearne's Journey from Hudson's Bay to the Northern Ocean]

This is not, of course, a shipwreck narrative, and it is hard to see why it appears in Duncan's book. The Dog Rib woman had been captured by the Athapuscow Indians and had escaped.

Narrative of Peter Serrano, who lived seven years on a sandy island, on the coast of Peru [related by Garcilasso de la Vega]

Serrano claimed to have been shipwrecked on a small island off the coast of Peru where he lived alone for a time, and then with another shipwrecked sailor. After three years they were taken off the island.

Sufferings of an Englishman, cast upon a small island between Scotland and Ireland, in 1615

This unnamed Englishman was a passenger on a ship captured by pirates between Scotland and Ireland. He and a companion were put off in a small boat and landed on an island near Scotland. The other man died, and the Englishman lived alone on the island for a year before he was taken off by a Fleming.

Loss of the Dromedary Store-Ship, Captain B. W. Taylor, which was wrecked on her passage to Trinidad, August 10, 1800

The *Dromedary,* carrying stores to Trinidad, struck on rocks in the Gulf of Paria and was lost. All five hundred on board were saved.

Loss of His Majesty's Ship Danae. By a conspiracy, commanded by Lord Proby, March the 14th, 1800

There was a mutiny on the *Danae* March 14, 1800, led by a crew member named Jackson. The mutineers ran the ship into Camaret Bay and surrendered her to the French. According to this narrative, Jackson had been secretary to Parker, the leader in the mutiny of 1797.

Loss of His Majesty's Ship Nassau, of 64 guns, Captain George Tripp, Commander, which was wrecked on the North Haak Sand-Bank, off the Texel, October 25, 1799

The *Nassau* struck on the North Haak in a heavy gale. She put over one boat, but that capsized and all in her were lost. The next day the weather moderated, and ship's boats from the *Jealouse* took off 206 men. About 100 died.

Perilous situation of the American, Samuel (now Sir Samuel) Standige, Captain, in a voyage to Rhode Island, 1749

The *American* set sail from Hull for Newport in very bad shape, leaking and with an unwilling crew. Pumping all the way, she crossed the Atlantic, escaped the shoals of Nantucket and Block Island, and sailed into the harbor of Newport.

Narrative of the shipwreck of Mons. Pierre Viaud, and his consequent embarrassments, with Madame la Couture, on a desart island, February 1766

See 80C, 1768.

Loss of the Dutton East India ship, on the S.W. part of Mount Batten, January 26, 1796

The *Dutton* was caught in a very bad storm while at anchor at Plymouth, and was driven ashore. The ship of course broke up, but under the leadership of Sir Edward Pelew the rescue of the crew was very well handled. Only about three or four were lost of five hundred.

Account of the loss of His Majesty's Ships, the Porpoise and Cato, on a sand bank, off the coast of New Holland, Aug. 17, 1803. Communicated by Captain Flinders, of His Majesty's Ship the Investigator

These two ships, in company with Flinders's *Investigator,* struck together on a coral reef 700 miles north of Sydney. All the men were rescued, and Flinders set out for help in a cutter. The crews were taken off without trouble. See 142C.

Volume V

A Preface to this volume is dated Portsmouth, July 31, 1808, and refers to "The unparalleled reception which the Mariner's Chronicle has met with . . . (numerous and extensive impressions of the Work having been sold in a short space of time) has induced the Editor to increase the number of his volumes . . ."

Narratives of shipwrecks, &c. &c. Relation of the wreck of His Majesty's Ship, Porpoise, on a reef of coral in the Pacific Ocean, August 17, 1803. Lieutenant Robert Fowler, Commander. Including an account of the extraordinary preservation of the crew

This is an enlargement of the last narrative in Vol. IV. The *Porpoise* and *Cato* succeeded the *Investigator* as survey vessels, but were lost on a coral reef near the Australian coast on August 17, 1803. Almost all the men reached a small island, where they lived well enough on the ships' stores while they built a small vessel. Captain Flinders, however, who had sailed for Port Jackson in one of the ship's boats, returned with three vessels and took everyone off in safety.

The whole business was very well managed by Flinders and Fowler, and the point underlined that a ship which struck in calm weather was far more likely to be available for stores and tools than a ship striking during a storm.

Loss of the Raven Brig, which was wrecked on an enemy's coast, January 29, 1804

This narrative is chiefly a letter from an officer imprisoned in Spain; few details of the wreck are given. The *Raven,* apparently with troops aboard, found itself embayed in the enemy harbor of Cadiz. The ship struck but held together, and only two were killed in the wreck. All the survivors became prisoners.

The imminent dangers and wonderful escapes of William Okely, John Anthony, William Adams, John Jepps, and the carpenter, on board the Mary of London, who made their escape from slavery in Algiers, in a boat of their own building, June 30, 1644

See 75C, 1764.

Narrative of the loss of His Majesty's Ship, Athénienne on her passage to Malta, 1806. Captain Raynsford, Commander

The *Athénienne,* Gibraltar for Malta, struck on a reef named the Esquerques near Sardinia, and finally broke up completely. Three hundred forty-seven of those on board died, and 123 were saved. Most of the survivors were in the launch and were rescued by a Danish brig.

Loss of the Duke William, Transport, Captain Nicholls, Commander, which foundered at sea in 1758, with upwards of 300 French prisoners on board. Including the miraculous escape of some of her crew in open boats

The *Duke William* was a member of a convoy of ships taking troops and French prisoners from Canada to Europe after the fall of Louisburg. Early in December the ship encountered a severe storm, and after some days of stress started a butt. The leak was too much for the pumps, and the ship became waterlogged. There were fine resolutions about staying with the ship to the bitter end, but Captain Nicholls and a French priest somehow found themselves in the longboat with some of the crew. They reached England; 360 sank with the ship.

Interesting account of the distresses and adventures of John Cockburn and his companions, who were taken by a Spanish Guarda Costa in 1730, and sent on shore at Tiger Island, near Porto Cavello, naked and wounded

The *John and Anne,* London for Jamaica, sailed January 18, 1730. She was captured by pirates in the Caribbean and the crew set on shore on an island. They reached the mainland, and a few of them began a trek that went through Mexico and Central America to Panama. Cockburn finally reached England in 1732.

Seizure of a British vessel, and the consequent sufferings of Thomas Lindley, and others, after a voyage to Brazil, in 1802

This narrative is much like Cockburn's except that Lindley had his troubles in Brazil. Lindley was attempting to trade in Brazil. He was accused of trying to evade the laws on trade, his ship was seized, and he and his wife were thrown in jail. After various vicissitudes, Lindley and his wife escaped. The fate of the crew is not reported.

Narrative of the shipwreck of the Amazon Frigate, Captain Reynolds, which was wrecked in a Bay called Hodierne, January 14, 1797, during an engagement with a French ship, the Droits de l'Homme. Including particulars of the seafight, and of the captivity of the English

See Vol. II, loss of the *Droits de l'Hommes.* The crew of the *Amazon* was captured after the ship went ashore, and was marched some hundreds of miles to a prison. C. S. Forester may have used this narrative in one of his *Captain Hornblower* series, though he probably depended most upon the manuscript *Adventures of John Wetherell,* who was captured in the *Hussar* and made the same journey.

Narrative of the loss of the Michael, of London, Richard Hutton, Commander, which struck upon the Caskets, near Alderney, January 7, 1701; and of the wonderful deliverance of nine of the crew

The *Michael* struck on the well-known reef in the Channel Islands, and broke up. Six of the fifteen on board were drowned. The nine others got on the rocks and stayed alive by eating shellfish and their dog, and drinking rainwater, till they were taken off by a small ship from Guernsey.

Narrative of the loss of the General Barker, East Indiaman, Captain James Todd, which was wrecked off Scheveling on the coast of Holland, February 17, 1781

The *General Barker* sailed from Madras for London in February, 1780, stopping at Madagascar, the Cape, and St. Helena. She touched at Crookhaven in Ireland, where Sir Thomas Rumbold and his family left the ship. She ran into a terrible storm in the Channel in February, 1781, dragged her anchors in the Downs, struck and drove over the Kentish Knock, and at last struck off Scheveling, on the Dutch coast. Most of those on board were taken off by two Dutch schutes, but twenty-five died. The survivors were made prisoners.

Loss of the ship Amicus, from Petersburgh, Captain Simpson, Commander which struck on the Holderness coast, December 8, 1807

This ship, of Hull, struck near Holderness. Four of those on board were rescued by people on shore, but five died.

Narrative of the loss of the Brig Ann, of Newcastle, Robert Potter, Commander, which was driven among mountains of ice, July 30, 1807, while on a voyage to Archangel. Including the miraculous preservation of the Captain and his crew, after being twenty-two days in an open boat at sea, in a frozen climate

The *Ann,* Newry in Ireland for Archangel, was caught in a bad storm and driven among icebergs. The ship struck on one, and sank. The crew put off in a small boat, hoping to make Jan Mayen or the Norwegian coast. They left their ship on July 30, 1807, and were rescued by Norwegian fishermen and taken to

Drontheim twenty-two days later. A number of the survivors had to have their legs amputated because of freezing.

Narrative of the shipwreck of M. Durand, formerly Governor of Isle St. Louis, in the Brigantine l'Aimable Marthe, on the coast of Wales, 1786

This French ship, Senegal for Le Havre, got off course in a bad storm and found herself in the Bristol Channel. She struck on the coast of Wales on September 13, 1786. All on board got ashore and were taken in at the country mansion of a Captain Trollope. M. Durand received much help from Captain Trollope, and reached France in safety.

Loss of the Brig Flora, of Philadelphia, on a whaling voyage to Cayenne and South America, 1804

The *Flora* ran into a terrible storm early in her cruise, and foundered. Five died, and the survivors tried cannibalism. They were rescued by the snow *Thames,* of London.

Loss of the Wakefield Merchantman, in 1806, commanded by Captain Bruce

The *Wakefield* lost touch with other ships in a convoy October 30, 1806. The next day the ship struck on the coast of Portugal, and only three of her complement survived.

Account of the loss of the Betsey Schooner, bound for New South Wales, William Brooks, Commander, November 24, 1805

The *Betsey,* Macao for New South Wales, with ten on board, struck a reef November 21, 1805. The crew left the wreck in a jolly boat and raft, but the raft was lost and never heard of again. Those in the jolly boat landed at Benguey, where Malays killed two of them including the captain. The others were captured and the three survivors were ransomed a month later.

Loss of His Majesty's Ship Boreas, upon the Hannois Rock, November 28, 1807. George Scott, Esq. Captain

The Hannois Rock is near Guernsey. Thirty were saved out of the *Boreas;* some were lost, including Captain Scott.

Account of the shipwreck of Jean Jacques Aymé, on the coast of Scotland, 1799

Aymé, imprisoned during the French Revolution, was sent to Guiana as a prisoner. After a year he escaped in an American ship bound for Gothenburgh. The ship encountered a very bad storm in the North Sea, and at last struck on the coast of Scotland, near Fraserburgh. Most of those on board were lost, but Aymé and a few others were taken off the wreck by a boat from shore. Aymé at last returned to France.

Loss of the Ter Schelling, including the various calamities of the crew during an unfortunate voyage to Bengal in 1661

This ship, Batavia for Bengal, struck on reefs and foundered. The crew put together a raft, but all on it were lost. Another raft, with twenty people on it, reached shore. After starvation and deaths, the survivors were forced into the Mogul's army. They were finally freed, and reached Holland in 1673. See 23C, 1675.

Narrative of Captain Kennedy's distresses, from losing his vessel at sea, December 23, 1768

Kennedy's ship, Port Royal for Whitehaven, with twelve on board, sank in a bad storm. All on board got off in a yawl with a little food, and the six survivors finally reached an island off Honduras, and safety.

Narrative of the loss of the Sidney, which ran upon a dangerous rock or shoal, May 20, 1806. A. Forrest, Commander, and of the subsequent preservation of the greater part of her crew. Copied from the Captain's account, as published in an Indian paper, called "The Asiatic Mirror," dated Calcutta, October 14, 1806

See 151C, 1806.

Account of the loss of the Hon. East India Company's Ship, Ganges, which foundered off the Cape of Good Hope, May 29, 1807. T. Harington, Commander, and of the miraculous preservation of all the crew

The *Ganges,* in bad shape with a leak, simply filled with water and sank on a fine clear day. The *St. Vincent,* in company, received first the passengers and then the crew. All 209 on board were saved.

Narrative of the loss of the Portuguese ship, Bowaniong, Captain John Nepremassena, which struck upon a narrow insulated rock on her passage from Calcutta towards China, June 17, 1807

This ship, Calcutta for China, with sixty on board, ran into two severe gales which strained the ship so badly that she had to be run on shore, apparently on the coast of Ava. The captain and a few others drowned when the ship broke up, but most of those on board escaped in the longboat and on rafts. They were made prisoners on shore, but most finally reached Calcutta.

Shipwrecks of James Sadeur, who was cast upon an unknown island, December, 1623, where he lived thirty-five years. Including a description thereof, and of its inhabitants

This narrative is said to have been printed in Paris in 1693. It may be the truth, but it certainly reads like fiction. Sadeur claimed that he had been captured by pirates, and that their ship had sunk and he had been saved by a Portuguese ship. He claimed to have visited the Congo, the Cape, and Madagascar, and to have been shipwrecked on what he claimed to be Australia. He escaped to Madagascar and eventually returned to France.

Loss of the Sussex Indiaman, in 1738; and the wonderful escape of John Dean, and four others of the crew

See 48C, 1740.

Famine on board the Dolphin Sloop, 1759, and the remarkable preservation of eight persons, who had been one hundred and fifteen days without food

The captain of the *Andalusia* reported finding the *Dolphin,* the Canaries for New York, dismasted and drifting. Those on the *Dolphin* had been without food for 115 of the 165 days of their voyage. They had cast lots, and killed and ate a passenger. A somewhat similar experience on the *Asia,* a Spanish ship in pursuit of Anson, completes the narrative.

Loss of the Pandora Frigate, Captain Edwards, Commander, which struck on a reef of rocks, Aug. 28, 1791

See 119C, 1793.

Sufferings of Captain Youl, &c. of the Fly Cruiser, in 1804

The *Fly,* an East Indiaman, was captured in the Gulf of Persia by a French privateer, *La Fortune.* Captain Youl, of the *Fly,* threw overboard a packet of dispatches, and after obtaining freedom went back to the Isle of Khen to retrieve the packet. He succeeded, but was captured by Arab pirates. Many of his crew, and Youl himself, died before some were rescued.

Shipwreck of Carl Ehric, a Prussian sailor, in the Snow Hope of Liverpool. And his wonderful preservation, Feb. 1, 1715

The *Hope* struck near Spurn Point and broke up. Ehric was the only survivor.

Narrative of the loss of the ship Fanny, Captain Robertson, Commander, November 29, 1803. Including the wonderful preservation of a part of the crew after remaining several weeks upon rocks in the centre of the Chinese Ocean

See 149C, 1805.

Brief but interesting narrative of the loss of His Majesty's Ship Flora, upon the Schelling Reef, Monday, January 18, 1808

The *Flora* struck on the Schelling Reef, got off, and was so badly damaged that she had to be run ashore. Apparently all on board were saved though the ship was lost.

Narrative of the loss of the American ship Golden Rule. Captain Austin, Commander, which sprung a leak, September 29, 1807, and of the sufferings of the crew

The *Golden Rule* sailed from Wiscasset with a cargo of lumber. She was caught in a severe gale, sprang a leak, and filled. Three of those on board died of hunger and thirst, but the ship *George* of Portland took off the survivors.

Narrative of the unfortunate loss of His Majesty's Ship, Ajax, by fire, February 14, 1807

The *Ajax* was cruising off the Dardanelles when there was an alarm of fire. Three hundred of the four hundred on board escaped before she blew up the next morning.

The sufferings of Captain Donald Campbell, in a journey overland to the East Indies. Including his disastrous shipwreck in his passage from Goa to Madras, May 12, 1782

See 123C, 1796.

Dreadful massacre of Captain Oliver Porter, and the crew of the Atahualpa, by the Indians, in the year 1805

See 152C, 1806. The story in *Mariner's Chronicle* states that ten of the twenty-three on board were killed, and nine wounded. These figures are somewhat different from those of the Hartford *Courant* story.

Interesting account of the shipwreck and subsequent melancholy fate of Machin discoverer of Madeira

This narrative is taken from J. S. Clarke's *Progress of Maritime Discovery*. In the time of Edward III, Robert à Machin is supposed to have fallen in love with Anna d'Arfet. They eloped from Bristol and discovered the Madeira Islands. The ship was later wrecked on the coast of Morocco, and both of the lovers died.

Hearne's relation of the shipwreck of Captain Knight, Captain Barlow, and Captain Vaughan, with several of their men, on Marble Island, Hudson's Bay, in the year 1719

The *Albany* and the *Discovery,* two small ships, sailed from Gravesend for Hudson's Bay in 1719 to look for copper mines reported by the natives. They were not heard from certainly until 1767, when evidence of settlement was discovered on Marble Island in northwest Hudson's Bay. Apparently the crews had lived there for some years and at last had all died.

Narrative of the adventures of Captain Robert Johnson, from his first leaving England for Madras, in the year 1768, to his return to England, in 1776

This is not a shipwreck narrative at all, though a storm at sea is described. Johnson saw much of India, hunted tigers, fought against the natives, and served as a judge. He died soon after returning to England.

Destruction of His Majesty's Sloop, Trincomalee, and the Iphigène, French Privateer, in October, 1799

The *Pearl,* a British ship, was captured by a French privateer, the *Iphigène*. A few days later the two ships encountered a British sloop, the *Trincomalee,* and a severe battle developed. The *Trincomalee* blew up, and the *Iphigène* was so damaged by the explosion that she also sank. The *Pearl* picked up a few survivors.

Volume VI

Narratives of shipwrecks, &c. &c. Affecting narrative of the loss of the Agatha, Captain Koop, Commander, which was stranded on the Suder Hacken, near Memel, April 7, 1808, by which unfortunate event, thirteen persons lost their lives

The *Agatha* left Liebau for Carlscrona April 3, 1808, and was caught in a bad storm soon after. The ship turned back to seek safety at Memel, but struck on Memel Bar and was lost. Many of those on board were washed off, and one boat was capsized. Eleven were saved by a lifeboat, and thirteen died, among them Lord Royston, son of the Earl of Hardwicke.

Interesting narrative of the sufferings of Mr. Hore, and his companions, on a voyage of discovery to Cape Breton and Newfoundland, in the year 1536

This expedition seems to have been as foolishly conducted as it could possibly have been. One hundred twenty people sailed from Gravesend for Cape Breton and Newfoundland in the 140-ton *Trinity* in April, 1536. Apparently Mr. Hore hoped to establish a settlement on Newfoundland. The supplies gave out, and the settlers were forced into cannibalism. At last they were able to steal supplies from a French ship, and got back to England in October, 1536.

Account of the remarkable manner in which His Majesty's Ship the Elephant, was struck by lightning, on the 21st of November, 1790. The following brief narrative is from the pen of one of the officers of the Elephant, who was on board at the time of the accident

The *Elephant,* apparently in harbor, was struck by lightning and the main mast shattered. No other significant damage was done.

Interesting narrative of the perilous voyage of Captain Norwood, as Officer in the Army under Charles I. And of the sufferings of him and his companions, on a desert island, on the coast of North America, in the years 1649–50. Written by Himself

Captain Norwood, a Cavalier, left England for Virginia in the ship *Virginia Merchant,* Captain Locker, about August 15, 1649. The ship was crank, and they ran into storm after storm, so that they were forced to eat rats, and some died of starvation. The ship at last reached Virginia, but Norwood left it and made his way to the settlements, with the help of Indians, by land and canoe.

Account of the loss of His Majesty's Frigate Anson. Captain Lydiard, Commander, which was run on shore, near Helstone, December 29, 1807

The *Anson* left Falmouth to join the blockade off Brest, but was embayed off the Lizard in a storm from the west. She anchored, but the cables parted and the ship ran aground on the bar at Loe Pool. She broke up, and many on board, including Captain Lydiard, were swept off and drowned. Some of the crew reached shore on the mainmast.

Remarkable preservation of the crew of a Danish vessel, from shipwreck

A Danish ship had struck on the coast of Norway. The British *Orpheus* happened upon the wreck, but could do nothing for five days. When the storm had subsided men from the *Orpheus* saved nine men; one had died.

Dangerous, and almost fatal voyage of Lord Hutchinson in the Astrea Frigate, in the year 1806

The *Astrea,* cruising off Denmark, was hit by a terrible storm in early December, 1806. The ship struck on a reef near the isle of Anholt, but she beat over the rocks, was jury-rigged, and limped into harbor on the Danish coast.

Loss of the Astrea Frigate, on the island of Anagada, in the year 1808

This same *Astrea* frigate was lost two years later in the West Indies. She was cruising in the Mona Passage, and struck on the isle of Anagada May 23, 1808. Four men were lost; and the rest were taken off the wreck by British ships.

Surprising heroism, and lamentable catastrophe of Captain Engledue, and his ship's crew, on the coast of Gambia, in the year 1759

Engledue was apparently the captain of a small ship engaged in the slave trade. He had sailed upriver to the country of the Cassinkas, where he was attacked. Engledue was wounded and the ship about to be taken when he had a powder train laid to the magazine and blew up the ship. Engledue and eight of his slave crew were killed, along with about forty of the Cassinka attackers.

Shipwreck, and extraordinary adventures, of Monsieur Saugnier, on the western coast of Africa, in the year 1784

See 114C, 1791.

Distressing account of the piratical seizure of the Brig, Admiral Troubridge, by part of her crew, in the Indian Seas, in the year 1807

The *Admiral Troubridge* was anchored off Sooloo August 21, 1807. The captain and some others of her complement were on shore when the ship set sail. The captain and first mate set off in a boat, but were fired at when they approached the ship. The lascars on board had mutinied under the sailing master, killed two officers and the gunner, and had made off with the ship.

Loss of the Queen, East Indiaman, by fire, on the coast of Brazil, in the year 1800

Fire broke out on the *Queen* at 2 A.M. on July 9, 1800. She blew up at 7 A.M. Seventy-six of her people died, and about three hundred were saved by the *Kent,* which sent off this report.

Historical and descriptive narrative of the shipwrecks, dangerous adventures, and imminent escapes of Captain Richard Falconer. Written by Himself. Part the first

Historical and descriptive narrative of the shipwrecks, dangerous adventures, and imminent escapes of Captain Richard Falconer. Written by Himself. Part the second

Historical and descriptive narrative of the shipwrecks, dangerous adventures, and imminent escapes of Captain Richard Falconer. Written by Himself. Part the third

See 40C, 1720.

Account of the perilous adventures of four Russian sailors, on the island of Unalaska, in the South Sea, in the year 1764

This narrative comes out of the Russian exploration of the Aleutians. The four men involved fought with the Eskimos and were caught on Unalaska when their boat was wrecked. They lived in a cave on the island and got off at last, probably reaching a ship.

Interesting narrative of the loss of His Majesty's Schooner, Felix, Captain Cameron, Commander, January 22, 1807, when every soul on board perished, except one

The *Felix* was ordered to Santander to pick up prisoners in an exchange. The Spanish authorities ordered the ship out of the harbor in spite of a very bad storm, and fired on the ship when the captain tried to stay at anchor. The *Felix* set sail, but was dismasted and driven on shore. Of seventy-nine on board only a Mr. Ellard survived.

Melancholy fate of the Cato, Admiral Sir Hyde Parker, on her passage to the East Indies, in the year 1783

The *Cato* sailed for the East Indies in October, 1782, and was never heard from until 1791 when a British captain saw a bucket in use in an Indian port with *Cato* on it. Natives reported that a large ship had struck on the Malabar coast, and that the survivors of the wreck were killed by natives.

Account of the loss of His Majesty's Ship Courageux, Captain Hallowell, with 470 of her crew, in the Mediterranean, in the year 1796

This ship was caught in a terrible storm at Gibraltar, and struck on the African shore December 18, 1796. One hundred twenty-two men got ashore, but about 470 were lost with the ship.

Account of the shipwreck of a Venetian ship, commanded by Pietro Quirino, on the island of the Saints, on the coast of Norway, in the year 1431. Related by Christoforo Fiorananti, and Nicholo di Michiel, two of the unfortunate sufferers

See 1C, 1550.

Account of the murder of Captain Johnstone, of the Perseverance; together with his officers and crew; and the destruction of that ship, by some Manilla men who were on board, in the year 1805

This ship, Penang for Pegue, was taken in a mutiny April 19, 1805. The Filipinos killed the officers and passengers, plundered the ship, and then set it on fire, burning to death all the lascar crew. One passenger, an Armenian, escaped and told the story.

Account of the sufferings and escape of Captain Woodard and four seamen, who lost their ship, while in a boat at sea, and afterwards endured a captivity of two years and a half, amongst the Malays

See 144C, 1804.

Critical situation and providential escape of Commodore Anson's ship, the Centurion, on the coast of South America

This narrative is a short section from Walter's narrative of Anson's voyage. The *Centurion,* its crew weakened terribly by scurvy, was caught in a hurricane off the coast of Chile and barely made the island of Juan Fernandez where the crew rested and recruited. See 57C, 1748.

Destruction of His Majesty's Ship Boyne, by fire, at Spithead, in the year 1795; with an account of a surprising instance of preservation, previously to her explosion

The *Boyne,* peacefully at anchor, caught fire, drifted ashore, and exploded at 6 P.M. on May 1, 1795. Only eleven men were lost.

Shipwreck of the Providence, Captain Broughton, in a voyage of discovery to the North Pacific Ocean, in the year 1797

This ship sailed from England on an exploring and surveying expedition to the Pacific, touching at the Sandwich Islands and surveying a part of the northeast coast of Asia. She struck on a reef near Formosa May 17, 1797, and broke up. All on board were taken off by an accompanying schooner.

Wonderful preservation of a seaman, on a shoal of ice, in the North Sea

A ship was wrecked on a sandbank off Cuxhaven and three seamen reached an ice flow on the bank. Two of them died but one was found on the drifting ice two months later.

Loss of the American ship, Rose in Bloom, on the coast of South Carolina, in the month of August, 1806

This ship sailed from Charleston and was caught in a very bad storm a week later. She went on her beam ends but righted when the masts were cut away. Her cargo of cotton kept the ship afloat. The *Swift* of St. John's, Captain Phelan, took off the survivors and reached New York with them. Apparently there was heavy loss of life, though this narrative does not give any numbers.

Extraordinary preservation of the life of Richard Devoe, a sailor lad on board the Schooner Mary, Seth Wadsworth, Master, which was lost on her passage from Curracoa for Greenock, in 1806

Devoe climbed on the booby hatch when the *Mary* capsized, and was picked up by a passing vessel. Apparently he was the only survivor of the wreck.

Shipwreck of the San Juan Principe, Captain Lobo, a Portuguese Frigate, off Gibraltar, in the year 1807

This story is told in a letter from Alexander Wilson, who helped to save a number of the survivors of this wreck. Nothing is told of the wreck itself, since Wilson became involved only after the ship had struck.

Dreadful consequences of the shipwreck of the Aeneas, transport, off Newfoundland, in the year 1805; from which, out of 347 souls, only seven were preserved

The *Aeneas* struck on a rock off Newfoundland, October 23, 1805. Only 7 of 354 on board survived; they were saved by hunters who found them on the shore.

Interesting narrative of the loss of the Glasgow Packet, of Leith, Captain Johnson, off Farn Island, in the year 1806

This ship struck on the Farn Islands, apparently because of the pigheadedness of an old sailor who was steering. Eleven died when the crew rowed away and left them on the wreck. The surviving passengers were taken off in a lifeboat.

Narrative of the loss of the Alexander, an English transport. From Monte Video, in the year 1807

The *Alexander* was carrying 110 people when she sprang a leak and foundered in the Atlantic. Thirteen were saved in one boat and 6 in another; all the rest were lost. There was cannibalism in one boat.

Loss of the Nymph Schooner, and singular preservation of one of her crew, in the year 1802

The *Nymph,* Philadelphia for Charleston, struck on the Cape Lookout Shoals and broke up. Of nine on board only one, John Kelly, was picked up and survived.

Adventures of Captain Keith, during his residence in North America

This is not a shipwreck narrative, and reads like fiction. Keith came to the United States to make his fortune, claimed to have been captured by Indians—a *very* unlikely story—and at last returned to England, where he found prosperity by winning a lottery.

Shipwreck of the Two Friends Transport

This ship, sailing for Canada, struck a rock on Cape Breton Island. Three died, and the others on board were saved by a boat from shore.

Account of the captivity of Mr. J. L. Turner, amongst the Ladrones, in the year 1807. Written by Himself

This is a narrative of some interest for its picture of life on the China coast. Turner was captured by the Ladrones, somewhat like a guild of pirates, and was ransomed for $2500 after 5 ½ months of captivity.

An account of the adventures of Captain Howel Davis; together with the daring piracies with which he was concerned in various parts of the world

This is not a shipwreck narrative at all. It seems to be taken from Johnson's *History of the Pyrates.*

Extraordinary escape of Captain Freeman, and five other Masters of vessels, from a Danish prison, in the summer of 1808

Freeman and twenty other captains of ships were in prison in Denmark, in North Jutland. They escaped June 20, 1808, and reached Heligoland in a stolen boat.

Distressing account of the voyage of the Schooner Little Patty. Greenman Grere, Master, with a melancholy relation of her foundering in the Gulph, and the sufferings of her unfortunate crew, in the year 1806

This small ship, Charleston for St. Mary's, was caught in a bad gale, developed leaks, and foundered. Seventeen of the crew got off in a boat and were picked up by the brig *Polly.* Four of the seventeen died.

Loss of the King George Packet. Off Parkgate, Ireland, in the year 1806

According to this somewhat confused account, the *King George* sailed from Parkgate for Dublin September 21, 1806. She struck on a sandbank and foundered. There were about 100 Irish harvestmen on board plus crew, under hatches, and according to this story they killed each other with knives to reach the deck. Six lived, and 125 died.

Account of Peter Serrano, who having escaped from shipwreck, lived seven years on a sandy island, on the coast of Peru

This is almost exactly the same story given in Vol. IV. The first line and the last paragraph have been slightly changed; otherwise the two accounts of Peter Serrano are exactly alike.

Capture of the General Washington, by two Barbary Galleys

This ship, New Orleans for Smurny [Smyrna?], was attacked by two galleys and captured. There ensued a bad storm, and both a galley and the *General Washington* were wrecked. The writer of the narrative was sold to a Jew at Tripoli, but he later stole a boat and reached Malta, from which he reached England.

Account of the loss of the Blanche Frigate, on the French coast, March 8, 1807. As communicated by her late Commander, Sir Thomas Lavie

The *Blanche* sailed from Portsmouth March 3, 1807. She struck on the French coast and was lost, with 250 saved out of about 300 on board. The survivors were captured and marched to Brest.

Remarkable escape from shipwreck, and preservation at sea, of Mr.
Dominicus, and a man named Wild French

This short anecdote tells of a shipwreck in 1729 or 1730 in the Mediterranean, in
which a Mr. Dominicus, later a captain in the service of the East India Company, saved an orphan boy called Wild French. The two floated on a plank to
the Barbary coast and were later released from captivity there. Wild French
became a captain in the Royal Navy, and a wealthy man.

144C.   WOODARD, DAVID [Vaughan, William, compiler and editor]
The narrative of Captain David Woodard and four seamen, who
lost their ship while in a boat at sea, and surrendered
themselves up to the Malays, in the island of Celebes; containing an interesting account of their sufferings from hunger and
various hardships, and their escape from the Malays, after a
captivity of two years and a half: also an account of the manners and customs of the country, and a description of the har-
bors and coast, &c. Together with an introduction, and an appendix, containing narratives of various escapes from shipwrecks, under great hardships and abstinence; holding out a
valuable seaman's guide, and the importance of union, con-
fidence, and perseverance, in the midst of distress. "There's a
sweet little cherub sits perch'd up aloft, To keep watch for the
life of poor Jack." Dibdin
London, printed for J. Johnson, 72, St. Paul's Church-Yard, by S.
Hamilton, Shoe-Lane, Fleet-Street, 1804

Woodard, an American, had sailed from Boston to India, and was appointed chief
mate of the American ship *Enterprise,* Captain Hubbard, on a voyage from
Batavia to Manila. In the Straits of Macassar the ship was held up by contrary
winds, and ran short of food. Woodard and five crewmen were accordingly
sent off in a boat to ask for food from a country ship in sight. While they were
on that ship, which had no extra food, the *Enterprise* sailed out of sight, and
they were unable to find the ship though they plied back and forth in the straits
for a week. They were finally forced to go ashore on Celebes, where one man
was killed and the others captured by natives. They were not badly treated after
the first few days, learned the language, were offered native wives, and could
have settled there. Woodard, however, kept trying to reach Macassar, and
after two years and five months of captivity he and the other four men landed
there on June 15, 1795. The Dutch governor provided them with clothes, food,
and money, and sent them to Batavia where they found an American ship.
Woodard later met the captain of the ship he had lost in the straits, who said
that he had waited for them for three days, and had then thought they must
have been captured by natives.

This narrative gives a good deal of material about the life of the natives of
the Celebes, but probably the most valuable portion of the book is the collection of narratives of shipwrecks and disasters at sea. Woodard's collection was
almost certainly used by Archibald Duncan for the later volumes of the
Mariner's Chronicle.

Appendix
No. I.   Robert Scotney's case. The following account was
received by Messrs. Peter and William Mellish, on the

A list of a number of accidents, shipwrecks, and escapes, where
   great hardships and difficulties have been encountered, and
   which many have survived by perseverance

	Accidents, &c. No. I. Loss of the Centaur man of war, Sept. 1782. Capt. Inglefield's account, printed for J. Murray, 1783
II.	Lieut. Bligh's narrative, from his quitting the Bounty Sloop, until his arrival at the island of Timor
III.	Genuine account of the loss of the Sussex Indiaman, off the coast of Madagascar, in 1738.—Vide John Dean's account, printed for T. Cooper in 1740
IV.	An account of the escape of Messrs. Carter, Shaw, and Haskett, from the coast of New Guinea, to Timor Island, in an open boat, in 1793.—Vide Oriental Repertory, vol. i. No. IX. March 17, 1795, and the Oriental Repertory, page 521
V.	Capt. Kennedy's narrative of the loss of his ship at sea, and of the distresses of himself and crew in an open boat; communicated to his owners.—Vide Annual Register, vol. xii, page 191, for 1769
VI.	Capt. Bartlett's account of a white man and a negro boy, taken up in a canoe, nineteen days from Grenada to Jamaica without food
VII.	The loss of the Pandora Frigate, on a voyage round the world in 1790 to 1792. By Mr. George Hamilton, the surgeon. Printed for W. Phorson of Berwick, and Law of London, 1793
VIII.	The case of Robert Scotney, seaman, 1803
IX.	The account of some deserters from St. Helena.—Calcutta Gazette, July 8, 1802
X.	Case of four seamen of the Randolph Frigate, picked up at sea on a raft, after being four days without food
XI.	Case of Mr. Dominicus, and of a boy called Wild French
XII.	Loss of the Wager Man of War, Capt. Cheap, in the South Seas, in May, 1740. Four separate accounts were published of this shipwreck. 1st. By John Bulkeley and John Cummins, late gunner and carpenter. Printed for Jacob Robinson, 1743
2d.	Isaac Morris's (midshipman) narrative of himself and seven others, left on shore in an uninhabited part of Patagonia, with their adventures. Printed for S. Birt, London; and A. Tozer of Exeter
3d.	Alexander Campbell's narrative; midshipman. Printed for W. Owen. 1747
4th.	Hon. John Byron's narrative; midshipman. Printed for Baker and Leigh, 1768

XIII.   Dampier's voyages.—Rogers's voyages

XIV.   Loss of the Investigator, the Porpoise, and the
           Cato.—Vide the Morning Herald paper in May or
           June, 1804

XV.   Narrative of the Deportment of Barthelemy and
           Pichegru, and others, to Cayenne, in 1797.—By
           General Ramel. Printed for Wright, 1799

XVI.   Loss of the Antelope Packet, Capt. Wilson, off the
           Pelew Islands, in 1783. Published by Keate

XVII.   Loss of the Doddington East-Indiaman, on a rock near
           the Cape of Good Hope, on the 17th of July 1755.—
           Vide Annual Register, vol. 1, page 297, for 1758

XVIII.   Loss of the Juno; wrecked on the coast of Pegou, June
           1797.—Vide William Mackay's second officer's ac-
           count. Printed for Debrett, 1798

XIX.   Loss of the Fazy Allum near Cape Orfoy, in
           1801.—Vide Asiatic Register, vol. i, page 17, for 1802

XX.   Loss of the Grosvenor Indiaman on the coast of
           Africa, 4th of August 1782.—Vide Alexander Dalrym-
           ple, Esq's. account, taken from four survivors. Printed
           for J. Sewell, Cornhill, 1785
           William Hubberley's account of ditto
           Narrative of two sailors' account of ditto. Printed for
               B. Pownall, 1783
           John Hyne's account of ditto. By George Carter.
               Printed for Lane, 1791

XXI.   Loss of the ship Hercules, Captain Benjamin Stout, on
           the coast of Caffraria, the sixteenth of June, 1796; with
           the travels of the survivors through the country.
           Printed for Johnson, 1798

XXII.   Shipwreck of the Nottingham Galley. By John Deane,
           commander. Printed in 1711 and 1726

XXIII.   Loss of the Litchfield Man of War, Capt. Barton, on
           the coast of Africa, and part of the crew carried into
           slavery. By Lieut. Sutherland. Published by T. Davis,
           1768

XXIV.   Capt. David Harrison's account of his distresses and
           deliverance in the Peggy, from Fayal to New-York.—
           Vide Annual Register, vol. ix, page 183, for 1766

XXV.   Loss of the Ann and Mary, of Galway, from
           Drontheim in Norway.—Vide Annual Register, vol. iii,
           page 75, for 1760

XXVI.   Loss of the Brig Sally, Capt. Fabray, from
           Philadelphia to Hispaniola.—Vide Annual Register,
           vol. x, page 211, for 1767

XXVII.   Loss of the Catharine, Venus, and Piedmont
           transports; and the Thomas, Golden Grove, and

XL.   Capt. Mears's voyage to the North-West coast of America

XLI.   An account of three persons buried in the snow at Bergemoletto, in the Valley of Stura, March 19, 1755.—Vide Philosophical Transactions, vol. xlix, part II, page 796, for 1756, for doctor Joseph Brune's (professor at Turin) account

XLII.   The case of Ann Woodcock, who was buried in a fall of snow, some years ago near Cambridge, for many days, and survived

Hardships on shore. Hardships.

XLIII.   J. Z. Holwell's esq. account of the Black Hole of Calcutta, in June, 1756.—Vide Annual Register, vol. i, page 278, for 1758

XLIV.   Sir William Hamilton's account of the earthquake at Calabria.—Vide Philosophical Transactions, 1783, vol. lxxxiii, page 169

XLV.   Dr. Percival's account of the effects of famine, in a communication to the Philosophical Society at Manchester, January 6, 1785.—Vide their Memoirs, vol. ii, page 483. Printed in 1789

XLVI.   The case of a dog shut up in St. Paul's church yard

XLVII.   The case of a cat

XLVIII.   Robert Eastburne's sufferings and escape from the Indians in North America.—Vide Annual Register, vol. i, page 301, for 1758

XLIX.   William Okeley's narrative of himself and four others, and their recovery from slavery at Algiers, in 1764 [1644]; or Ebenezer, or a small monument of great mercy in their delivery. Printed for Buckland, Keith, and Dilly, in 1764 [1664?]

L.   Sufferings of De St. Germain and his companions, in the desert of Egypt.—Annual Register, vol. xxiii, page 54, 1780

LI.   A Chinese contrivance to keep those above water who do not know how to swim.—Annual Register, vol. iv, page 141, 1761

LII.   Greathead's life boat

1 8 0 5

145C. ANONYOUS

God's wonders in the great deep, recorded in several wonderful and amazing accounts of sailors, who have met with unexpected deliverances from death, when in the greatest dangers; to which is added, the seaman's spiritual directory; showing what he ought to think and do. With forms of prayers, suited to their several circumstances, and various occasions. His way is in the sea, and his paths in the great waters, and his footsteps are not known.

Published at Newburyport, by Thomas & Whipple: sold wholesale and retail at their bookstore, sign of Johnson's Head, Market-Square. E. W. Allen, Printer. 1805

1. *Michael* of London, Captain Hutton, struck on the Caskets 1/5/1701
2. *John and Sarah,* Biddeford, ran on the Croskom near St. David's Head. One sailor was saved
3. Barkentine *Reformation,* Jonathan Dickenson's narrative
4. Adventure of Mr. Sturt, 9/21/1800
5. Captain Inglefield and the *Centaur*
6. Adventure of Ephraim How
7. Wreck in the Bahamas, 1638
8. Crew of an Irish ship saved by an American, 4/18/1681
9. A small boat from St. Christopher in the West Indies
10. Manuel Sousa
11. A ship bound for Newfoundland
12. A ship from Boston
13. The ship *Delight,* Captain Clark, with Sir Humphrey Gilbert
14. John Okley and his companions
15. The Portuguese *St. Iago,* 1585
16. Englishmen left on Greenland
17. Some Scotch ministers emigrating to America
18. Captain Frankmore swept overboard and saved
19. Fifteen ships of Hull lost off Holland

The seaman's spiritual directory
The seaman's devotions

146C. ANONYMOUS

The loss of the Earl of Abergavenny, East Indiaman, off Portland, on the night of fifth February, 1805 . . . corrected from the official returns at the East India House

London, John Stockdale, Feb. 13, 1805. Pamphlet, 49 pp.

This narrative was based primarily on testimony at East India House by Cornet Burgoyne of the Eighth Regiment Light Dragoons and by Mr. Gilpin, fourth officer of the ship. The *Earl of Abergavenny,* a richly laden East Indiaman, sailed from Portsmouth in convoy on February 1, 1805. Her captain was John Wordsworth, brother of the poet William Wordsworth, but in the Channel she was under the direction of a pilot. The ship was bearing up for Portland Roads with a steady wind when suddenly the wind slackened and the tide took her rapidly toward the Shambles, a much-feared reef. She struck about 2 miles off the Bill of Portland, beat part of her bottom out, and then cleared the rocks. They set sail for the land, but the ship took in so much water that she was obviously sinking. One boat was sent on shore, and a few passengers were taken off; many more could have been saved, apparently, but ". . . in the general distress and agony of the moment, the ship's boats were not hoisted out, when every soul on board might possibly have been saved." At eleven o'clock the ship gave a surge and sank in 12 fathoms. About 180 people climbed into the tops and rigging still above water, and some of these were taken off by boats from another vessel. One hundred thirty-nine people were eventually saved out of 402. Captain Wordsworth died with his ship; his brother wrote three important poems about his death.

147C. ANONYMOUS
> An authentic narrative of the loss of the Earl of Abergavenny East Indiaman, Captain John Wordsworth . . . by a gentleman in the East India House
> London, Minerva Press, Feb. 21, 1805

See 146C, 1805.

148C. CLARKE, JAMES STANIER
> Naufragia or historical memoirs of shipwrecks and of the providential deliverance of vessels by James Stanier Clarke F.R.S. Chaplain of the Prince's Household and Librarian to His Royal Highness
> London, printed by I. [Joyce] Gold, Shoe Lane, Fleet Street, for J. Mawman, 22 Poultry, MDCCCV [1805]. 2, xvi, 421, 2
> Chapter I. Section I.   Dissertation on Alexander Selkirk, and on the real author of Robinson Crusoe
> Section II.   First discovery of Juan Fernandez-Indian who lived there above three years—Account of the island—A seaman shipwrecked on its coast, who lived there for five years
> Section III.   Commodore Anson's providential escape, and arrival at the island of Juan Fernandez
> Chapter II.   North Atlantic. Section I.   Singular preservation of Robert à Machin, and the ship's crew; which led to the first discovery of the island of Madeira, by the Moderns
> Section II.   Perilous situation of some seamen, who appear to have visited Puerto Santo prior to the Portuguese
> Section III.   Shipwreck of the Toby from Hakluyt—Liberality of the Irish merchants
> Section IV.   Notice of the Earl of Cumberland's twelve voyages, from Purchas—Perils which his Lordship endured
> Section V.   Shipwreck of Monsieur Saugnier on the western coast of Africa
> Chapter III.   North Atlantic. Section I. I. A shipwreck the origin of Lord Duncan's Crest   II.   Providential escape of some Scotch seamen, and of a sailor who had been cast away on the ice—III. Sir Humfrey Gilbert's shipwreck in 1583, from Hakluyt
> Section II.   Abstract of a briefe Note of a voyage to the East Indies, begun the 10th of April, 1591; wherein were three tall ships, the Penelope of Captaine Raimond, Admirall; the Merchant Royall, whereof was Captaine, Samuel Foxcroft, Vice Admirall; the Edward Bonauenture, whereof was

Captaine, M. James Lancaster, Rere Admirall, with a small Pinnesse. Written by Henry May, who, in his returne homeward, by the West Indies, suffred shipwracke upon the Isle of Bermuda

Section III.   A true reportory of the wracke, and redemption of Sir Thomas Gates, Knight, upon, and from the Ilands of the Bermudas, written by William Strachy, Esquire.—A most dreadful tempest, the manifold deaths whereof are here to the life described

Section IV.   Shipwreck of the Captains, James Knight, George Barlow, and David Vaughan, on Marble Island in Hudson's Bay, 1719. Extracted from Hearne's journey from Prince of Wales's Fort in Hudson Bay, to the Northern Ocean, for the discovery of copper mines, and a North West Passage, 1769–1772

Section V.   Loss of His Majesty's Ship La Tribune, Captain S. Barker, off the Harbour of Hallifax in America, 1797

Chapter IV.   North Atlantic. Abstract of the adventures, shipwreck, and distresses of Monsieur Pierre Viaud, a Captain in the French Service, and a native of Bourdeaux, 1766. In a letter to a friend. Translated from the original, by Mrs. Griffith. 8vo 4s. Davies. 1771

Chapter V.   North Atlantic. The dangerous adventures, and imminent escapes of Captain Richard Falconer

Chapter VI.   Pacific Ocean. Shipwreck of Captain Flinders and Lieutenant Fowler, in His Majesty's Armed Vessel, Porpoise, and of Mr. Park, Commander of the ship Cato, on a coral reef, as represented in the Frontispiece. From MSS. and other information furnished by the Officers

Appendix.   View of the different methods that have been suggested to assist the crews of vessels in distress

CLARKE, JAMES STANIER F.R.S.

Naufragia or historical memoirs of shipwrecks and of the providential deliverance of vessels. By James Stanier Clarke F.R.S. Chaplain of the Prince's Household and Librarian to His Royal Highness. Vol. II

London, printed by I. [Joyce] Gold, Shoe Lane, Fleet Street, for J. Mawman, 22 Poultry, MDCCCVI [1806]. 2, xvii, 445, 3

Dedication: to the Rev. Dr. Vincent, Dean of Westminster

Preface: [Clarke states that he is continuing his original plan in consequence of the reception of the first volume of Naufragia.] "The whole, should it be called for in the same flattering manner, will be comprised in about four Volumes.

"... and the Utility which I had in mind, was to inculcate the lesson of Resignation and Perseverance; to point out the Resources which shipwrecked, or distressed Mariners, had discovered; the Ability and Industry which naval Officers, now almost forgotten, had exerted in the service of their King and

Country: And in a more general point of view, to form a Work, which yielding not in point of interest to the Horrors, and unnatural Incidents of the modern Novel, might engage even the female Mind, without poisoning its principles, or tainting its purity.

I.   The shipwreck of Pierre Viaud, and the imminent escapes of Captain Richard Falconer, were inserted in the first volume; as following with some degree of similar interest, and a display of valuable resource, the philosophical Romance of Crusoe. . . .

The present Earl of Oxford, since the publication of this Volume, had done me the honor of informing me, That the family had always considered the first Earl of Oxford to have been the Author of Robinson Crusoe.''

Introductory Chapter—Section I—*Histoires des Naufrages*—Par M.D. . . . Avocat. Three volumes, 8vo. Paris. Chez Cuchet, An 3me. de la Republique. Section II—Iceland, Greenland, Spitzbergen, Nova Zembla, and Baffin's Bay. From Churchill's *Voyages*—2 letters from Mons. la Peyrere on Iceland, dated Copenhagen 1644, and Greenland, from the Hague, 1646

Chapter II—North Atlantic. The Ship-wracke of Master Piero Quirino, described by Christoforo Fioravanti, and Nicolo Di Michiel, who were present there, 1431

Note—Purchas (Vol. iii, p. 611) who adds "There is also the Relation hereof by Quirino himselfe, extant together with this in Ramusio, Tom. ii, out of which I have here added divers annotations.''

Chapter III

The Journall of Master Henry Hudson for the Discourie of the North West Passage, begunne the seventeenth of Aprill, 1610, ended with his end: being treacherously exposed by some of his Companie. Written by Abacuk Pricket. (Purchas, Vol. iii. Page 597)

Chapter IV.   God's power and providence shewed in the miraculous preservation and deliverance of eight English-men, left by mischance in Greenland, Anno 1630, nine months and twelve days. (Churchill's Collection, Vol. iv, Page 750) The first account was published by Dr. W. Watts. With a true relation of all their miseries, the shifts and hardships they were put to, their food; such as neither Heathen nor Christian ever before endured. Faithfully reported by Edward Pelham, one of the eight men aforesaid

The eight men had gone hunting for deer in Greenland [?] and had been left by their ship, a whaler from London, May 1, 1630. They showed considerable courage and ingenuity in building a shelter and finding food, and survived their ordeal in good shape.

Chapter V.   Captain Thomas James's strange and dangerous voyage, in his intended discovery of the N.W. Passage into the South Sea, in the years 1631, and 1632. wherein the miseries endured, both going, wintering, and returning, are related at

large. Published by the special command of King Charles the
First, in quarto, 1633; reprinted in Churchill's Collection,
1732; and published in a third edition, octavo, in 1740 [by Olive
Payne]

Chapter VI.   A true and short account of forty-two persons, the
greater part of whom perished by shipwreck, near Spitzbergen,
in the year 1646. (Churchill's Collection, Vol. ii, page 381)

John Cornelius of Muniken sailed from the Texel in a galliot, May 6, 1646, for
whales off Spitzbergen. While after whales in a small sloop, they saw
something on an iceberg, and eventually took off four Englishmen who had
lost their ship and had been living, and starving, in a cave they had cut in the
berg. They were apparently the last survivors of forty-two men of an English
ship. Three of the four died in spite of all the Dutch could do, and the single
survivor, not named, was taken in the galliot *Delft* to the Meuse, whence he set
out for England.

Chapter VI.   The perilous voyage of Captain Norwood, an officer
in the army of Charles the First. With an account of the sufferings, which that officer, and his companions endured, when
left on a desert island, belonging to the Kickotank North
American Indians, 1649–1650 (Churchill's Collection, Vol. vi)

Norwood, a supporter of Charles I, left England for Virginia after the execution of
the King. The ship, *The Virginia Merchant,* Captain John Locker, sailed from
the Downs about the middle of September, 1649. She was not in good condition, and not well supplied for the voyage. When off the coast of Virginia, trying to make Chesapeake Bay, a storm from the northwest blew her offshore,
and so delayed the ship that both water and food ran out. The ship rats were
caught and eaten, and were bought for sixteen shillings. At last the ship made
an island on what seems to have been the Delmarva Peninsula, where Norwood
and some others were left ashore by accident. They killed waterfowl and found
oysters, but as winter came on they found less and less food on the island, and
were at last reduced to cannibalism. They were rescued by Kickotank Indians,
who cared for them very well, and at last the survivors reached the English settlements at Jamestown.

Appendix—1.   The Hon. R. Boyle's History of Cold
2.   Captain James's observations on a N. passage into
the South Sea
3.   Captain James's remarks on the accumulation of ice
in Hudson's Bay (Jan. 1632)
4.   The effects of cold; with observations of the
longitude, latitude, and declination of the magnetic
needle, at Prince of Wales' Fort, on Churchill River
in Hudson's Bay, North America. By Captain
Christopher Middleton, F.R.S. 1741–2. Philos.
Trans. No. 465. Baldwin's Abridgement, Vol. VIII,
P. 591

149C.   PAGE, THOMAS
Narrative of the loss of the ship Fanny on her passage from Bombay
to China &c. In a letter from Thomas Page, Second Officer
London, 1805 [2d edition], iv, 36 pp., 8vo

Page sailed out to India, and sought a position on a ship there. He finally was hired as second mate of the ship *Fanny,* Captain Robertson, bound for China. They sailed August 8, 1803. About two weeks later they encountered a very severe typhoon, in which the foremast fell, the rudder was torn away, and a bad leak developed. The ship finally anchored off Hainan, but the natives there were under orders to supply nothing for foreign ships, and provisions grew very short. They repaired the ship, and set sail, but on November 26 the *Fanny* struck on an unknown reef 250 miles off Cochin-China, and was firmly aground. The weather was good and the ship filled with water only slowly, but the crew became sick and a number died during the next month. On December 22 a sail was seen, which turned out to be an American vessel, the *Pennsylvania* of Philadelphia, which offered to take them off. Captain Robertson made the almost insane decision to try to get off in rafts, and Page stayed with his commander. Four Portuguese passengers were transferred to the *Pennsylvania.* The crew of the *Fanny* built two scows in which they sailed all the way to Malacca, with some losses. Of seventy-one on board at the start of the voyage, thirty-six died in various ways, and ten were missing.

150C. STEEL, DAVID
>Naval chronologist of the war, 1793–1801, an account of the ships lost, taken or destroyed of the British, French, Dutch, Spanish and Danish navies, with five engraved plans of engaging tactics
>London, 1805. 8vo

Another volume of the series begun in 98C, 1783. Presumably there was at least one other volume published between these two.

1 8 0 6

151C. FORREST, CAPTAIN A.
>*Asiatic Mirror,* Calcutta, October 14, 1806

The *Mariner's Chronicle* narrative of the loss of the *Sidney* on a reef in the East Indies gives this article as the source. The *Sidney* left Port Jackson for Bengal on April 12, 1806. She was attempting to go through Dampier's Strait when she struck an uncharted reef, was holed, and broke up. The 108 on board left the wreck in three boats on May 21, but the jolly boat soon sank and 16 were drowned. The other two boats landed on an island and were threatened by natives, but got off and obtained food and water on the island of Ceram. From there they reached Bencoolen, and were taken to Calcutta. A number of the lascar sailors stayed on the islands they visited, and at least a few died of starvation or thirst, but apparently about 75 survived the wreck.

152C. ISAACS, CAPTAIN
>Massacre of crew of ship Atahualpa
>Connecticut *Courant,* April 16, 1806. P. 3, col. 4.
>Fairfield, Washington, Galleon Press, 1978

Captain Isaacs, of the ship *Montezuma,* reported that the *Atahualpa,* lying in Sturgis Cove, Milbank Sound, on the coast of British Columbia, was attacked by Indians who were driven off. Nine of the crew were killed.

1 8 0 7 – 1 8 1 0

153C. ANONYMOUS

Mariner's Marvelous Magazine or wonders of the ocean
London, Thomas Tegg, 111 Cheapside, 1807–1810

In 1807 Thomas Tegg began issuing a series of twenty-eight-page pamphlets, ten a year, of narratives of shipwrecks and disasters at sea. Each pamphlet had a folding aquatint as frontispiece. This series was apparently issued as individual pamphlets at sixpence each, but, like the Cundee pamphlets which made up the *Mariner's Chronicle,* they could be collected into individual volumes. The four bound volumes in the National Maritime Museum Library at Greenwich have no title pages and no dates, but all the aquatints are dated; the spine titles are uniform—*Mariner's Magazine,* I, II, III, IV. The *Catalogue of the John S. Barnes Memorial Library* contains one entry for a collection of these Tegg pamphlets, but there are fourteen pamphlets in this volume instead of ten, and the individual items are from three of the volumes from the National Maritime Museum; presumably a purchaser could have any pamphlets bound up in any order he chose. I have seen many bookseller's advertisements for these Tegg pamphlets, but no such offerings of units from Cundee's collection. The four National Maritime Museum Library volumes contain the following items:

Vol. I [1807]
1. Loss of Lord Royston in the Agatha; loss of the Bowaniong
2. Voyage of Lord Anson; loss of the Sidney
3. Loss of the Ganges; loss of the Winterton
4. Adventures of Captain Robert Johnson
5. Loss of the Porpoise and Cato; loss of the Doddington
6. Struggles of Captain Thomas Keith in America
7. Shipwreck of Dr. Archibald Thompson, on board the Sympathy, in 1777 off Algiers
8. Loss of the Grosvenor
9. Shipwreck and capture of Captain Donald Campbell; loss of the Sidney
10. Loss of the Fanny

Vol. II [1808]
1. Adventures of Captain Woodard
2. Destruction of the Boyne
3. Loss of the Antelope
4. Loss of the Halsewell
5. Loss of the New Hoorn
6. Loss of the Ville de Paris; the Amethyst against the Thetis
7. Loss of the Earl of Abergavenny; the shipwreck of Occum Chamnan
9. Loss of the General Washington
10. Loss of the St. Lawrence

Vol. III [1809]
1. Ship Industry; dealings with Eskimoes
2. Loss of the Admiral Trowbridge; adventures of Mr. Brisson
3. Loss of the Centaur; loss of the Prince

  4. Loss of the Lady Hobart; shipwreck and death of E. Sosa
  5. Loss of the Turner and the Tay; adventures of Peter Serrano
  6. Loss of the Hindostan
  7. Losses of the Apollo and the St. Peter
  8. Loss of the Thames Smack; story of Alexander Selkirk
  9. Loss of the Guardian
  10. Loss of the Hercules

Vol. IV [1810]
  1. Adventures of Captain Stedman
  2. Loss of the Crescent; story of Captain Uring
  3. Loss of the Sceptre; story of Joseph Pizarro
  4. Loss of the Wager
  5. Loss of the Cumberland; loss of the Fattysalem
  6. Loss of the Phoenix; adventures of F. P. De Laval
  7. Adventures of Captain Wallis
  8. Loss of the Amphion; loss of a Spanish frigate
  9. Loss of the Litchfield; adventures of the Countess de Bourk
  10. Loss of the Travers Indiaman; loss of the Sparrowhawk

154C. ANONYMOUS [James, Captain Thomas?]
       The voyages and distresses of . . . T. James and Mr. H. Ellis, for
          the discovery of a north-west passage to the South Seas
       London, 1807

155C. JEWITT, JOHN R.
       A journal kept at Nootka Sound
       Boston, 1807, 1931
Jewitt was born in Boston, Lincolnshire, England, the son of a reasonably prosperous blacksmith. The father moved his business to Hull, and there did a good
deal of work for shipmasters and owners. In 1802 the American ship *Boston,*
Captain John Salter, put into Hull to take on a cargo of trade goods for a
voyage to the North-West coast of America, thence to China, and back to the
United States. Young Jewitt was signed on as an armorer on board the *Boston,*
and the ship sailed from the Downs September 3, 1802. Nothing of importance
occurred in the voyage round the Horn, and the *Boston* reached Nootka Sound
March 12, 1803. Relations with the Indians were apparently friendly, but
Jewitt later heard that another ship captain, incensed at Indian thefts, had fired
into the canoes and killed many Indians. In any case, on March 22 the Indians
under Chief Maquina attacked the crew and killed all except Jewitt and a man
named Thompson. The major part of this book is given up to the life that
Jewitt led with the Indians for the next few years. Jewitt was finally able to get
in touch with Captain Samuel Hill, of the brig *Lydia* of Boston, off Nootka,
and to arrange that he and Thompson should be rescued. After sailing to China
in the *Lydia,* Jewitt landed in Boston, Massachusetts. He eventually settled in
Middletown, Connecticut, and died at Hartford January 7, 1821.
       This narrative can be compared with the attacks on the *Tonquin* (171C),
1813, and the *Atahualpa* (152C), 1806.

156C. [MARTIN, MRS. MARIA?]
       History of the captivity and sufferings of Mrs. Maria Martin, who
          was six years a slave in Algiers, two of which she was confined

in a dark and dismal dungeon, loaded with irons. To which is annexed a history of Algiers; a description of the country, the manners and customs of the natives—their treatment of their slaves—their laws and religion

Boston, W. Crary [1807?], 40 pp.; same, except for wording of title, Boston, W. Crary, 1807, 72 pp.; same, Philadelphia, printed and sold by Joseph Rakestraw, 1809, 107 pp.; same, Boston, Lemuel Austin, 1810, 67 pp.; same, except wording of title, Philadelphia, published by Jacob Meyer, No. 177 north Second Street, 1811, 107 pp.; same, Trenton, N.J., printed by James Oram, 1811, 106 pp.; same, Sidney's Press, for Increase Cooke & Co., booksellers, Church-street, New Haven, 1812, 107 pp.; same, New York [1812?], 108 pp.; same, New York, published by Evert Duyckinck, J. Oram, printer, 1813, 108 pp. Bound with Life of Mahomet; same, St. Clairsville, Ohio, printed by John Berry, 1815, blue wrappers; same, Brookfield [Mass.?] Ptd. by E. Merriam, 1818. 125 pp.

This book begins with about forty pages of history of the Barbary States, chiefly of Algiers, borrowed from some other source. Mrs. Martin claimed to have married a sea captain in England and to have sailed with him for Minorca, but the ship got off course and struck on the coast of Africa. Two black slaves swam underwater for a quarter-mile and got lines ashore, and most of those on board reached the beach. She makes no mention of wreckage, or Arabs pillaging the cargo or taking the clothes of the survivors. Those who reached shore blundered in and out of forests and swamps [!], but were finally seized and enslaved in Algiers. Mrs. Martin was bought by a Turk, who after two years demanded that she become his mistress. She of course refused him, was loaded with chains, and was thrown into a dungeon where only the consciousness of her virtue sustained her. Word of her imprisonment at last reached the ears of the English consul in Algiers, and she was ransomed. Her husband reached England six months after she did.

Though Mrs. Martin was said to be English, and to have been ransomed by an English consul, there is no English edition of this book. Almost certainly the whole thing is a fabrication, probably put together by W. Crary of Boston to take advantage of the American interest in the Barbary States because of the wars with Tripoli and Algiers, and to inject a little sex into a familiar enough story of ransom. The shipwreck narrative is absurd. This book should be classified as fiction, like the similar book by Eliza Bradley (202C), 1820. See also 141C, 1804.

157C. SHAW, THOMAS

Melancholy shipwreck. The following lines were occasioned by the loss of the schooner Charles, Captain Adams, of Portland, which was wrecked on Richmond's Island, . . .

Portland, 1807

A broadside, 45.8 × 16.6 cm, double columns, black border, 16 woodcut coffins. Story of the wreck at the bottom. Richmond's Island is off Cape Elizabeth, Maine.

1 8 0 8 [?]

158C. ANONYMOUS

Shipwreck and death of Lord Royston, and other persons of distinction, in the Agatha, commanded by Captain Coop, which was unfortunately stranded near Memel, April 7 [1808], when near 20 persons perished. The wonderful preservation of some of the crew, particularly the women and children

Thirsk, H. Masterman, n.d. [1808?]. 8pp., 2 woodcuts

See 143C, Vol. VI.

159C. GILPIN, WILLIAM

Memoirs of Josias Rogers, Commander of His Majesty's ship Quebec, by the late Wm. Gilpin, Prebentary of Salisbury, and Vicar of Boldre in New Forest. Published by his trustees, for the benefit of his school, at Boldre

n.p., 1808

Bookseller's note: "Contains a curious account of his shipwreck in Virginia . . . Williamsburg during the Revolutionary War . . . Siege of Charleston . . . Block Island."

160C. RAY, WILLIAM

Horrors of slavery: or, the American tars in Tripoli. Containing an account of the loss and capture of the United States frigate "Philadelphia" . . . interspersed with interesting remarks, anecdotes and poetry, on various subjects. Written during upwards of nineteen months' imprisonment and vassalage among the Turks

Troy [New York], printed by Oliver Lyons for the author, 1808. 280 pp., 12mo

The *Philadelphia* grounded in the harbor of Tripoli, and was captured by the Tripolitans with all on board. Stephen Decatur led a small boat attack to burn her as she lay aground, and first achieved fame through this exploit. Attacks on the Barbary pirates eventually led to freeing the captured American sailors.

1 8 1 0

161C. ANONYMOUS

Narrative of calamitous and interesting shipwrecks &c., with authentic particulars of the sufferings of the crews . . .

Philadelphia, published by Mathew Carey, printed by A. Small, 1810. iv, 92 pp.

162C. KIRBY, JOHN (Comm.)

Narrative of the wreck and loss of the ship Albion of London and of the circumstances of her being found at sea

[London?], 1810. Fldg. plate, 8vo

163C. LARCOM, CAPTAIN HENRY
        Captain Larcom's narrative
        Connecticut Courant, Wed., August 15, 1810. Page 2, cols. 1–3
This narrative of the loss of the ship Margaret, which foundered west of Gibraltar,
     is stated to be taken from the Salem *Gazette.*
        This is one of two narratives on the loss of the *Margaret.* This one, by
     Captain Larcom, who was a passenger on the *Margaret,* is very critical of the
     conduct of Captain Fairfield, of the *Margaret,* who wrote the narrative that ap-
     pears in R. Thomas's *Remarkable Shipwrecks* (280C). According to Captain
     Larcom, the *Margaret* went on her beam ends in a squall, and when she righted
     after the masts were cut away was so full of water that nothing could be done
     with her and little food or drink could be salvaged. Fifteen men got into the
     longboat and repaired her; they refused to take in any more from the ship
     though Larcom thought she could have taken in at least ten more people and
     should have stood by the derelict. The longboat sailed away and was eventually
     picked up by another ship after four days. Five of those who remained on the
     wreck sailed off in the repaired yawl, and three of those survived when they
     were picked up by a ship twenty-three days after they had left the *Margaret.*
     They left ten men alive on the wreck, who were never heard of again. Forty-six
     people had left Naples in the ship on April 10, 1810, and twenty-eight died.

164C. LARCOM, CAPT. H.
        Distressing narrative of the loss of the ship Margaret of Salem, by
            Capt. H. Larcom
        n.p. [1810]. 2. 12 pp.
See 163C.

1 8 1 2

165C. ANONYMOUS
        Narratives of shipwrecks and other calamities, incident to a life of
            maritime enterprise: comprising authentic particulars of the
            loss of the Wager man of war one of Commodore Anson's
            squadron, and the subsequent distresses suffered by the crew,
            during a period of more than five years. By the Honourable
            John Bryon [Byron]. Also, the loss of the Halsewell East-
            indiaman, wrecked off Seacombe, in the Isle of Purbeck, on
            the coast of Dorsetshire, January 6, 1786
        Sidney's Press. For Increase Cooke & Co. Book-sellers, Church-
            Street, New Haven, 1812. 107 pp., 16mo
        Contains also:
        Loss of the *Prince George,* by fire, April 13, 1758. Letter from Mr.
            Sharp, Chaplain. 715 hands and 30 passengers to Gibraltar.
            260 saved, 485 lost

166C. ANONYMOUS
        Tales of the sea, or, interesting narratives of shipwrecks,
            engagements, and other perils of the ocean
        William Strange [London?], n.d. [ca. 1812]. 60 woodcut engrav-
            ings, 1 colored
        Contains:

1. Adventures of John Cockburn, taken by a Spanish Garda Costa in 1730
2. Loss of the Russian *St. Peter,* Bering's Island, 1741
3. Sufferings of Alexander Selkirk, 1704
4. Loss of the *Cumberland* packet on the coast of Antigua, 1804
5. Sufferings of Thomas Lindley after a voyage to Brazil, 1802

167C. [DALYELL, SIR J. G.]
Shipwrecks and disasters at sea; or historical narratives of the most noted calamities and providential deliverances, which have resulted from maritime enterprise: with a sketch of various expedients for preserving the lives of mariners. In three volumes
Edinburgh, printed by George Ramsay & Company, for Archibald Constable and Company, Edinburgh, and Longman, Hurst, Rees, Orme, and Brown, London, 1812

This collection of narratives seems to have been less popular than the Mariner's Chronicle, but was probably used as a source for borrowings exactly as that collection was. Both books owed something to Hakluyt and a great deal to Deperthes. These narratives tend to be somewhat longer than those in Duncan's collection; there was a considerable advantage for the editor in not having to fit his items into monthly parts.

Volume I
1. Quirini, 1431
2. Famine in *Le Jacques,* for Brazil, 1558. By John Lery
3. Loss of Sir Humphrey Gilbert, with the *Squirrel* and *Delight,* 1583
4. Shipwreck of the Portuguese Admiral, Fernando De Mendoza, 1585
5. Wreck of the *Tobie* of London, near Cape Espartel, 1593
6. Shipwreck of Henry May, on the Bermuda islands, 1593
7. Wintering of the crew of a Dutch vessel in Nova Zembla, 1596
8. Shipwreck of Francis Pyrard, in the *Corbin,* 1601; with an account of his subsequent misfortunes
9. Wreck of the *Sea Venture,* an English vessel, on the Bermuda Islands, 1609
10. Destruction of the *New Horn,* by fire, 1619
11. Shipwreck of two Dutch vessels on the coast of Madagascar, 1600–1620
12. Shipwreck of Francis Pelsart, on the coast of New Holland, 1629
13. Preservation of eight seamen accidentally left in Greenland, 1630
14. Fate of seven sailors left in the island of St. Maurice, 1633; and of other seven sailors left in Spitzbergen, 1634
15. Shipwreck of the *Spitzbergen,* 1639
16. A small monument of great mercy, in the miraculous deliverance of five persons from slavery at Algiers, in a canvas

boat; with an account of the great distress and extremities which they endured at sea. By William Okeley, 1644

17. Providential escape of several Frenchmen banished to the Virgin Islands, 1647
18. Narrative of a great deliverance at sea, 1648. By Dr. William Johnson, Chaplain and Subalmoner to King Charles II
19. Condition of Olave and Andrew Engelbrechtsen on a barren island, 1652
20. Loss of the *Bleeker,* a Dutch whale ship, 1670
21. Dangers and distresses of the Dutch in the Greenland Seas, 1675, 1678
22. Shipwreck of Captain John Wood, 1676
23. Shipwreck of Hanjemon, a Japanese, on a rock near Visia Grande, 1682
24. Shipwreck of King James II, while Duke of York, 1682
25. Shipwreck of Occum Chamnam, a Siamese Mandarin, near Cape Needles, 1686. By Father Tachard
26. Shipwreck of M. De Serres, near the island of Martinique, 1687
27. Explosion of a French vessel, commanded by the Sieur De Montauban, on the coast of Guinea, 1695
28. Wreck of two English vessels on the island of Mayotta
29. Loss of the *Degrave* East Indiaman, off the coast of Madagascar, 1701
30. Preservation of nine men in a small boat, surrounded by islands of ice, on a voyage to Newfoundland, 1706. By Allen Geare

Volume II
31. Shipwrecks and disasters at sea. Loss of the *Nottingham* Galley, 11th December 1710. By Captain John Dean
32. The voyage, shipwreck, and escape of Richard Castleman, 1710
33. Wreck of a Genoese Tartan on the coast of Algiers, 1719
34. Condition of M. De Belleisle, abandoned on the coast of Mexico, 1719
35. Loss of the *Speedwell* on the island of Juan Fernandez, May 25, 1720
36. Adventures of Philip Ashton, who, after escaping from pirates, lived sixteen months in solitude on a desolate island, 1723
37. Loss of the *Sussex* East Indiaman, near the coast of Madagascar, 1738. By John Dean
38. Loss of the *Wager* Man-of-War, on the coast of Patagonia, 14th May 1741
39. Hardships suffered by part of the crew of the *Wager* Man-of-War, after their departure from Wager Island, 1741
40. Adventures of Alexander Campbell, and some of the officers of the *Wager,* 1741
41. Dangers and distresses of Isaac Morris, a midshipman of the

Wager, and seven companions, abandoned on the coast of Patagonia, 1742

42. Account of four Russian sailors abandoned on the island of East Spitzbergen, 1743
43. Wreck of the *Inspector* Privateer in Tangier Bay, 4th January, 1746
44. Burning of the *Prince,* a French East Indiaman, 1752. By Lieutenant De La Fond
45. Burning of an East India Ship, 1754. Written by the mate
46. Wreck of the *Doddington* East Indiaman, on a rock in the Indian Ocean, 17th July, 1755
47. Shipwreck of Philip Aubin, on the coast of Guiana, 16
48. Escape of eight persons from the Adu Isles, 1757
49. Loss of the *Duke William* Transport, 1758
50. Wreck of the *Litchfield* Man-of-War, on the coast of Africa, 29th Nov. 1758. By Lieutenant Sutherland
51. Loss of the Brig *Tyrrel,* and subsequent distresses of the crew, July 1759
52. Famine in the *Dolphin* Sloop, Captain Barron, 1759
53. Shipwreck of a Russian crew, on the Aleutian Islands, 1758–1760
54. Loss of the *Ann* Frigate, 1760. By Seth Houghton
55. Shipwreck of the *Utile,* commanded by M. De La Fargue, on Sandy Isle, 1761
56. Famine suffered on board of the *Peggy,* 1765
57. Loss of three of the Dutch Fleet in Greenland, 1777
58. Wreck of the Brigantine *St. Lawrence,* on the island of Cape Breton, 5th December 1780. By S. W. Prenties, Ensign of the 84th Regiment of Foot

Volume III
59. Wreck of the *Grosvenor* East Indiaman, on the coast of Caffraria, 1782
60. Loss of the *Centaur* Man-of-War, 1782, by Captain Inglefield
61. Wreck of the *Antelope* Packet, 1783
62. Loss of the *Halsewell* East Indiaman, on the coast of England, 1786
63. Dangerous voyage by Captain Bligh, in an open boat, from Tofoa to Timor, 1789
64. Wreck of the *Pandora* Frigate, 28th August 1791
65. Loss of the *Winterton* East Indiaman, near the coast of Madagascar, 20th August 1792
66. Hardships suffered by David Woodard, and five seamen, on separation from an American vessel, 1793
67. Shipwreck of the *Juno,* on the coast of Aracan, June 1795, by John Mackay

168C. LUCE, JOHN
   Narrative of a passage from the Island of Cape Breton across the Atlantic Ocean, with other interesting occurrences in a letter to a friend . . .
   London, 1812
Barnes Catalogue: ". . . case of shipwreck, disasters, and rescues."

169C. PELLHAM, EDWARD [fl. 1630, author of first item only]
   Narrative of the adventures, sufferings, and deliverances of eight English seamen, left by accident in Greenland in the year 1630. To which is added, the loss of the Lady Hobart . . . adventures of four Russian sailors, and the loss of the ship Litchfield
   Philadelphia, Bennett & Walton, 1812. 105 pp.
For the Greenland narrative, see 143C, Vol. III; for the *Lady Hobart,* 139C, 1803; for the four Russian sailors, 84C, 1774; for the *Litchfield,* 73C, 1761.

1 8 1 3

170C. ANONYMOUS

Analectic Magazine: containing selections from foreign reviews and magazines, together with original miscellaneous compositions and a naval chronicle

Philadelphia, 1813–1820

171C. ANONYMOUS

Loss of the ship Tonquin, near the mouth of the Columbia River

National Intelligencer, Washington, D.C., June 22, 1813

The *Tonquin,* Captain Thorn, was trading with Indians on Vancouver Island. Captain Thorn attempted to get furs cheaply from the Indians on board the ship, and when they refused to trade he drove the chief off the ship with some violence. The next day Indians boarded the ship, and, on signal, attacked the crew. Four sailors and two wounded officers finally drove the Indians off the vessel with gunfire from the cabin. Captain Thorn and Clerk Lewis, both convinced that they were mortally wounded, told the sailors to leave the ship in a boat, invited the Indians on board again, and, when the ship was crowded, blew it up by firing the mgazine. Many Indians and the two Americans were killed. The four sailors who had left the ship were captured by the Indians and also killed.

The story of the loss of the *Tonquin* is told in Washington Irving's *Astoria,* Vol. I, p. 116, and also in Edmund Fanning's *Voyages to the South Seas, . . . between the years 1830–1837 . . . ,* New York, 1838. Fanning's narrative was said to be based on an interview with Lamazee, an Indian who had served as an interpreter for Captain Thorn of the *Tonquin,* and was the only survivor of the ship's complement.

172C. ANONYMOUS

Narrative of the capture of the United States brig "Vixen" of 14 guns, by the British frigate "Southampton," and of the subsequent loss of both vessels on a reef of rocks off Conception Island: with some account of the sufferings of the crew, their manner of deliverance and final deposit in the prison ships at Port Royal, Jamaica. The whole interspersed with various remarks, relative to the treatment shown to and conduct observed by the prisoners. By one of the "Vixen's" crew, in a letter to his friend

Charleston, S. C., *Gazette* Office, printed and published by the author, 1813. 35 pp., 8vo

Barnes Catalogue

173C. ANONYMOUS

Remarkable shipwrecks and naval disasters

Hartford Industrial Fair, 1813

Bookseller's catalogue gives no other information. This item appears to be the same as the Andrus and Starr anthology (174C).

174C. ANONYMOUS

Remarkable shipwrecks, or a collection of interesting accounts of naval disasters with many particulars of the extraordinary adventures and sufferings of the crews of vessels wrecked at sea, and of their treatment on distant shores together with an account of the deliverance of survivors. Selected from authentic sources

Hartford, published by Andrus and Starr, John Russell, Jr., printer, 1813

1. Loss of the brig *Sally,* with the sufferings of her crew, on the wreck

2. Shipwreck of the Countess de Bourk, on the coast of Algiers; and the adventures of her daughter, Mademoiselle de Bourk, in 1719

3. Narrative of the loss of the American ship *Hercules,* on the coast of Caffraria, June 16th, 1796

4. Loss of the *Grosvenor* Indiaman, on the coast of Caffraria, August 4th, 1792; with the particulars relative to the unfortunate survivors of the wreck

5. Shipwreck of the English East-Indiaman, the *Fatty-salem;* on the coast of Coromandel, on the 28th of August, 1761

6. The loss of His Majesty's ship *Litchfield,* of fifty guns, on the coast of Barbary, on the 30th of November, 1758

7. Shipwreck of the Portuguese vessel *St. James,* off the coast of Africa, in 1586

8. The loss of an English sloop, on the coast of the island of Cape Breton, in 1780 [the *St. Lawrence*]

9. The loss of His Majesty's ship *Centaur,* of seventy-four guns, September 23rd, 1782; and the miraculous preservation of the pinnace, with the captain, master, and ten of the crew

10. Shipwreck of the sloop *Betsy,* on the coast of Dutch Guiana, August 5th, 1756

11. The shipwreck of a Portuguese vessel, with Emmanuel Sosa, and his wife Eleonora Garcia Sala, on the east coast of Africa, in 1553

12. Narrative of the loss of the brig *Tyrrel,* which was overset in a gale of wind, on her passage from New York to Antigua, in 1759

13. Narrative of the sufferings and extraordinary adventures of four Russian sailors, who were cast away on the desert island of East-Spitsbergen, in 1743

14. Loss of the *Halsewell* East Indiaman, wrecked off Seacombe, in the isle of Purbeck, on the coast of Dorsetshire, January 6th, 1786

15. Loss of the *Nottingham* galley, of London; wrecked on Boon-Island, near New-England, December 11th, 1710; with the sufferings, preservation, and deliverance of the crew

16. Narrative of the shipwreck of M. De Brisson, on the coast of Barbary; and of his captivity among the Moors, in 1785

17. Shipwreck of the *Jonge Thomas,* a Dutch East-Indiaman, at the Cape of Good Hope, on the 2d of June, 1773

18. Loss of the *Apollo* frigate, and twenty-nine sail of West-Indiamen, near Figuera, on the coast of Portugal, April 2d, 1804

19. Shipwreck of the French ship *Droits de L'Homme,* of seventy-four guns, driven on shore, on the 13th of January, 1797

20. The loss of His Majesty's ship *Phoenix,* off the island of Cuba, in 1780

21. The sufferings of Robert Scotney, second mate of the brig *Thomas,* Captain Gardner, who survived by himself seventy-five days, on a perfect wreck in 1803

22. The sufferings of Ephraim How, of New-Haven, who set sail for Boston in a small ketch, which on its return was wrecked near Cape Sable, in the year 1676

23. Loss of His Majesty's ship *La Tribune,* off Halifax (Nova Scotia) November, 1797

24. Shipwreck of Captain George Roberts, on his passage from Virginia to the coast of Guinea, in the year 1721

25. Narrative of the loss of the *Earl of Abergavenny,* East Indiaman, Captain John Wadsworth [Wordsworth], which drove on the Shambles, off the Bill of Portland, and sunk in twelve fathom water, on the 5th of February, 1805

26. Loss of the *Corbin,* commanded by Francis Pirard de Laval, on the Maldivia Islands

27. Loss by fire, of the French East-India Company's vessel, the *Prince,* bound from L'Orient to Pondicherry, July 26th, 1752

28. Shipwreck of the *Degrave* East-Indiaman, on the coast of Madagascar, in 1701

29. An extraordinary famine in the American ship *Peggy,* on her return from the Azores to New-York, in 1765

30. The loss of the American sloop *Thetis,* which was upset in a gale of wind, on the 23d of November, 1809, on her passage from New-Bedford to Savanna

The *Thetis,* with thirty-four on board, sailed from New Bedford November 16, 1809. She was thrown on her beam ends by a white squall, and only ten survived. They cut away the mast, and the ship righted but was full of water. The last five survivors were starving and buffeted for seventeen days before they were rescued by Captain Hudson of the ship *William and Henry.*

31. A brief sketch of the engagements that have taken place between the public vessels of the United States and those of Great Britain, since the commencement of the present war

32. [35 pages of names of subscribers, about 4,000 in all]

1 8 1 4

175C. [ANONYMOUS?]
The duty and reasonableness of prayer . . . loss of the Lady Hobart . . .
Boston, 1814

176C. FLINDERS, CAPTAIN MATTHEW, R.N.
       A voyage to Terra Australis; undertaken for the purpose of com-
          pleting the discovery of that vast country, 1801–1803, in
          H.M.S. "Investigator" . . . with an account of the ship-
          wreck of the "Porpoise"
       [London?], 1814. Two vols. with 8 plates, plus atlas with 16 large-
          scale maps

177C. JACKSON, JAMES GREY
       An account of the empire of Morocco, and the districts of Suse and
          Talilelt . . . an account of shipwrecks on the west coast of
          Africa . . .
       London, William Bulmer and Co., 1814. Port., 2 maps, 12 pl., 3
          colored
I have not seen this book. In view of the date and the listed material, this might have
    been a source for some of the other books published about shipwrecks on the
    Moroccan coast—by Riley, for instance. See 190C.

178C. O'BRIEN, DONAT H.
       Narrative of Captain O'Brien, R.N., containing an account of the
          shipwreck, captivity, and escape from France . . . the
          "Hussar," 1804
       London, 1814; 2 vols., 1839
The *Hussar* was on blockade duty, in the Western Approaches, when she was
    ordered to England. The course she followed was too far to the east, and the
    ship ran on the rocks of the Saints, near L'Orient. Most of the crew reached
    shore and were captured and imprisoned for years in France. The story of the
    wreck of the *Hussar,* and of experiences in French prisons, has been published
    recently in *The Adventures of John Wetherell,* N.Y., 1953. This book, and
    probably O'Brien's as well, were used by C. S. Forester in writing the Horn-
    blower stories.

179C. SWETT, SAMUEL
       Interesting narrative of the loss of the ship Milo of Newburyport,
          November 13, 1813, and the preservation of her company after
          being 18 days in the long boat
       Newburyport, 1814. 14 pp., 8vo

                                  1 8 1 5

180C. ANONYMOUS
       Narrative of the heroic enterprise of William Hanson . . . also,
          the shipwreck and sufferings of Occum Chamnan, a Siamese
          mandarin, in 1674
       London, Champante and Whitrow [1815?]

181C. JEWITT, JOHN R. [really written by Alsop, Richard]
       A narrative of the adventures and sufferings of John R. Jewitt; only
          survivor of the crew of the ship Boston, during a captivity of

nearly three years among the savages of Nootka Sound: with an account of the manners, mode of living, and religious opinions of the natives

Middletown, printed by Seth Richards, 1815 [March]. Other editions: Middletown, July 1815; New York [1815?], 1816; Wakefield, 1820; Edinburgh, 1824; Ithaca, 1840, 1849, 1851; London, 1896; in German, Leipzig, 1928

See 155C, 1807.

1 8 1 6

182C. ADAMS, ROBERT

The narrative of Robert Adams, a sailor, who was wrecked on the western coast of Africa, in the year 1810, was detained three years in slavery by the Arabs of the great desert, and resided several months in the city of Tombuctoo. With a map, notes, and an appendix

London, printed for John Murray, Albemarle-Street, by William Bulmer and Co., Cleveland-Row, 1816 [edited by S. Cock]; Boston, Wells and Lilly, 1817; Paris, Michaud, 1817; Stockholm, 1817

Robert Adams claimed to be an American sailor of Hudson, New York, the son of a sail-maker father and a mulatto mother, who had left New York in the 280-ton ship *Charles,* James Horton, Master, on June 17, 1810, for Gibraltar. There were eleven in the crew, and after discharging cargo at Gibraltar the ship set sail for the Isle of May for salt, and to trade along the African coast. Like so many other ships, the *Charles* was caught in unknown currents and was carried ashore about 400 miles north of Senegal on October 11, 1810. The whole crew reached shore, but all were made slaves by the Arabs, and the captain and mate killed. Adams was taken far to the eastward and visited Timbuctoo on a trading expedition; he may have been only the second or third European or American to describe that city. He was transferred from owner to owner, and at last reached Mogadore where he was ransomed by Mr. Dupuis, the British Consul there. He was sent to Cadiz and then London, where he told his story to the editor of this book.

Adams was illiterate, but must have been of high intelligence to have kept events and dates as straight as he did for the quite long period, 1810 to 1814, during which he was a slave. According to his narrative he was much more combative, much less overwhelmed by his situation, than Riley or Robbins or Paddock, who wrote parallel accounts at nearly the same time. Adams once attacked a cruel Arab, and survived, and he frequently refused to work, telling his owners that they could kill him if they chose. He even had an affair of some length with the young wife of one of his owners, and was discovered only through the jealousy of an older wife. The young wife was divorced, and Adams handed over to another owner.

Adams had shipped on board the *Charles* under the name Benjamin Rose, and he was obviously uncomfortable in London and feared the press gang. Probably he had served in the British Navy and had deserted. It is interesting to note that a young black from Hudson, New York, Jack, had been captured by Arabs from the wreck of Captain Paddock's ship *Oswego* (see 193C). One wonders if perhaps Adams might have been Jack, and that there were other cruises and adventures that he preferred not to mention to Mr. Cock. How many blacks from Hudson, New York, would be likely to be roaming around the Sahara?

183C. ALLEN, MRS. SARAH
>   A narrative of the shipwreck and unparalleled sufferings of Mrs. Sarah Allen
>   Boston, Benjamin Marston, 1816, 24pp.; Boston, M. Brewer, 1816

184C. CAMPBELL, ARCHIBALD
>   A voyage round the world, from 1806 to 1812, in which Japan, Kamschatka, the Aleutian Islands and the Sandwich Islands were visited, including a narrative of the author's shipwreck on the Island of Sannack, and his subsequent wreck in the ship's long-boat; with an account of the present state of the Sandwich Islands, and a vocabulary of their language
>   Edinburgh, 1816; New York, Van Winkle, Wiley & Co., 1817; Jena, August Schmid & Co., 1817; Amsterdam, J. C. Van Kesteren, 1817; New York, Broderick and Ritter, 1819; Charleston, S.C., Duke & Browne, 1822; Roxbury, Mass., Allen & Watts, 1825; Univ. of Hawaii Press, 1967 (1822 ed.); Da Capo Press, N.Y., 1971

Campbell, a Scots seaman, entered on the Indiaman *Thames* for a voyage to China in May, 1806. They reached Whampoa in January, 1807, where Campbell and some others deserted to an American ship, the *Eclipse,* which had been chartered by the Russian American Company. In the *Eclipse* Nagasaki, Kamschatka, and the Aleutians were visited in order, and among these last islands the ship struck a rock and was lost. The entire crew escaped safely in a longboat to the island of Sannack, where natives and some Russians offered help. Since some of the cargo of the *Eclipse* could be saved, the men in the longboat set out to inform officials on Kodiak Island, which they did, but on the return voyage to Sannack the longboat was wrecked and the men had to make a terrible trek through the snow to seek help. Campbell froze both feet, parts of which had to be amputated when they at last reached a settlement. Campbell was eventually taken to Hawaii, where he settled down for a time and did well; but he left the islands on a whaler which took him to Rio de Janeiro, where he lived for two years. He then returned to Scotland, where he stayed for four years, but left on an American ship, hoping to return to Hawaii. According to the text, he published the book to get funds for the journey.

Campbell's is one of the best of shipwreck narratives, with good pictures of life in the Aleutians and in Hawaii. The story has been retold by Stanley D. Porteous, in *The Restless Voyage,* London, 1949.

185C. FOSS, DANIEL
>   Brig Negociator, of Philadelphia, which foundered in the Pacific Ocean on the 26th November, 1809—and who lived five years on a small barren island . . .
>   Boston, printed for N. Caverly, Jr., 1816. Another edition, New York, W. Abbatt, 1914

The *Negociator*—strange name for a ship—was out of Philadelphia on a sealing voyage in 1809, with twenty-one men on board. She struck an iceberg somewhere in the far north Pacific on November 25, 1809, and sank almost at once. All on board escaped in the longboat with scanty provisions and water, and sailed south to escape the cold. After about two months only three men survived, Captain Nicoll, a seaman named Jones, and Foss. These three drew lots, and Jones was the unlucky man. Neither Nicoll nor Foss could kill him, and Jones cut his own wrist, bled to death, and was eaten. In February, 1810, the two survivors saw an island and ran the boat ashore; it capsized, and Foss alone survived. He remained on this unnamed dot of land, eating seals and fish, and drinking rainwater caught in hollows, for five years. He was at last picked up by the bark *Neptune,* Captain Call, Batavia for New Bedford, and brought back to the United States.

Since Foss was the only survivor of the crew of the *Negociator,* we must accept his word on what happened. One wonders why the men in the longboat did not try for either Kamchatka or Alaska, rather than sailing south after the ship was wrecked. But if Foss did not tell the truth of his adventures, no one will ever know.

186C. PLOWMAN, WILLIAM
A full account of the dreadful shipwreck of the Comus and Harponeer, in Shot's Bay, Newfoundland, Jan. [1816] by William Plowman, and how 110 out of 400 passengers were saved by means of a Newfoundland dog
n.p., n.d. [1816?] A broadside

1 8 1 7

187C. CORRÉARD, ALEXANDRE, AND SAVIGNY, HENRI
Naufrage de la frégate le Meduse faisant partie de l'expédition du Senegal en 1816 . . .
Paris, Corréard, 1817; 4th edition, 1821; London, H. Colburn, 1818; Haarlem, Loosjes, 1818

The wreck of the *Medusa* is one of the best known in the whole history of maritime enterprise, primarily because of Géricault's famous painting, "The Raft of the Medusa." It was also one of the worst examples of leadership ever given, in which panic drove out every vestige of common sense. The *Medusa* sailed on June 17, 1816, from Rochefort for Senegal. She carried M. Schmaltz, who had been appointed Governor of Senegal, and was commanded by Captain La Chaumareys. Schmaltz wished only to reach Senegal as soon as possible; La Chaumareys had been chosen for his position primarily because he had opposed Napoleon. For some reason La Chaumareys refused to trust the officers of the ship and followed the directions of a passenger, M. Richefort, who claimed to know all about navigating on the dangerous northwest coast of Africa. The result was that the *Medusa,* in perfectly clear weather, struck upon the Arguin Bank and could not be freed. A fraction of those on board were placed in the ship's boats. Most of the rest were ordered on board a hastily built raft, so inadequate that all those on it were partly in the water all the time, which the boats were to tow to shore. A few people were left on the *Medusa.* In short order the cable by which the raft was towed was cut, and the boats set off. Of the more than 150 people on the raft, only a dozen survived. Corréard

and Savigny, the authors of this account, were on the raft. The boats did reach
the shore of Africa, and most of those in them survived to reach Senegal. The
story of those in the boats was well told by Charlotte Dard in her *La Chaumiére
Africaine* (218C). When the *Medusa* was finally reached by ships sent from
Senegal, it was discovered that the ship had not broken up, and that all those
on the raft might have stayed on the ship in relative safety. The narrative by
Corréard and Savigny created a great furor when it was published, and many
denials, but the best evidence indicates that their account is essentially accurate. A modern summary is Alexander McKee's *Death Raft: The Human
Drama of the Medusa Shipwreck,* Scribner's, New York, 1976.

188C. McLEOD, JOHN
>   Narrative of a voyage in H.M.S. Alceste along the coast of Corea to
>   the island of Lewchew, with an account of her subsequent ship-
>   wreck
>   London, John Murray, 1817, 1818; Philadelphia, Carey, 1818

The *Alceste,* with two other ships, sailed from Spithead on February 9, 1816, for
China. She carried Lord Amherst, who had been named Ambassador Extraordinary for the King of Great Britain to the Emperor of China. All went well on
the cruise out, and China, Korea, and Manilla were visited by the small fleet.
This book contains a good deal of material about the contemporary life in
China and Korea. On the return voyage the ship was on the way through the
Straits of Gaspar, near Borneo, when she struck on an uncharted reef. There
was no hope of getting the ship off, so all on board were taken in boats to a
small island, Pulo Leat, where stores from the ship were deposited and a well
dug. Since the boats could hold only half the ship's company, it was decided to
send a group in the barge and cutter to Java for help, and Lord Amherst and
forty-six others set off, leaving about two hundred men and one woman on the
island. Natives threatened those left on Pulo Leat, but Captain Maxwell and
the other officers kept morale high and discipline effective. The ship was lost
on February 19, 1817; in early March the ship *Ternate,* which had been lying at
Batavia, turned up at Pulo Leat and took in everyone. The voyage to Batavia
was uneventful.

189C. MARINER, WILLIAM
>   An account of the natives of the Tonga Islands, in the South Pacific
>   Ocean, with an original grammar and vocabulary of their
>   language, compiled and arranged . . . by John Martin, M.D.
>   London, 1817, 2 vols., 8 vo, portrait; Boston, 1820, 1 vol.; 3rd edi-
>   tion, 2 vols., Edinburgh, 1827

Mariner was a sailor on board the *Port-au-Prince,* 500 tons, Captain Duck, which
sailed from Gravesend on February 12, 1805. The cruise was a strange one, for
the *Port-au-Prince* carried letters of marque allowing her to serve as a warship
against Napoleon and his allies, and the ship was also prepared for whaling and
sealing. There were a number of conflicts with Spanish ships and settlements in
the Pacific, and some whales and many seals were captured. In late November,
1806, the ship anchored off Lefooga, in the Tonga group. Captain Duck had
died, and the new captain, one Brown, foolishly allowed the Tonga natives to
come on board ship in large numbers, and armed. On the first of December the
natives killed about half the crew, including Brown, captured the rest, and
burned the ship. Mariner lived reasonably well with the natives for several
years, learning the language and the details of their life. He still wished to
escape, however, and eventually was able to take his canoe off to the brig

Favourite, of Port Jackson. That ship took Mariner to Macao, and he finally reached England in June, 1811. Dr. Martin put the narrative together; it is considered an authoritative account of life in the Tonga Islands just as European and American influences were first felt.

190C. RILEY, JAMES

An authentic narrative of the loss of the American brig Commerce, wrecked on the western coast of Africa, in the month of August, 1815. With an account of the sufferings of her surviving officers and crew, who were enslaved by the wandering Arabs on the great African desart, or Zahahrah; and observations historical, geographical, &c. made during the travels of the author, while a slave to the Arabs, and in the Empire of Morocco. By James Riley, late Master and Supercargo. Preceded by a brief sketch of the author's life; and concluded by a description of the famous city of Tombuctoo, on the river Niger, and of another large city, far south of it, on the same river, called Wassanah; narrated to the author at Mogadore, by Sidi Hamet, the Arabian merchant. With an Arabic and English vocabulary. Illustrated and embellished with ten handsome copperplate engravings

Hartford, published by the author, 1817; New York, 1817; London, J. Murray, 1817; New York, bound together with Paddock's *Narrative,* Collins & Co., 1818; Paris, 2 vols., 1818; Chillicothe [Ohio?], Bailhache & Scott, 1820; Lexington, Ky., 1823; Hartford, 1828, 1829, 1831, 1836; New York, 1839; Hartford, 1843, 1844, 1846, 1847, 1848, 1850, 1851; New York, Leavitt & Allen, 1859; New York, 1965

There was also a *Sequel,* by William Willshire Riley, Columbus, 1851. James Riley named his son for William Willshire, the British consul at Mogadore who was so kind to suffering Americans.

James Riley was a native of Middletown, Connecticut. Brought up a farmer, he became a sailor and learned enough to become first a mate and then a master of vessels. On May 6, 1815, he set sail in the *Commerce,* 220 tons, from the Connecticut River for New Orleans. That voyage completed, he loaded tobacco and flour for Gibraltar, where he arrived on August 9, 1815. There he loaded brandy and wine, and decided to complete his cargo with salt from the Cape Verde Islands. On this last voyage Riley failed to make enough allowance for currents—the common cause for shipwreck on the coast of Morocco—and the *Commerce* struck near Cape Bojador on August 28, 1815. The whole crew reached shore with the longboat, but Arabs attacked them and forced them back to the wreck. They repaired the boat and set off in it to the south, but were forced to land again because of thirst and starvation. After this second landing, near Cape Barba, they were captured and enslaved by Arabs. Riley and a few others of his crew were sold from master to master until he became the property of one Sidi Hamet, who undertook to send him to Mogadore where he could be ransomed. After many adventures and much suffering Riley reached Mogadore in October, 1815, and was ransomed with his fellows by William Willshire, the British Consul there, for $1,852.45. Riley reached New York on March 20, 1816. Other crew members, including Archibald Robbins (see 194C), were later ransomed, but four of Riley's crew were still slaves when the book was published.

Riley's *Sufferings in Africa* was one of the most popular books of the nineteenth century in the United States, probably because of interest in the Arab countries developed in the wars with the Barbary States, and because of its interesting reverse view of slavery—Moors were considered Blacks, and in this narrative they were the owners of white Americans. Abraham Lincoln read Riley's book as a boy, and the book is said to have influenced his attitudes on slavery.

191C. TERRY, EZEKIEL [papers and recollections of Patterson, Samuel]
Narrative of the adventures and sufferings of Samuel Patterson, experienced in the Pacific Ocean, and many other parts of the world with an account of the Feegee, and Sandwich islands
From the press in Palmer [Mass.], May 1, 1817; Providence, printed at the *Journal* office, 1825; Fairfield, Washington, Galleon Press, 1967

This narrative is one of the best of the "mendicant" books, printed by poor wretches who then peddled them wherever they could for whatever they could get. The narrative of Israel Potter is another good example. Patterson's experiences, on the other hand, were a good deal like those of Archibald Campbell (184C), with visits to the northwest American coast and to Hawaii; like Campbell, Patterson claimed to own land in Hawaii. Patterson was born in North Providence, Rhode Island, on August 16, 1785. His father was a sailor, and Patterson himself went to sea when he was 14. He later was a sailor in the United States Navy, and visited Algiers and Constantinople in the *George Washington*. Cruises in merchant vessels took Patterson to Havana, the American Northwest, and Hawaii. Patterson moved from ship to ship, and at last became a seaman on board an unnamed American ship commanded by Captain E. H. Corey. That ship, in the Fijis, picked up two men from the *Port-au-Prince*, which had been captured by the natives; this was William Mariner's vessel (189C). On June 20, 1808, Patterson's ship struck on a reef near Nirie. The crew reached the island and got along reasonably well with the natives. Patterson had earlier had a stroke, and was sick a good deal of the time. Some months later he and a fellow castaway reached an Australian vessel. After some other adventures Patterson found an American ship and returned to his native Providence on June 9, 1810. The chief impression one gets from his narrative is that American ships were everywhere in the Pacific, and that a Rhode Islander in the Fijis could count on finding a neighbor from home on the next island.

1 8 1 8

192C. FRACKER, GEORGE
Narrative of the shipwreck of George Fracker and the loss of the ship Jane at the mouth of the Rio de la Plata, September, 1817 . . .
First published in 1818 by George Fracker [Boston?], 51 pp., 24mo. Republished by A. H. Fracker, Philadelphia, E. C. Markley and Son, Printers, 422 Library St., 1870.

There was another edition, probably identical with that of 1818, *A Voyage to South America, with an Account of a Shipwreck in the Rio Plata in 1817* . . . , Boston, 1826. The 1870 reprint was in wrappers, and I have seen a copy signed by George Fracker, "The Survivor," which means that Mr. Fracker lived for at least fifty-three years after the wreck.

Fracker, from Boston, signed on as mate on the *Jane* in the summer of 1817. The ship made a voyage from Buenos Aires to Rio de Janeiro and back, and then was caught in a terrible storm while at anchor in the Rio Plata off Montevideo. The ship dragged her anchors, struck on a reef, and broke up. Fracker was at last swept ashore, the only survivor of twenty-three on board when the storm struck. He was badly injured, and had difficulties with lawless gauchos, but was at last carried to civilization, nursed back to reasonable health, and sent off to his Boston home.

193C. PADDOCK, JUDAH

> A narrative of the shipwreck of the ship Oswego, on the coast of South Barbary, and of the sufferings of the Master and the crew while in bondage among the Arabs; interspersed with numerous remarks upon the country and its inhabitants, and concerning the peculiar perils of that coast

> New-York, published by Captain James Riley, J. Seymour, printer, 1818; London, 1818

The *Oswego* was a ship of 260 tons, of Hudson, New York. Captain Paddock sailed in her from New York for Cork on January 8, 1800, with a crew of thirteen. From Cork the *Oswego* sailed for the Cape Verde Islands to pick up salt and skins for New York, but the ship was caught in an east-running current and struck on the coast of Morocco, near Cape Nun, on April 3, 1800. The crew was soon captured by Arabs, and separated, but Captain Paddock and some companions were fairly soon taken to Mogadore and ransomed there, about May 17, 1801. He had some difficulty in getting passage back to the United States, but eventually arrived home at Hudson on December 1, 1801. Obviously Paddock published this account because of the success of Captain Riley's *Sufferings in Africa,* and Riley used some of his profits to bring out this parallel account. Paddock refers in his narrative to one of his crew, ". . . a black man Jack of Hudson. . . ." This Jack was later separated from Captain Paddock and never seen again. It seems possible that this Jack may have been the Robert Adams, of Hudson, who was the narrator of another story of an Arab captivity (182C).

194C. ROBBINS, ARCHIBALD

> A journal comprising an account of the loss of the brig Commerce, of Hartford, (Con.) James Riley, Master, upon the western coast of Africa. August 28th, 1815; also of the slavery and sufferings of the author and the rest of the crew, upon the Desert of Zahara, in the years 1815, 1816, 1817; with accounts of the manners, customs, and habits of the wandering Arabs; also a brief historical and geographical view of the continent of Africa

> Hartford, published by Silas Andrus, 1818; 20th edition, 1829; Greenwich, Conn., 1937

Robbins was an able seaman on board the *Commerce,* and endured the same sufferings as Captain Riley described (190C). Obviously Robbins wished to cash in on the interest shown in Riley's adventures, and rushed his narrative into print soon after the captain's. At least eight editions of this book appeared in the year of first publication, 1818; it must have been popular, but I suspect that the editions must have been very small.

1 8 1 9

195C. ANONYMOUS
> Wonderful escapes! containing the narrative of the shipwreck of the
> Antelope packet. The loss of the Lady Hobart packet, on an
> island of ice. The shipwreck of the Hercules, on the coast of
> Africa. An extraordinary escape from the effects of a storm, in
> a journey over the frozen sea, in North America
>
> Dublin, W. Espey, 1819, pp. 3, 6–180, illus. Dublin, printed by
> Richard Grace, 3 Mary-Street, 1822

The narratives of the *Antelope,* the *Lady Hobart,* and the *Hercules* are standard
shipwreck stories. The last narrative is attributed to ". . . an Englishman who
emigrated to America" and tells of a sledge journey over sea-ice with Eskimos,
on the coast of Labrador in 1782. I have not seen this narrative anywhere else.

196C. ANONYMOUS [a main-top-man]
> The fate of Myra, or, a cruise to the westward. A poem in four
> parts. By a main-top-man
>
> Chiswick, press of W. Whittingham, published for the author by
> W. H. Reid, 1819. 130 pp., 8vo

I have not seen this book, but a bookseller stated that it is about a shipwreck. I do
not know whether the account was factual or invented.

197C. DE MAY, R.
> Narrative of the sufferings and adventures of Henderick Portenger,
> a private soldier of the Lake Swiss Regiment de Mueron, who
> was wrecked on the shores of Abyssinia, in the Red Sea (ship
> "Weissheld") Capt. Baer
>
> London, 1819

198C. DUMONT, PIERRE JOSEPH
> Narrative of thirty-four years slavery and travels in Africa. By P. J.
> Dumont. Collected from the account delivered by himself, by
> J. S. Quesne
>
> London, printed for Sir Richard Phillips and Co., Bride-Court,
> Bridge-Street, 1819

Dumont claimed to have been born in Paris in 1768, and to have served as an officer
in the French Navy during the American War. He was present at the Battle of
the Saints, April 12, 1782, and afterward returned to France. He sailed for
Mahon in the *Lievre* in late October, 1782, and the ship was caught in a bad
storm and wrecked on the coast of Africa, between Oran and Algiers. Dumont
and others were made slaves by the Koubals, and were imprisoned at Mount
Felix by Sheik Osman along with other European slaves to the number of
2,000. After many years of hard labor, severe punishments, and sufferings,
Dumont was one of a group of slaves traded to the Bey of Titre for some
Koubal prisoners, and he was at last freed when Lord Exmouth bombarded
Algiers and demanded that the Christian slaves there be freed. Dumont reached
Marseilles in a British vessel, and made his way to Paris, where he told his
story.

199C. FRANCKEN, C. W., CHIEF OFFICER [Sixth Officer]
> A narrative of the loss of the Hon. East India Company's ship

Cabalva, which was wrecked on the morning of July 7, 1818, upon the Cargados Garragos Reef, in the Indian Ocean
London, printed for Black, Kingsbury, Parbury, and Allen, Leadenhall Street, 1819

On the flyleaf of the National Maritime Museum Library's copy of this book: "The author of this pamphlet, C. W. Francken, reached the rank of Captain in the Honorable East India Company's Service, and afterwards became a clergyman in the Church of England. His son, W. H. Francken, who died at Scarborough in 1922, a retired Indian civilian, left me his father's sword in his will."

The *Cabalva,* 1200 tons, Captain Dalrymple, sailed from Gravesend for China, April 14, 1818, with about 130 people aboard. On April 17 the ship struck on the Ower Bank in the English Channel but was got off with only minor damage; later it was discovered that the Ower Lightship had been driven from its post, and that the pilot was not at fault in this grounding. The ship leaked fairly badly as a result of striking, and the crew had to work at the pumps quite steadily, which may have contributed to bad feeling. There was a near mutiny at one time. On July 7, 1818, while the ship was bound from Cape Town for Bombay for repairs, she struck on the Cargados Garragos Reef, about 250 miles from the Isle de France. About ten of the crew were drowned, including the captain; all the rest reached rocks and sandbanks. About half the crew, well supplied with beer and wine and brandy, spent their whole time in getting and being drunk. The others repaired the large cutter, set sail for Mauritius, and reached Port Louis, where a ship was immediately dispatched to rescue the others on the reef. The loss of the *Cabalva* is a story of very bad discipline and very good luck, an illustration of the fact that it was probably better to suffer shipwreck on a distant reef in good weather than to be wrecked in familiar waters in a bad storm.

1 8 2 0

200C. ANONYMOUS [and Stout, Captain Benjamin?]
Cape of Good Hope and its dependencies. An accurate description of those . . . regions. . . . Likewise a detail of Captain S's travels through the deserts of Caffraria . . . to the Cape
London, 1820. 8vo

See 127C for Captain Benjamin Stout's narrative of the loss of the *Hercules.*

201C. ANONYMOUS
The shipwreck: showing what sometimes happens on the seacoasts, etc.
New York, American Tract Society, 1820; London, 1830

In verse. This may be part or all of Falconer's *The Shipwreck,* or something quite different.

202C. BRADLEY, ELIZA [?]
An authentic narrative of the shipwreck and sufferings of Mrs. Eliza Bradley, the wife of Captain James Bradley of Liverpool, commander of the ship Sally which was wrecked on the coast of Barbary, in June, 1818 . . . Written by herself. . . .
Boston, printed by James Walden, 1820; Boston, G. Clark, 1821, 1823; Exeter, Abel Brown, 1824, 1826; Concord, L. Roby,

1829; Boston, John Page, 1832; Ithaca, Mack, Andrus &
Woodruff, 1835, 1837; Lowell, H. P. Huntoon, 1848

According to the narrative, Eliza Bradley set sail with her husband in the ship *Sally,*
Liverpool for Teneriffe, May, 1818. About five weeks later the ship was lost on
the coast of Morocco, and all on board became prisoners of the desert Arabs.
Mrs. Bradley, sustained by her Bible, endured her captivity for about six
months, and then was ransomed by William Willshire, British Consul at
Mogadore, who had already rescued Captain Bradley. Husband and wife
reached England in February, 1819.

   This narrative is almost certainly spurious, another in the succession *Cap-
tivity and Sufferings of Mrs. Mary Velnet,* and *Captivity and Sufferings of
Maria Martin* (141C and 156C). This book is stated to be the "First American
Edition." I have searched diligently and can find no English edition at all. The
wreck is not recorded at Lloyd's, or in the Custom House records. Parts of
Mrs. Bradley's *Narrative* are taken directly from Captain Riley's *Sufferings in
Africa,* a best seller of those years. Since James Walden never published
another book, I believe that he too was probably invented, and that G. Clark,
the second publisher, used his name on a manufactured book.

203C. [BUCHAN, G.]
       Narrative of the loss of the "Winterton" East Indiaman, wrecked
          on the coast of Madagascar in 1792, and of the sufferings con-
          nected with that event, with a short account of the natives of
          Madagascar, etc. By a passenger of the ship
       Edinburgh, 1820. Frontis., fldg. map, and plate

The loss of the *Winterton* was described by the third mate of that ship in his narrative published by Archibald Duncan.

204C. RALFE, J.
       The naval chronology of Great Britain, or an historical account of
          naval and maritime events from . . . 1803 to . . . 1816
       London, 1820. 3 vols., 59 hand-colored plates

                              1 8 2 1

205C. CHASE, OWEN
       Narrative of the most extraordinary and distressing ship wreck of
          the whale ship Essex of Nantucket
       New York, W. B. Gilley, 1821

The *Essex,* Captain George Pollard, sailed from Nantucket on August 12, 1819, for
a sperm whaling cruise in the Pacific. Nothing of importance occurred until
November 20, 1820, when a pod of whales was seen and two were struck. One
whaleboat was damaged by a whale, and while Chase was repairing it he saw a
whale, whether one of those struck or not he could not know, a few ship's
lengths away and swimming directly at the ship. While he watched, the whale, a
large one, rammed the ship at the fore-chains and almost certainly broke in her
timbers. While the crew stared aghast, the whale flurried on the surface, and
then charged the ship once more. This time the whale struck the *Essex* just
below the cathead and completely stove in her bow, when the *Essex* went over
on her beam-ends. All boats returned to the ship and they got out what food
and water and equipment they could; they then decided to make for the coast
of South America in the three boats. En route they landed at Henderson Island,

but could not stay there for lack of water and food, though three sailors were left. One boat was lost halfway to Chile, and two were picked up by ships near Juan Fernandez. There were five survivors in the boats and three on Henderson Island, of twenty-one men who had set out from the wreck of the *Essex.*

In all three boats the survivors had resorted to cannibalism, and in Captain Pollard's whaleboat, Owen Coffin, a relative of the captain, was killed and eaten. Herman Melville used Chase's narrative as a source for his *Moby Dick,* and thus made the whale ship *Essex* a part of world literature. See 241C and 246C.

206C. COCHELET, CHARLES
> Naufrage du brick français La Sophie, 1819, sur la côte occidentale
> d'Afrique . . .
> Paris, 1821. 2 vols., map, plates. *Narrative of the shipwreck of the
> Sophia* . . . , by Charles Cochelet, Ancient Paymaster-General in Catalonia and one of the sufferers. London, printed for
> Sir Richard Phillips and Co., Bride-Court, Bridge-Street, 1822

M. Cochelet sailed from Nantes in the *Sophia,* Captain Scheult, on May 14, 1819, with thirteen on board. The Captain tried to sight the Madeiras and the Canaries, but was baffled by the winds and let the currents sweep his ship too far to the eastward. On May 30 the ship struck on the coast of Africa. M. Cochelet and his companions were captured by the desert Arabs, and enslaved. They were sold and resold, and at last reached Mogadore, where M. Cochelet was ransomed. He arrived back in France, at Marseilles, February 8, 1820. Captain James Riley's *Sufferings in Africa* is mentioned twice by Cochelet, so this story of the loss of the *Sophia,* like the narratives of Paddock and Robbins, was probably published because of the popularity of Riley's story.

207C. EYRIES, J. B.
> Histoire des naufrages
> Paris, 1821. 3 vols., engravings, 16mo

See 88C, 1781

[1 8 2 2]

208C. ANONYMOUS
> Chambers's Edinburgh Journal, Vol. V, p. 252 [1822?]

Cited by J. G. Lockhart as a reference to the loss of the *Blenden Hall.* See 350C.

209C. J[ACKSON], N[OAH]
> A brief narrative of the most distressing shipwrecks, and the sufferings of their crews, in 1815, 16, 17, 18, 19, 20, and 21. By N. J.
> T. George, n.p., n.d.

210C. PEPPER, LIEUTENANT JOHN
> Asiatic Journal, Vol. 14, p. 119, 1822

J. G. Lockhart cites this article in his book on the loss of the *Blenden Hall.* Pepper was a lieutenant in the East India Company's Bombay Marine, and a passenger on board the ship. See 350C.

1 8 2 3

211C. ANONYMOUS [Allen, William]
    Accounts of shipwrecks and other disasters at sea, designed to be in-
        teresting and useful to mariners . . . compiled by a friend to
        seamen
    Brunswick, Maine, published by Griffin, 1823
The introduction gives some statistics on shipwrecks. Allen quotes Benjamin
Franklin, and mentions the loss of the *Essex.* Refers in the introduction to
Riley's narrative, and to the *Blenheim, Java, Wasp,* and *Epervier,* all lost with-
out trace.
        1. *Albion*
        2. *Confiance,* 1822. All lost
        3. Liverpool packet, 1822, iceberg
        4. *Thomas and Ann,* 1649
        5. *Lady Hobart*
        6. *Jupiter,* 1805
        7. *Sally,* 1805
        8. *La Lutine,* 1799
        9. *William* of Boston, 1822
        10. *Boston,* 1802, Nootka Sound
        11. *Tonquin,* 1811–12. Pacific Northwest
        12. *Industry,* 1805
        13. *Sarah,* 1805
        14. *Jane,* 1805
        15. *Margaret*
        16. *Essex,* 1819
        17. Boat of the Franklin, 1822
        18. *Macedonian*—not a shipwreck
        19. *Little William,* 1822
        20. *Rolls*
        21. *Henry*
        22. *Philip and William*
        23. *Nautilus*
        24. *L'Africaine*
        25. *Luxemburg* [*Luxborough*] Galley
This anthology contains a great many more very short narratives of disasters at sea.

212C. ANONYMOUS
    Loss of the ship Enterprise
    New Hampshire *Patriot and State Gazette,* August 4, 1823

213C. CRAMP, W. B.
    Narrative of a voyage to India; of a shipwreck on board the Lady
        Castlereagh; & a description of New South Wales
    London, 1823

214C. HURD, SETH T.
    Shipwreck! A memorial account of the unfortunate and distressing
        catastrophe of Captain Samuel Soper and his crew of the brig

Ardent, from Boston . . . shipwrecked on 28th September, 1823 . . . poetical reflections
[Boston, 1823?] Broadside

215C. VEALE, JARVIS, AND PETHERBRIDGE, EMANUEL
Morning Herald [London], Nov. 24, 1823
Cited in Goodridge's *Narrative* (297C) as containing the first report of the loss of the *Princess of Wales* cutter off the Crozets.

1 8 2 4

216C. ANONYMOUS
Slaves wrecked in the Portuguese ship called the "Donna Paula" . . . in the neighborhood of Tortola
n.p., 1824. Two reports, 10 pp., map

217C. C**T, ANT.
Nouvelle histoire des naufrages anciens et modernes, ou tableau des malheurs, captivité et délivrance d'un grand nombre de marins, avec une notice exacte sur le naufrage de la Meduse, et la mort de Mungo-Parck. Par Ant. C**t, membre de l'ancienne Université Paris, chez Corbet Aine, Libraire, Quai des Augustins, N. 61
1824; 1825
  1. Preface. Reflexions sur les naufrages
  2. Naufrage du Vénitien Quirini
  3. Emmanuel Sousa—1552
  4. Le *Santiago*—1586
  5. Vaisseau Hollandais—Nouvelle Zemble—1596/7
  6. Vaisseau Hollandais—L'Isle de Quelpaert—1653
  7. Marins Hollandais—Spitzberg—1634/5
  8. Frégate Anglaise—Nouvelle Zemble—1676
  9. *William et John,* et un navire Danois—1648
10. Le *Batavia*—1630
11. Du *Taureau,* near Cape Verde—1665
12. *Sea Venture*—1609
13. Frégate Espagnole, Nouvelle-Espagne, 1678
14. Naufrage d'Occum-Chamnan—1686
15. *Degrave,* Robert Drury, 1701
16. Le *Nottingham,* 1710
17. Naufrage de la Comtesse de Bourk—1719
18. Naufrage de la Capitaine Bering—1711
19. Quatre matelots Russes, Spitzberg—1743
20. Madame De Noyer—1776
21. Madame Godin Des Odonais—1769
22. Un vaisseau Hollandais—1773
23. Un vaisseau Français, Dieppe, 1777
24. *Grosvenor*—1782
25. *Juno*—1795

218C. DARD, CHARLOTTE (née Picard, Charlotte Adelaide)
   La chaumière Africaine; ou, histoire d'une famille française jetée
      sur la côte occidentale de l'Afrique, à la suite du naufrage de la
      frégate la Meduse
   Dijon, 1824

For the loss of the *Medusa,* see 187C. Mlle. Picard was one of the fortunate few
   taken off the *Medusa* in the boats, and reached the coast of Africa safely with
   her family. Her account supports the narrative by Corréard and Savigny.

219C. FELLOWES, FRANCKEN, INGLEFIELD, SUTHERLAND
   Narratives of shipwrecks. Loss of the Lady Hobart packet; of the
      Hon. East India Company's ship Cabalva; and of the Centaur
      and Litchfield men-of-war
   London, printed for C. & J. Rivington, booksellers to the Society
      for Promoting Christian Knowledge, No. 62 St. Paul's Church-
      yard, and No. 3 Waterloo-Place, Pall-Mall, 1824

220C. KIRKHAM, SAMUEL, JR.
   Remarkable shipwrecks and chronological tables
   Harrisburg, Pennsylvania, John S. Wiestling for the author, 1824.
      98 pp.
   Contains:
   Loss of the *Carmul,* Ajan, October 2, 1819. "This narrative is given
      in a letter from Cyrus Lansington to his mother in America,
      dated St. Petersburg, Russia, August 4, 1821"
   Loss of the steamboat *Tennessee,* February 8, 1823
   Loss of the *Alert* packet, April 5, 1823
   Loss of the *St. James* [1552]

This was apparently the first book by Samuel Kirkham, Jr., whose *Grammar* was
   one of the most popular textbooks of the nineteenth century.

221C. POTTER, ISRAEL
   Life and remarkable adventures of Israel R. Potter
   Providence, printed by Henry Trumbull, 1824

Potter claimed to have been a soldier at Bunker Hill, and a sailor in the Navy during
   the Revolution. In the narrative he tells of the loss by fire of an unnamed
   vessel. This book supplied Herman Melville with material for *His Fifty Years
   of Exile (Israel Potter).* It is a mendicant book of some interest. Potter claimed
   to have made a whaling voyage to the South Seas in 1773. This he could not
   have done—the earliest such cruise was in the 1790s—so his tale of having
   fought at Bunker Hill may also be false.

222C. STANWOOD, JOHN [?]
   Aetna. A discourse . . . May 23, 1824 . . . occasioned by the
      bursting of the boiler of the steamboat Aetna . . . by John
      Stanwood
   New York, 1824. 21 pp., 8vo

The *Aetna,* Philadelphia for New York, blew up in New York harbor at 7:00 P.M. on
   May 15, 1824. There were supposedly thirty-four people on board, and ap-

parently about half of these lost their lives. Ships were near and aid was provided as quickly as could be expected, but still some people were drowned. Most of those who died were scalded to death. No cause was assigned for the explosion.

1 8 2 5

223C. ANONYMOUS
        Eighteenth and nineteenth century shipwrecks
        Paris, 1825. 2 engr. plates
There is no indication in the bookseller's catalogue whether this item is printed in English, or whether the title was translated.

224C. ANONYMOUS
        Narrative of the loss of the Comet steam-packet, on her passage
            from Inverness to Glasgow, on Friday, the 21st October 1825;
            including an account of attempts made to raise the wreck
        Hanover Street, Edinburgh, William Hunter, and London, James
            Duncan, MDCCCXXV [1825]. Frontis.
My copy of this narrative has eighty-two pages of text, and about forty pages not printed on at the end. On the eighty-third page, in longhand, is the following note in ink: "The Author of the foregoing narrative, and of the poems which follow, died of the bursting of a blood vessel—the effect of sea sickness on the —June—1831." Three poems follow, again in longhand. The first, "The loss of the Abeona," seems to be in the same handwriting as that of the note, and is about a ship that sailed for "Caffraria's strand" and caught fire. The other two poems are "The Land I Love," and "Chorus," and seem to be in a different hand, perhaps that of the author. The verses are *very* feeble.
    The *Comet* sailed from Inverness for Glasgow on October 18, 1825, under the command of Captain M'Innes. There were thirteen crewmen on board, and about seventy passengers when she approached Glasgow. As the *Comet* steamed up the Clyde off Kempoch Point, she was rammed by the steamer *Ayr*. The *Comet* sank in a few minutes, and the *Ayr*'s captain, in panic, set off for Greenock without attempting to save anyone from the sunken ship. Only thirteen people were saved, some by small boats from Gourock, and some by drifting ashore. The state of river navigation and regulation of the time is indicated by the fact that the *Ayr* was carrying a light, but the *Comet* was not because of a shortage of candles. This narrative concludes with excerpts from a number of newspapers concerning the tragedy.

225C. ANONYMOUS
        On the means of assistance in cases of shipwreck
        Norwich, England, 1825

226C. COLLINS, DANIEL
        Narrative of the shipwreck of the brig Betsy, of Wiscasset (Maine),
            and murder of five of her crew, by pirates on the coast of
            Cuba, Dec. 1824 . . . by Daniel Collins, one of the only two
            survivors
        Wiscasset [Maine], printed by John Dorr, 1825
Reprinted in Wiscasset *Seaside Oracle,* 3/20 to 4/24, 1875.

227C. A PASSENGER [Servatus] [McGregor, Sir D.]
      A narrative of the loss of the Kent East Indiaman, by fire, in the
      Bay of Biscay, on the 1st March, 1825. In a letter to a friend.
      By a passenger
  Edinburgh, published by Waugh & Innes, Edinburgh; M. Ogle,
      Glasgow; R. M. Tims, Dublin; Hatchard & Son, J. Nisbet, and
      James Duncan, London, MDCCCXV [1825], pp. (2) 3–61, ap-
      pendixes 63–78 (4). Second edition, 1825; third edition, with
      additions, 1825. Other editions: Edinburgh, 1826; Dublin,
      before 1837; London, 1837; Boston, Henry Hoyt, n.d.
The letter that is the main part of the narrative is signed Servatus, identified in
    bookseller's catalogues as Sir Duncan McGregor. He was major of the Thirty-
    first Regiment.
        The *Kent*, 1,350 tons, Captain Henry Cobb, sailed from the Downs for
    Bengal and China on February 19, 1825. She carried 20 officers, 344 soldiers,
    43 women, and 66 children of the Thirty-first Regiment, and 20 private
    passengers, with a crew numbering 148. The ship encountered a storm in the
    Bay of Biscay, and on March 1 an officer checking the spirit room dropped a
    light just as a cask stove. The spirits at once caught fire and the flames were
    soon out of control. Fortunately the brig *Cambria*, 200 tons, Captain Cook,
    was soon sighted, and three of the six boats on the *Kent* were used to transport
    her people to the brig. The first boat was sent out with ". . . all the ladies,
    and as many as the soldiers' wives as it could safely contain. . . . " When all
    who could be got into the boats had been saved, about 20 men were still on the
    Kent. They got into the chains, and then, after the magazine exploded, on the
    wreckage; 14 of them were finally taken off by a boat from the *Caroline*, Cap-
    tain Bibby, which had seen the explosion. Apparently 568 out of 637 people
    were saved from the *Kent*, a very good record in view of the stormy weather
    and the difficulty of reaching small boats from a large ship. One soldier's wife
    gave birth to a child an hour or two after reaching the *Cambria*, and both
    mother and child were doing well when they reached Falmouth on March 4,
    1825.

1 8 2 6

228C. BYRON, REAR-ADMIRAL GEORGE ANSON, SEVENTH BARON, ET AL.
      Voyage of HMS Blonde to the Sandwich Islands, in the years
      1824–25. Captain the Right Honorable Lord Byron, Com-
      mander
  London, John Murray, 1826. iii–xi, 260 pp., 15 engr., pl., 4to
This Admiral Byron was a cousin of the poet. On the return voyage from the Sand-
    wich Islands the *Blonde* rescued the survivors from the *Frances Mary*, as told
    by Ann Saunders (234C).

229C. HANNAH, REV. JOHN, D.D.
      The story of the wreck of the Maria mail boat, with a memoir of
      Mrs. Hincksman, the only survivor
  London, Wesleyan Conference Office, from "The Loss of 5
      Wesleyan Missionaries in the Maria Mail-Boat, off Antigua in
      the West Indies, Feb. 28, 1826," n.d. [1826]
See 346C, 1846.

1 8 2 7

230C. ANONYMOUS
Seaman's recorder, or authentic and interesting narratives of remarkable shipwrecks
London, 1827. 2 vols., illus.

231C. ANONYMOUS
Constable's miscellany of original and selected publications in the various departments of literature, science, and the arts. Vol. XI. Perils and captivity
Edinburgh, printed for Constable & Co., 1827
I. History of the sufferings and misfortunes of the Picard family, after the shipwreck of the Medusa, on the western coast of Africa, in the year 1816. From the French of Madame Dard, one of the sufferers. By P. Maxwell, Esq.
II. Narrative of the captivity of M. De Brisson in the deserts of Africa, in the year 1785. Translated from the French.
III. Account of the adventures of Madame Godin Des Odonais, in passing down the river of the Amazons, in the year 1770.

232C. [MAMPEL, JOHAN G.]
The young rifleman's comrade: a narrative of his military adventures, captivity, and shipwreck
Philadelphia, H. C. Carey and I. Lea, Chesnut Street, 1827
Mampel was drafted into the French Army as a youth, and was captured with Dupont's army in Spain. After a good deal of suffering as a prisoner he joined the British forces and was finally discharged from the army. He then became an officer's servant, and at last was employed by Captain Dalrymple of the *Cabalva,* which was shipwrecked in the Indian Ocean (199C). The report by Mampel appears to have been copied from C. W. Francken's. There must have been both German and English editions of this book. There is a preface by Goethe.

233C. MURRAY, H.
Adventures of British seamen in the Southern Ocean
Edinburgh, 1827
1. Mutiny on the *Bounty*
2. Bligh's voyage in the open boat
3. Cruises of the *Pandora* and the *Briton*
4. Barry's account of the massacre of the crew of the *Boyd,* New Zealand, 1809
The *Boyd,* 500 tons, Captain Thompson, sailed from Port Jackson for England late in 1809. She intended to call at New Zealand to take on some timbers of New Zealand pine. Among the seventy people on board was a young Maori, Tarrah, who refused to work and was twice flogged by the captain. Apparently this ill treatment was the cause of the massacre. When the ship reached New Zealand Tarrah persuaded the captain to put in at Wangarooa Bay, where he was known. There he told his story to the local chief, who agreed to attack the ship. First the captain and part of the crew were persuaded to land and were killed ashore; then the ship was attacked from canoes and all on board except one young boy and a woman with two children were killed. Some time later these survivors were rescued with the help of friendly natives.

234C. SAUNDERS, ANN [?]
  Narrative of the shipwreck and sufferings of Miss Ann Saunders,
  who was a passenger on board the ship "Francis Mary,"
  foundered at sea on the 5th of February, 1826. Survivors sub-
  sisted 22 days on the dead bodies of the crew who died of starvation, one of whom she was engaged in marriage.
  Providence, printed for L.S. Crossman, 1827

The ship *Frances Mary* [*sic*], Captain Kendall, sailed from St. Johns, New
Brunswick, for Liverpool on January 18, 1826. She carried a cargo of lumber,
and was therefore unsinkable. On February 1 the *Frances Mary* was caught in a
terrible storm which so battered the ship that she filled and became unmanageable. The people on board were able to get some provisions and water from
below decks, but still suffered greatly from hunger and thirst. Two ships were
seen and hailed but both claimed the weather was too severe to provide help.
On February 22 John Wilson, a seaman, died; he was cut up and eaten by the
survivors, and the same horrid pattern was followed with a half-dozen others.
James Frier, cook, was engaged to marry Ann Saunders, a passenger. When he
died his fiancée, who was among the strongest of those who lived, ". . .
shrieked a loud yell, then snatching a cup from Clerk, the mate, cut her late intended husband's throat and drank his blood! insisting that she had the greatest right to it." The six survivors were taken off the derelict by H.M.S. *Blonde*
on March 7, 1826. Ann Saunders's narrative is much less detailed and horror-
filled, and more sanctimonious, than the report of Captain Kendall which is
printed in R. Thomas's *Remarkable Shipwrecks,* pp. 295–298.

235C. SAUNDERS, MISS ANN
  "There is nothing true but Heaven!" Lines composed by Miss Ann
  Saunders on the melancholly death of JAMES FRIER, to
  whom she expected to be married in a few weeks; but who, with
  fourteen of his ship companions perished on board the ship
  Francis Mary
  [Providence, 1827] Broadside verse, 11½ by 18½ inches

See 234C. Miss Saunders not only mourned the unfortunate James Frier, she also
helped to eat him, and claimed first rights to his blood because he was her
fiancé.

1 8 2 8

236C. ADAMS, WM., M.A. [editor]
  The modern voyager & traveller through Europe, Asia, Africa, S.
  America
  Vol. 1—Africa
  London, Henry Fisher, Son, and P. Jackson, 38 Newgate Street,
  1828
  Contains:
  The narrative of Robert Adams, a sailor, who was wrecked on the
    western coast of Africa, in 1810 . . . pp. 135–165
  An authentic narrative of the loss of the brig *Commerce,* wrecked
    on the coast of Africa in August, 1815 . . . [by Captain
    James Riley] pp. 165–199
  Narrative of P. G. DuMont . . . pp. 313–337

Narrative of a voyage to Senegal, in 1816. By J. B. H. Savigny and Alexander Corréard, pp. 327–341

237C. LAY, WILLIAM, AND HUSSEY, CYRUS M.
A narrative of the mutiny on board the ship Globe, of Nantucket, in the Pacific Ocean, Jan. 1824 and the journal of a residence of two years on the Mulgrave Islands; with observations on the manners and customs of the inhabitants. By William Lay, of Saybrook, Conn. and Cyrus M. Hussey, of Nantucket: the only survivors from the massacre of the ship's company by the natives

New-London, published by Wm. Lay and C. M. Hussey, 1828; another edition, N.Y., Abbey Press, n.d. [1912?]

The stories of the mutiny on the *Globe* and the wreck of the *Essex* are the best-known narratives of the American whaling industry. The *Globe* was commanded by Captain Worth, was owned in Nantucket, and sailed from Edgartown for the Pacific on December 15, 1822. She reached the Sandwich Islands on May 1, 1823. There five men jumped ship—as Herman Melville and Toby Green did later at Nukahiva—and had to be replaced by men off the beach, some of whom were "abandoned wretches." One of the boatsteerers was Samuel B. Comstock, who must have been a good whaleman to have reached officer's rank, but had been in trouble, apparently, since childhood. Comstock joined with four of the men newly enrolled at Oahu, and murdered the captain and the three mates, killing each man himself. A little later Comstock had one of the mutineers hanged for disloyalty. The ship was sailed to the Mulgrave Islands, where Comstock proceeded to antagonize the natives and make the surviving crewmen, conspirators and innocents, fearful for their lives. Silas Payne, who had been Samuel Comstock's chief lieutenant in the mutiny, led a group that shot Comstock. Some of the innocent crew, left aboard the *Globe,* cut her loose and sailed to Valparaiso, where they reported the mutiny. Meanwhile Mulgrave natives had killed all those on the island except Lay and Hussey, who were adopted into native families. These last two survivors were rescued by the American ship *Dolphin,* John Percival, which had been dispatched to capture the mutineers and rescue any other members of the crew. See also 247C and 312C.

1 8 2 9

238C. ANONYMOUS
The sailors' Magazine and Naval Journal, published by the American Seamen's Friend Society . . . monthly
New York, published at the Society's office, 1829–1849

Barnes Catalogue: ". . . replete with naval anecdotes . . . shipwrecks . . ."

239C. BARNARD, CHARLES H.
A narrative of the sufferings and adventures of Capt. Charles H. Barnard . . . seizure of his vessel at the Falkland Islands, by an English crew whom he had rescued . . . and of their abandoning him on an uninhabited island . . .
New York, for the author, 1829. 296 pp., plates, a map

240C. BURT, LLOYD B.
        An account of the loss of the ship Rose in Bloom, by Lloyd B. Burt
        n.p. [Feb. 12, 1829] 12 pp., 8vo

The *Rose in Bloom* sailed from Charleston, S.C., on August 16, 1806, for New York. On the nineteenth a storm began which grew steadily worse; probably it was a full-scale hurricane. On the twenty-sixth the ship went over on her beamends, and filled. Many of the passengers were drowned in their berths. Some of the crew, with pocketknives, cut the lanyards of the masts on the weather side, and at last all the masts broke off short, and the ship, though waterlogged, righted. Her cargo of cotton probably gave her some buoyancy. On the next day the ship was sighted by the British brig *Swift,* Captain Phelan, and the surviving passengers and crew were taken off. The narrative I quote gives no numbers.

1 8 3 0

241C. CHAPPLE [Chappell?], THOMAS
        Loss of the Essex [?]
        London, Religious Tract Society, 1830 [?]

Chapple was a seaman on board the *Essex* when it was sunk by a whale (205C). He was one of three men left on Henderson's Island, and was taken off by the English ship *Surrey*. Edouard A. Stackpole, in a pamphlet, "The Loss of the Essex," gives the date 1830 for Chapple's story of the wreck. This narrative has been reprinted with the stories of Owen Chase and Captain Pollard in a book published by the Golden Cockerel Press.

242C. SMITH, JOHN
        Narrative of the shipwreck and sufferings of the crew and
        passengers of the English brig "Neptune," which was wrecked
        in a violent snowstorm on the 12th of January, 1830, on her
        passage from Bristol, England, to Quebec
        New York, 1830. Woodcut frontis., 36 pp.

1 8 3 1

243C. BAYS, PETER
        A narrative of the wreck of the 'Minerva' whaler of Port Jackson,
        New South Wales, on Nicholson's Shoal, 24 S. 179 W. . . .
        Cambridge, B. Bridges, 1831

The *Minerva* struck on the shoal in September, 1829. The crew reached Vatoa Island, where they were well treated by the natives. This account is one of the first descriptions of the Lau Islanders. This listing is taken from H. E. Maude's *Of Islands and Men,* OUP, Melbourne, 1968. See 372C.

244C. BEECHEY, CAPTAIN F. W.
        Narrative of a voyage to the Pacific and Beering's Strait to co-
        operate with the polar expeditions, performed in H.M.S.
        Blossom, 1825–28
        [London?], 1831. 2 vols., 3 charts, 23 plates

Bookseller's note: "While in Pitcairn Beechey met John Adams, the "Bounty" mutiny survivor, who gave him a long account of the mutiny."

245C. FOWLER, J.
> Journal of a tour in the state of New York in the year 1830: remarks
> on agriculture in those parts most eligible for settlers and a
> return to England by the Western Islands in consequence of be-
> ing shipwrecked in the Robert Fulton . . .
> London, Whittaker, Treacher and Arnot, 1831. 333 pp.

246C. MONTGOMERY, JAMES [compiler; Tyerman, Daniel, and Bennet,
> George, authors]
> Journal of voyages and travels . . . of Daniel Tyerman and
> George Bennet . . . deputed from the London Missionary
> Society, to visit their various stations in the South Sea islands,
> China, India, &c. 1821–1829
> London, compiled by James Montgomery, 1831. 2 vols., 14 plates

While Tyerman and Bennet were at Raiatea they encountered Captain George
Pollard, Jr., of the American whaleship *Two Brothers,* which had been lost on
an uncharted coral reef. Pollard was, of course, the unfortunate master of the
Essex, sunk by a sperm whale in 1820. The two missionaries talked with the
discouraged captain, and recorded in their journals what he said of the loss of
the *Essex.* The details of the killing of Owen Coffin, who was shot and eaten by
his shipmates, are known only from this account. See 205C and 241C.

247C. PAULDING, LIEUTENANT HIRAM
> Journal of a cruise of the United States schooner Dolphin among
> the islands of the Pacific Ocean and a visit to the Mulgrave
> Islands, in pursuit of the mutineers of the whale ship
> Globe . . .
> New York, 1831

The *Dolphin* rescued Lay and Hussey from natives of the Mulgraves, now Mili
Atoll, and discovered that the other members of the crew of the *Globe* who had
stayed on the island had been killed by the natives. Paulding gave many of the
details included in the book by Lay and Hussey. See 237C and 312C.

248C. [PORTER, JANE?]
> Sir Edward Seaward's narrative of his shipwreck, and consequent
> discovery of certain islands in the Caribbean Sea: with a detail
> of many extraordinary and highly interesting events in his life,
> from the year 1733 to 1749, as written in his own diary. Edited
> by Miss Jane Porter
> London, Longman, Rees, Orme, Brown, and Green, Paternoster-
> Row, 1831, 1841, 1852, 1878, 1879; 1883, 3 vols.; New York,
> 1831, 3 vols.

The British Museum Catalogue states of this book, "Edited [or rather written] by
Miss J. Porter." Jane Porter is best remembered as the author of the historical
novel *The Scottish Chiefs. Sir Edward Seaward's Narrative* . . . is an imita-
tion of *Robinson Crusoe* with Utopian overtones. Sir Edward and his wife
leave England for a voyage to the West Indies, stop at Jamaica, and are cast
away on an island near the mainland of Central America. Their adventures
with black slaves, Spanish vessels, and English administrators make up the
three volumes of the novel. The shipwreck is handled with reasonable realism,
but the discovery of the Seaward Islands in the thoroughly explored Caribbean

is a false note. One of the author's repeated theses is the iniquity of work on Sunday in a Christian country.

1 8 3 2

249C. ADAMS, WM., M. A. [editor]
The modern voyager and traveller, through Europe, Asia, Africa, & America
Vol. II—Asia
London, printed for Fisher, Son & Co., 1832
Contains:
Journal of the proceedings of the late embassy to China: . . . by Henry Ellis, pp. 304–370
Narrative of a voyage in His Majesty's late ship *Alceste* to the Yellow Sea . . . by John M'Leod, pp. 370–385
See 188C.

250C. ANONYMOUS
Horrible shipwreck and dreadful loss of lives . . . [*Helen McGregor*]
London, J. Catnach [1832?]
The *Helen M'Gregor*—the name is spelled in both ways—stopped at Memphis to land passengers and take on freight on the morning of February 24, 1830. As the ship moved away from the shore, with four or five hundred passengers and crew, the boilers blew up. One guess was that between forty and fifty people were killed by the explosion, by scalding, and by drowning after they were blown overboard. The ship did not sink. Apparently there was no certainty about the reason for the explosion, but one guess was that water had drained from one boiler while the ship was stopped, and that a sudden influx, changed to steam almost instantly, was too much for a cracked boiler-head.

251C. ANONYMOUS
The Nautical Magazine for 1832. . . . A journal of papers on subjects connected with maritime affairs in general. There are no charts of any part of the world so accurate and no directions so perfect as not to furnish frequent occasion for revision and amendment
Published by Simpkin and Marshall and by R. B. Bate agent for the sale of the charts and published by the direction of the Lords Commissioners of the Admiralty
I have not seen the volume for 1832. That for 1833 contains many charts, suggested sailing routes, and notes about changes in lighthouses or sailing marks, along with all kinds of papers on maritime affairs. Among the items in the volume for 1833 are the following:
Admiralty Court Decisions. No. IV. His Majesty's ship *Thetis*. This decision concerned the rewards for salving the treasure lost in the *Thetis* when it sank off Cape Frio; $750,000 was recovered. See 275C.
Lists of English ships lost or damaged, from *Lloyd's List*
A list of sixteen ships of the Royal Navy wrecked after January 1, 1816
Massacre of the crew of the ship *Oldham* by the natives of Wallis Island. The *Oldham,* a whaler of London, anchored at Wallis Island with three other

whalers, English and American. Native women were taken on board, but one ran away and the drunken captain of the ship threatened the natives. A party of islanders went on board the *Oldham* and eventually killed twenty-eight men, including eight seamen from two other ships who were ashore.

Particulars relating to the loss of H.M. ship *Saldanha,* commanded by the Hon. W. Pakenham, on December 2, 1811, in Ballymastoka Bay, Lough Swilly. The *Saldanha,* caught in a violent gale, apparently struck on Swilly Rock and then drifted ashore at Ballymastoka Bay, where she broke up. There were no survivors.

Loss of the ship *Flora,* Sheriff, Commander, on the Barrier Reefs, in May, 1832. The *Flora,* Port Jackson for Java, was embayed on the Barrier Reef in a storm and was lost. The crew, chiefly lascars, repaired the damaged longboat, touched at various islands, and eventually reached Timor, covering part of the route followed by Captain Bligh of the *Bounty.* Apparently there were no casualties in the loss of the *Flora.*

252C. SHAW, LEONARD
"A brief sketch of the sufferings of Leonard Shaw on Massacre Island"[1832?]

This sketch was published in Benjamin Morrell, Jr.'s *A Narrative of Four Voyages, to the South Sea. . . . From the year 1822 to 1831. . . .* New York, J. & J. Harper, 1832. In that book Captain Morrell states that the Shaw narrative was taken from a pamphlet published by Shaw himself, but no such pamphlet has been discovered. Shaw was captured by natives of Kalinailau Island in the Solomons, and was going to be eaten when he was rescued. This listing is taken from H. E. Maude's *Of Islands and Men.*

1 8 3 3

253C. ADSHEAD, JOSEPH
The wreck of the "Rothsay Castle" . . . steam packet on her passage in 1831 . . . with 127 lost out of 150

London, Hamilton, 1833; 1834. 6 engravings

The *Rothsay Castle* sailed from Liverpool for Beaumaris and Bangor on August 17, 1831. There had been a storm that morning, but the weather had moderated and there was no reason to expect trouble on the short voyage—only fifty miles. The steamer was old, however, and the engine weak. Through strain from the waves some seams opened, the coal was wetted, and power was lost. The ship drifted on a bank near the shore of Anglesey, and broke up. The only survivors were those who kept their holds on wreckage until small boats reached them. One account of the tragedy states that both captain and mate were drunk. Among those who drowned were many women and children. The account of this wreck in the *Mariner's Chronicle* (259C) is by John A. Tinne, Esq., one of the few survivors.

254C. ANONYMOUS
Constable's miscellany of original and selected publications in the various departments of literature, science, & the arts. Vol. LXXVIII. Shipwrecks & disasters at sea

London, printed for Whittaker, Treacher & Co. and Waugh & Innes, Edinburgh, 1833

Volume I
Chapter I
Introductory remarks. Nobility of East Friesland, 900; Prince William, 1120; Nicolo Zeno, 1380; Pietro Quirino, 1431
Chapter II
Brothers Cortereals, 1500; *Minion* and *Trinity,* 1536; Sir Hugh Willoughby, 1553; Sir Humphrey Gilbert, *Delight* and *Squirrel,* 1583; Barentz, Heemskirk, and De Veer, Nova Zembla, 1595; John Knight, 1606
Chapter III
Henry Hudson, 1610; Munk, 1619
Chapter IV
Salutation, 1630
Chapter V
Captain James, 1631
Chapter VI
Dutch seamen, Spitzbergen and Jan Mayen, 1633–34; Dutch whaler, 1639; forty-one Englishmen on the ice, 1646
Chapter VII
Dr. Johnson's deliverance, 1648
Chapter VIII
Dutch whalers; *Speedwell,* 1678; Allen Geare, 1706
Chapter IX
Nottingham Galley, 1710; Knight and Barlow in Marble Island, 1719
Chapter X
Behring's shipwrecks, 1741; four Russian sailors, Spitzbergen, 1743; Russian crew on the Aleutians, 1758
Chapter XI
Loss of the *St. Lawrence,* 1780
Chapter XII
Loss of the *Lady Hobart,* 1803

Volume II [also 1833]
Chapter I
Toby of London, 1593; *New Horn,* fire, 1618
Chapter II
Captain Norwood, 1649
Chapter III
Spanish vessel, America, 1678
Chapter IV
Speedwell, 1719, at Juan Fernandez; *Prince,* fire, 1752
Chapter V
Doddington, 1755; *Utile,* 1761; famine in the *Peggy,* 1765
Chapter VI
Peter Viaud's shipwreck, 1766; Madame Denoyer, 1766
Chapter VII
Grosvenor, 1782

Chapter VIII
Centaur, 1782
Chapter IX
David Woodward [Woodard], 1793; *Dutton,* 1796; *Nautilus,* 1807
Chapter X
Commerce, 1815.

255C. ANONYMOUS
Disasters at sea, a history of calamities from 900 A.D. to 1815, from
the most authentic sources
London, 1833–1835. 2 vols., 19 engravings
May be another edition of 254C.

256C. ANONYMOUS
Perils of the sea being authentic narratives of remarkable and affecting disasters on the deep
New York, 1833. 205 pp. Boys and Girls Library XIV. 12mo, chap-
book

257C. ANONYMOUS
Shipwreck of the schooner Mechanic and loss of lives
Salem Gazette Extra, Feb. 1, 1833. Broadside

258C. ANONYMOUS
Stories of voyages: being authentic narratives of the most celebrated
voyages from Columbus to Parry, with accounts of remarkable
shipwrecks and naval adventures . . .
Boston, 1833. Illustrated, 12mo
Barnes Catalogue.

1 8 3 4

259C. ANONYMOUS
The mariner's chronicle: containing narratives of the most
remarkable disasters at sea, such as shipwrecks, storms, fires,
and famines: also, naval engagements, piratical adventures, incidents of discovery, and other extraordinary and interesting
occurrences
New Haven, stereotyped by A. Chandler, published by Durrie and
Peck, 1834
  1. Loss of the *Kent*
  2. Loss of the *Grosvenor*
  3. Loss of the *Hercules*
  4. Loss of the sloop of war *Hornet* [Really a history of the ship.
    The *Hornet* was lost with all on board in early September, 1829,
    off the coast of Mexico in a very severe hurricane.]
  5. Shipwreck of the Countess De Bourk
  6. Loss of the *Rothsay Castle*
  7. Four Russian sailors, Spitzbergen, 1743
  8. English sloop [*St. Lawrence*], Cape Breton, 1780

9. Ephraim How, Cape Sable, 1676
10. Voyage of the packet-ship *President,* 1831
11. Loss of the *Centaur*
12. Loss of the *Prince* by fire
13. Loss of the *Hibernia* by fire [No date given. *Hibernia* was bound for Van Diemen's land; about 80 survived of 232 on board.]
14. *Nottingham* galley lost on Boon Island
15. Shipwreck of M. De Brisson on the coast of Barbary
16. Famine in the *Peggy*
17. Loss of the *Magpie* [No date given. This account, complete with dialogue, may be fiction.]
18. Adventures of Mme. Denoyer
19. Shipwreck of a Spanish frigate on the coast of Mexico, 1678
20. Loss of a Jamaica sloop, Captain Uring
21. Loss of the Russian ship *St. Peter,* 1741
22. Shipwreck of the *Medusa*
23. Destruction of the *Essex* by a whale [This short account contains material from Captain Pollard and from Thomas Chapple. See 241C and 246C.]
24. Wreck of the *President,* off New York City, Dec. 4, 1831. All were saved
25. A tragical tale of the sea [Fiction]
26. The whale; the Greenland whale fishery; the polar bear
27. Loss of the *Phoenix*
28. Loss of the *Jonge Thomas,* Cape of Good Hope, June 2, 1773
29. Polar ice; the Maelstrom; Captain Ross's narrative—the Arctic
30. Shipwreck of the *Albion*
31. Explosion of the *Helen M'Gregor,* Memphis, Feb. 24, 1830
32. Explosion of the steam-boat *Aetna,* New York Harbor, May 15, 1824
33. Burning of the *Phoenix* on Lake Champlain, Sept. 5, 1819
34. Explosion of the steam frigate *Fulton,* Brooklyn, June 4, 1829
35. Explosion of the steamboat *New England,* Essex, Conn., Oct. 9, 1833
    Captures of the *Guerriere, Macedonian, Java;* Battle of Lake Erie; Battle of Lake Champlain; piracy; Kidd's money; outrage of the Malays; poem on a shipwreck in the Scillies, Dec., 1813, by Nathaniel Ogle, Esq.

This is not a reprinting of the original *Mariner's Chronicle* (142C) in spite of the title. Many of the shipwrecks listed occurred after 1810, and Duncan's book did not tell of piracies or of American victories in the War of 1812—of course.

260C. ANONYMOUS

The mariner's chronicle

Boston, printed and published by Charles Gaylord, 1834–1840. 2 vols.

I have not seen this collection. Probably it is different from the other *Mariner's Chronicle*s, of 1804, 1834, and 1849.

261C. ANONYMOUS [Mrs. Mathews]
   Melancholy shipwreck and remarkable instance of the interposition
   of divine providence, in the preservation of the lives of 12 unfortunate persons, who were shipwrecked on the 3d of
   December last, (1833,) on their passage from Portsmouth,
   (Eng.) to Bombay, and after being 17 days in an open boat,
   subsisting on an allowance of half a biscuit to each per day,
   were providentially picked up by an English homeward bound
   whaleman
   n.p., 1834. Wrappers, 2 plates, 24 pp.
The ship is not named in this narrative. Mrs. Mathews was sailing to meet her husband, a missionary in Hindostan. The ship encountered a severe storm and
sprang a leak. Of twenty-three on board only twelve could be taken in the yawl,
and the eleven others went down with the ship. After sixteen days the castaways
planned to draw lots and kill and eat one of their number, but Mrs. Mathews
persuaded them to wait for twenty-four hours, and the English whaler picked
them up. This book is three-fourths religious exhortation and one-fourth shipwreck narrative.

262C. ANONYMOUS [Quillinan, Edward]
   Mischief [Second section]
   London, Edward Moxon, Dover Street, 1834
Contains "Sequel," pp. 34–40, and "Note on the loss of the *Amphitrite*," pp.
45–48. This "Second section" is, in the copy I have seen, bound with *Mischief*,
London, Edward Moxon, 64 New Bond Street, 1831.
  The subject of "Sequel" was the loss of the *Amphitrite* convict ship in the
harbor of Boulogne on August 31, 1833. Like all the other poems in both sections, it is an exercise in the Spenserian stanza. Halkett and Laing identifies the
author as William Wordsworth's son-in-law. The loss of the *Amphitrite* was a
miserable business from beginning to end, one of the worst examples of in-
competence and stupidity in the whole history of shipwrecks. The ship, with
108 female convicts, 12 of their children, and a crew of 16, sailed from
Woolwich for New South Wales on August 25, 1833. She immediately ran into
a severe Channel storm and was driven on a lee shore at Boulogne, well inside
the harbor. A pilot boat reached the stranded ship and offered to take everyone
off, but the captain refused. A little later a brave French sailor swam off to the
ship and tried to take a line ashore, but the captain again refused to allow the
line to be carried all the way in, and almost drowned the would-be rescuer. The
miserable convicts and their children had been confined under the hatches, and
the captain apparently preferred that everyone on board drown rather than let
his charges reach the shore. When the tide came in the ship broke up and only
three sailors were saved of the 136 on board, the captain deservedly dying with
the poor women and their guiltless children.

263C. ANONYMOUS [By an officer of the ship]
   Narrative of the loss of the Honorable East India Company's ship
    Duke of York in the Bay of Bengal, on the 21st May, 1833
   Edinburgh, Waugh and Innes; W. Curry & Co., Dublin; London,
    Whittaker & Co. and Richardson, 1834

264C. BOURCHIER, CAPTAIN W., R.N.
   Narrative of a passage from Bombay to England, describing the

author's shipwreck in the Nautilus, in the Red Sea; journies across the Nubian Desert; detention in the lazaretto at Leghorn, &c.

London, Whittaker & Co., Ave-Maria Lane, 1834; second edition, 1834

Bourchier made a whirlwind journey from Liverpool to India in only a little over three months, found that his hopes would not be answered there, and set out immediately to return to England. He sailed in the East Indiaman *Nautilus,* Captain Lowe, on a passage up the Red Sea; he planned to go overland to Alexandria and there find a ship for England. The *Nautilus* reached the Red Sea, stopped at Mocha, and took on an Arab pilot. On December 5, 1833, the ship struck on a coral reef not far from the Nubian shore. All those on board, about eighty, left the ship in four boats. They slept on various small islands on the way to shore, but at last reached the island of Suakin, where they were welcomed. One group sailed in the gig for Mocha, Captain Lowe returned to the *Nautilus* to try to salvage the cargo, and Captain Bourchier, with three other Europeans, set out across the Nubian desert for Berber. His narrative is mostly about travel to Berber, Kroosko, Cairo, Alexandria, Leghorn, and London. The book ends with a subscribers' list of about 250.

265C. RILEY, JAMES

The story of Captain Riley, and his adventures in Africa

Philadelphia, Henry F. Anners, 1841 [copyright, 1834]. With engravings

This book is a condensation of Captain Riley's narrative (190C) published by Peter Parley (S. G. Goodrich) in a series for juveniles. Another similar narrative, in the same series, was *The Story of John R. Jewitt, the Captive of Nootka Sound* (269C). This version of Captain Riley's story is 18mo, 240 pages, and has nine engravings.

1 8 3 5

266C. ANONYMOUS

The mariner's chronicle . . .

New Haven, George Gorton, 1836

Printed from the same plates as 259C. Perhaps Durrie and Peck went out of business and Gorton took over from them.

267C. MCCOSH, J., ASSISTANT SURGEON, HONORABLE EAST INDIA COMPANY

Narrative of the wreck of the Lady Munro, on the desolate island of Amsterdam, October, 1833

Glasgow, printed by W. Bennet, Free Press Office, 1835

268C. MACY, OBED

The history of Nantucket; being a compendious account of the first settlement of the island by the English, together with the rise and progress of the whale fishery . . .

Boston, Hilliard, Gray, 1835

This history contains a few individual narratives, including accounts of the *Globe* mutiny and the loss of the *Essex.*

269C. GOODRICH, S. G. [Parley, Peter]
The captive of Nootka
New York, 1835; Philadelphia, 1837, 1841, 1854, 1861, 1869
See 155C, 1807. This adaptation of the Jewitt narrative was made by Peter Parley
from Alsop's version of 1815.

270C. REDDING, CYRUS [editor]
Newberry Library card says that two more volumes of Redding's anthology (254C)
were published in 1835.

271C. WILSON, T. B., M.D., SURGEON R.N., MEMBER OF THE ROYAL
GEOGRAPHIC SOCIETY
Narrative of a voyage round the world; comprehending an account
of the wreck of the ship "Governor Ready," in Torres Straits;
a description of the British settlements on the coasts of New
Holland . . . with an appendix, containing remarks on
transportation, the treatment of convicts during the voyage . . .
London, printed for Sherwood, Gilbert, & Piper, Paternoster Row,
1835. First edition, full page frontispiece plate, and two other
full page plates, with tissue guards. With folding map of
Australia, errata leaf, and 10 pp. publisher's catalogue dated
Sept. 1831

1 8 3 6

272C. ANONYMOUS
The book of shipwrecks
Boston, 1836. 492 pp., 12mo

273C. ANONYMOUS
Diary of the wreck of His Majesty's ship Challenger, on the western
coast of South America in May, 1835, with an account
of . . . encampment of the officers and crew . . . on the
south coast of Chile
London, Rees, 1836. 8vo, 160 pp., 4 pl.

274C. ANONYMOUS
Histoire complète des naufrages événements et aventures de
mer . . .
Paris, 1836. 2 vols., 12mo, 267, 275 pp., 6 engr. pl., large fldg. map
Bookseller's note: "Most wrecks are 19th century, hence *not* Deperthes."

275C. DICKINSON, CAPTAIN THOMAS, R.N.
A narrative of the operations for the recovery of the public stores
and treasure sunk in the H.M.S. Thetis, at Cape Frio, on the
coast of Brazil, on the 5th of December, 1830. To which is
prefixed a concise account of the loss of that ship
London, Longman, Rees, Orme, Brown, Greene, and Longman,
MDCCCXXXVI [1836]

There was a court case concerning the recovery of treasure from the *Thetis*. The decision of the court was given in the *Nautical Magazine,* 1833 (251C).

276C. ELLMS, CHARLES [compiler]

Shipwrecks and disasters at sea; or historical narratives of the most noted calamities, and providential deliverances from fire and famine, on the ocean. With a sketch of the various expedients for preserving the lives of mariners, by the aid of life-boats, life-preservers, &c.

Boston, S. N. Dickinson, 1836; New York City, I. J. Rouse, 1860

Ellms, like R. Thomas (280C), put together a book on pirates and piracies as well as this anthology of shipwrecks and disasters at sea. The collections must have been quite popular.

1. Riley's narrative of the loss of the *Commerce*
2. Loss of the *Centaur*
3. Loss of the *Albion*
4. Captain Cazneau and the *Peggy*
5. Loss of the *Lady Hobart*
6. Loss of the *Halsewell*
7. Fate of La Perouse
8. Loss of the *Helen MacGregor*
9. Burning of the *Kent*
10. Loss of the *Grosvenor*
11. Famine in *Le Jacques*
12. Loss of the *Phoenix*
13. Loss of the *Alceste*
14. Loss of the *Blendenhall*
15. Loss of the *Juno*
16. Loss of the *Amphitrite*
17. Loss of the *Doddington*
18. Loss of the *Margaret*
19. Loss of the *Prince*
20. Loss of the *Isabella*
21. Loss of the *Amphion*
22. Loss of the *Cumberland*
23. Narrative of Archibald Campbell, shipwreck on the Isle of Sannac
24. Loss of the *Logan*
25. Loss of the *Medusa*
26. Loss of the *Rothsay Castle*
27. Captain Samuel Standige's voyage to Rhode Island, 1749
28. Life boats, life preservers, etc.

277C. HOLDEN, HORACE

A narrative of the shipwreck, captivity and sufferings of Horace Holden and Benj. H. Nute; who were cast away in the American ship Mentor, on the Pelew Islands, in the year 1832; and for two years afterwards were subjected to unheard of sufferings among the barbarous inhabitants of Lord North's Island.

Boston, Russell, Shattuck, and Co., 1836; Boston, Weeks, Jordan, 1839; Cooperstown, N.Y., H. & H. Phinney, 1841, 1843; Fairfield, Washington, Galleon Press, 1975

The *Mentor,* a New Bedford whaler, struck on a reef in the Palaus on May 21, 1832. The crew reached Babelthuap, the largest island of the group, and eventually settled down quite comfortably with the natives there. They wanted to reach their homes, however, and set out from the island in a patched-up whaleboat and a leaking native canoe. Short of food and water, they had to put ashore on Tobi, a small island near New Guinea. There all suffered dreadfully, and about half the group died. Horace Holden and Benjamin Nute were finally taken off the island by the British *Britannia,* Captain Short, on November 27, 1834, which landed them at Canton. They reached New York May 5, 1835. Holden, who became an early settler in Oregon and died there in 1904, wrote one of the better shipwreck narratives in this account. Herman Melville probably used this narrative in his description of native tattooing in *Typee.*

278C. O'CONNELL, JAMES F.

A residence of eleven years in New Holland and the Caroline Islands: being the adventures of James F. O'Connell. Edited from his verbal narration

Boston, B. B. Mussey, 1836. 12mo, 265 pp., 2 woodcuts

Bookseller's note; "He was later wrecked in the Carolines."

279C. RENEY, WILLIAM

A narrative of the shipwreck of the Corsair; in the month of January, 1835, on an unknown reef near the Kingsmill Islands, in the South Pacific Ocean; with a detail of the dreadful sufferings of the crew

London, Longman, Rees, Orme, Brown, Green and Longmans, 1836

This listing is from H. E. Maude's *Of Islands and Men.*

280C. THOMAS, R., A.M. [editor]

Interesting and authentic narratives of the most remarkable shipwrecks, fires, famines, calamities, providential deliverances, and lamentable disasters on the seas, in most parts of the world

New-York, published by Ezra Strong, 1836 [copyright, Conn., 1835]; Hartford, published by Silas Andrus & Son, 1855

This seems to have been the most popular of the American anthologies pirated from the *Mariner's Chronicle* or from Sir J. G. Dalyell's collection. Thomas also edited a collection of piracy narratives, and that book and the shipwreck volume were apparently published both separately and together.

1. Loss of the *Grosvenor*
2. Loss of the *Fattysalem*
3. Loss of the ship *Hercules*
4. Loss of the ship *Litchfield*
5. Loss of the *St. James*
6. Loss of the *Centaur*
7. Loss of the *Betsy*
8. Loss of the *Tyrell*

9. Loss of the *Prince,* by fire
10. Loss of the *Phoenix*
11. Loss of the *La Tribune*
12. Famine in the *Peggy*
13. The wrecked seamen [*Magpie*]
14. Loss of the *Peggy*
15. Loss of the *Halsewell*
16. Loss of the *Nottingham* galley
17. Loss of the *Droits de L'Homme*
18. Loss of the *Earl of Abergavenny*
19. Loss of the *Catherine, Venus,* and *Piedmont,* and three merchant ships
20. Loss of the *Sidney*
21. Loss of the *Ramillies*
22. Preservation of nine men
23. Loss of the *Aeneas*
24. Loss of the *Nautilus*
25. Loss of the *Amphion*
26. Loss of the *Helen M'Gregor*
27. Loss of the *Beverly*
28. Loss of the *Frances Mary* [page 295—omitted in index]
29. Loss of the *Albion*
30. Loss of the *Logan,* by fire
31. Loss of the *Margaret*
32. Loss of the *Kent,* by fire
33. Loss of the *Boston*
34. Loss of the *Essex*
35. Loss of the *Isabella*
36. Loss of the *Rothsay Castle*
37. Loss of the *Sally*
38. Sufferings of Ephraim Howe
39. Loss of the *Harpooner*
40. Loss of the *Polly*
41. Loss of the *Queen Charlotte*
42. Loss of the *Amphitrite*
43. Loss of the *Lady of the Lake*
44. Loss of the *Jesse*

1 8 3 7

281C. ANONYMOUS
Loss of the ship Home
Christian Witness, Boston, October 27, 1837

The steam packet *Home* sailed from New York for Charleston October 7, 1837. She carried a crew of forty-five and about ninety passengers. The *Home* was a fast ship but apparently weakly built, and her engines were unreliable. She was caught in a storm as she approached Cape Hatteras, and sprang a leak. The water from the leak wetted the coals, and there was trouble with one of the waterlines to the boiler. Captain White decided that the only hope for the ship was to run her ashore. The ship struck on October 9, and broke up almost at once. About ninety-five of the passengers and crew were drowned.

282C. ANONYMOUS
       Shipwreck of Mrs. Fraser and the loss of the Stirling Castle
       London, Dean and Munday, 1837. Plates
See 294C.

283C. ANONYMOUS
       Tales of travellers or a view of the world
       n.p., September, 1837
Cited in Michael Alexander, *Mrs. Fraser on the Fatal Shore* (N.Y., S. & S., 1971, p.
    29) as presenting one version of Mrs. Fraser's story. See 294C.

284C. ANONYMOUS [Fraser, Mrs. Eliza?]
       Narrative of the capture, sufferings and miraculous escape of Mrs.
           Eliza Fraser
       New York, Charles Webb, 1837. Plates
See 294C. The American publisher obviously knew nothing of Australian
    aborigines, but a good deal about American stories of Indian captivities. One
    of the illustrations shows Mrs. Fraser being led by an American Indian in full
    costume, including feathers, and the text has her captor demanding that she
    become his *squaw.*

285C. KING, CAPTAIN PHILLIP P.
       A voyage to Torres Strait in search of the survivors of the ship
           Charles Eaton, which was wrecked upon the Barrier Reefs, in
           the month of August, 1834, in His Majesty's colonial schooner
           Isabella, C. M. Lewis, Commander.
       Sydney, George William Evans, 1837
See 295C.

286C. [MANBY, GEORGE W.]
       Reflections on shipwreck, with historical facts and suggestions for
           diminishing that calamity . . .
       Yarmouth [1837]. 8vo, 31 pp., 4 pl.

287C. PALMER, JOHN
       Awful shipwreck. An affecting narrative of the unparalleled suffer-
           ings of the crew of the ship Francis Spaight . . . by . . . one
           of the survivors
       Boston, G. C. Perry, 1837. 24 pp., wraps., woodcut frontis.
The *Francis Spaight,* caught in a bad storm in the Atlantic, was dismasted and
    became waterlogged. The crew could not get at any of the stores, and at last
    lots were drawn and one of the ship's boys was killed and partly eaten. All
    other crew members were at last rescued by another ship. The woodcut frontis-
    piece must be one of the most unpleasant—and worst done—of all book il-
    lustrations, I believe. It pictures a few of the survivors on the hulk's deck,
    weeping, praying, and eating the severed arm of a nearby corpse.
        Jack London must have seen this pamphlet. In his *When Gods Laugh,*
    New York, 1911, there is a short story, "The 'Francis Spaight,' " which retells
    the story of this wreck. London used the subtitle "(A true tale retold)" and
    added little to the narrative except dialogue and his guess about the vindictive
    selection of one of the ship's boys as the victim.

288C. PATON, ALEXANDER

Narrative of the loss of the schooner "Clio," of Montrose, Captain George Reid; containing an account of the massacre of her crew by the Indians, on the north coast of Brazils in October, 1835, with other interesting particulars relative to the subsequent adventures and miraculous escape of the author from the hands of a savage people, by Alexander Paton, a native of Ferryden, the only survivor

Montrose, published by Alex. Burnett, 2 High Street [third edition, 1879, but preface dated October 31, 1837]

The *Clio* sailed from Liverpool on August 9, 1835, bound for Para in Brazil with a general cargo of dry goods and arms. There were only seven men in the crew. The vessel made the island of Salinas on September 29, and sent a boat ashore for a pilot. The *Clio*'s crew apparently stumbled into a revolt of the Indian population against the Portuguese rulers, and the arms in the ship's cargo were important to the rebels. A man who called himself John Priest, who said he was an American, led a group of Indians who killed all the crew except two who were drowned, and Paton. Paton escaped the massacre and hid in the jungle until he was found by Indians who protected him until he was rescued by H.M.S. *Racehorse,* Captain Sir Everard Home. Priest and a number of Indians were captured by the crew of the *Racehorse* and turned over to the Portuguese; Priest starved to death aboard a prison ship. Paton arrived back in Montrose in the spring of 1837, the only survivor of the *Clio*.

1 8 3 8

289C. ANONYMOUS

Broadsides and ballads

J. Catnach and other cheap publishers

On September 6, 1838, the *Forfarshire* was wrecked on a voyage from Hull to Dundee, thirty-eight out of fifty-three people being drowned. James Darling, lighthouse keeper on Outer Fern Island, and his daughter Grace put off in a coble to attempt a rescue. Grace Darling became a widely renowned heroine, the subject of innumerable street ballads and pamphlets. (Charles Hindley, *The Life and Times of James Catnach,* London, 1878, p. 343)

1 8 3 8

290C. ANONYMOUS

Burning of the Canadian steamer Sir Robert Peel on the St. Lawrence

Times and Commercial Intelligencer, New York, June 4, 1838

291C. ANONYMOUS

Chronicles of the sea; or, faithful narratives of shipwrecks, fires, famines, and disasters incidental to a life of maritime enterprise; together with celebrated voyages, interesting anecdotes . . .

[London?] 1838–1840. Portrait and 119 finely engraved text illus., 2
vols., 4to

Bookseller's note: "119 weekly numbers beginning on Jan. 6, 1838, and published
every Saturday, price one penny." There were 442 narratives.

This publication was obviously modelled on Tegg's magazine (153C) and
perhaps on the *Mariner's Chronicle.* I have not seen this item; it would be interesting to know which sources were copied from.

292C. ANONYMOUS
Loss of the ship Pulaski
Times and Commercial Intelligencer, New York, June 23, 1838

The *Pulaski* sailed from Charleston for Baltimore on June 14, 1838. That night, at
about 11:00 P.M., the starboard boiler exploded. Many of the passengers and
crew were killed by the escaping steam, and when the ship broke up many
others were drowned. A few people reached the shore in two boats, and a larger
number drifted for days on part of the bow, and were picked up by a sailing
vessel. There were about 165 passengers and crew on board, and 59 were saved.
The cause of the explosion was supposedly the second engineer's letting the
boiler run low on water, and then letting in a large amount which instantly
became steam.

293C. ANONYMOUS
Wreck of the Stirling Castle
London, J. Catnach, 1838

This item is a broadside sheet with a woodblock illustration and seven dreary stan-
zas of verse about Mrs. Fraser. See 294C. James Catnach was a very successful publisher of broadside ballads and prints, many of them about murders
and executions.

294C. CURTIS, JOHN
Shipwreck of the Stirling Castle, containing a faithful narrative of
the dreadful sufferings of the crew, and the cruel murder of
Captain Fraser by the savages. Also, the horrible barbarity of
the cannibals inflicted upon the Captain's widow, whose unparalleled sufferings are stated by herself, and corroborated by
the other survivors
London, George Virtue, 1838. Many plates

The *Stirling Castle,* after a successful voyage from London to Hobart and Sydney,
sailed from the latter port for Singapore on May 13, 1836. On May 22 the ship
ran on a coral reef, an outlier of the Great Barrier Reef, and broke up. All on
board got off in small boats, and they set out for the Australian coast. There
they became the captives of groups of aborigines. Captain Fraser was speared
to death soon after their capture, and the others, including Mrs. Fraser, suffered severely. Eventually most of the castaways were rescued, and Mrs. Fraser
became something of a heroine in the press. As in the narrative of the wreck of
the *Grosvenor,* the possibility of miscegenation seems to have titillated the fan-
cy of both Australian and English readers.

The story of the *Stirling Castle* and poor Mrs. Fraser is well told in
Michael Alexander's *Mrs. Fraser on the Fatal Shore,* New York, 1971.

295C. CURTIS, JOHN AND [?]
The shipwreck of the Stirling Castle, containing a faithful narrative
of the dreadful sufferings of the crew, and the cruel murder of

Captain Fraser by the savages. . . . To which is added the narrative of the wreck of the Charles Eaton, in the same latitude

London, George Virtue, 1838. 8vo, embellished with engravings, pp. viii, 376

I have not seen this book, and cannot identify the writer of the narrative of the wreck of the *Charles Eaton.*

296C. FERRAR, LIEUT. W.A., R.N.

Narrative of a shipwreck on the coast of North America, in 1814 . . .

Falmouth, printed for the author, 1838. 2d edition, 23 pp., wraps.

American schooner *Post-Boy,* captured, wrecked on voyage to Bermudas.

297C. GOODRIDGE, CHARLES MEDYETT

Narrative of a voyage to the South Seas, and the shipwreck of the Princess of Wales cutter with an account of a two years residence on an uninhabited island, by Charles Medyett Goodridge, of Paignton, Devon, one of the survivors

Exeter, printed and published by W. C. Featherstone, and sold by the author, 1838, 1839, 1841 [4th], 1847

This is one of the liveliest and best of the shipwreck narratives, and almost the only one with a happy ending. Goodridge shipped on board the *Princess of Wales* for a sealing cruise, and sailed from Limehouse on May 9, 1820. They touched at a few places, did some sealing at Prince Edward's Island, and then set sail for the Crozets. There they did some sealing, but on March 17, 1821, they had to slip their cable when an unfavorable wind sprang up. The wind died suddenly, no anchor could touch bottom, and the currents swept the ship on the rocks of the island. Since there was no storm, all on board were able to get ashore, and a good deal of material from the wreck was saved. The Crozets are bleak and unpleasant, but there were many seals, sea lions, elephant seals, birds, penguins' eggs, and fish to be had, and the men did a better job of making their exile bearable than most shipwrecked mariners. About two years later they were taken off by the American schooner *Philo,* Isaac Perceval, Master. Goodridge, after some further vicissitudes, became a ferryman and sailor at Hobart Town, Tasmania, and the latter part of the book is mostly about his experiences there. He returned to Paignton, however, married, lost his Tasmanian fortune, and depended on this book for his livelihood. The fourth edition contains eighteen pages of names of purchasers of the book, and many testimonials to its value. Goodridge had much to say of the value of a Bible to the shipwrecked men, and this emphasis doubtless helped his sales.

298C. REID, LIEUT.-COLONEL W., C.B. (of the Royal Engineers)

An attempt to develop the law of storms by means of facts, arranged according to place and time; and hence to point out a cause for the variable winds, with the view to practical use in navigation

London, published by John Weale, 59 High Holborn, 1838

Reid, a genuine scientist, had discovered from the study of logbooks and sailing records that major storms were "rotatory and progressive." This book cites hundreds of such records. Reid was attempting to reach conclusions that would enable the captains of ships encountering storms to determine the general direction of the storm and the patterns followed by the winds. This knowledge would enable a captain to decide early which course would take him away from the worst winds; in earlier times ships attempting to escape from storms had frequently sailed into still worse conditions.

299C. SPOLASCO, (Baron)
> Narrative of the wreck of the Killarney steamer, with interesting details not yet published relative to the sufferings of those who were left desolate upon the rock in Renny Bay
> Cork, 1838. 2 litho. plates, 8vo, wraps.

The *Killarney,* 200 tons, Cork for Bristol, sailed from Cork on January 19, 1838, with forty-three on board, twenty-one passengers and twenty-two crew. She carried 650 pigs, some in the hold and some on deck. The ship encountered a severe storm, coals clogged the pumps, and the fires were put out. She drifted helpless before the gale and finally struck; some of those on board reached a rock, but most were swept overboard and drowned. Only twelve people survived of the forty-three on board.

1 8 3 9

300C. ANONYMOUS
> Minute and circumstantial narrative of the loss of the steam packet Pulaski . . . on the coast of North Carolina, June 14, 1838
> Providence, 1839. Woodcut frontis.

See 292C.

301C. ANONYMOUS
> Stories of voyages, being authentic narratives of the most celebrated voyages from Columbus to Perry, with accounts of remarkable shipwrecks and naval adventures
> Boston, 1839. 288 pp., illus., 18mo

Mostly narratives of voyages:
> Ship *Antelope*
> Captain Riley's narrative, *Commerce*
> Ship *Bounty*

302C. BINGLEY, THOMAS
> Tales of shipwreck and other disasters at sea . . . embellished with engravings from drawings by E. Landells
> London, Tilt, 1839; Boston, Weeks, Jordan & Co., 1839; London, 1864; Boston, 1842, 1847, 1850, 1851, 1859

This book, which was designed for younger readers, was reviewed by Edgar Allan Poe in *Burton's Magazine,* September, 1839.

> 1. Adventures of Captain Richard Falconer
> 2. Wreck of the *Vryheid,* near Hythe
> 3. Mutiny on the *Bounty*
> 4. Loss of the *Kent*
> 5. Wreck of the *Medusa*
> 6. Loss of the *Winterton*
> 7. Loss of the *Royal George*
> 8. Loss of the steamers *Killarney* and *Forfarshire*
> 9. Loss of the *Albion*
> 10. Loss of the *Doddington*

303C. FAIRLAND, T., AND WALTERS, S. [artists]
The loss of the *Pennsylvania,* New York packet ship; the
Lockwoods, emigrant ship. The *St. Andrew* packet ship, and
the *Victoria* from Charleston, near Liverpool, during the hur-
ricane on Monday and Tuesday, Jany. 7th and 8th, 1839
Lithograph in colors by T. Fairland and S. Walters. 1839

1 8 4 0

304C. ANONYMOUS
Awful calamities: or, the shipwrecks of December, 1839, being a
full account of the dreadful hurricanes of Dec. 15, 21, & 27, on
the coast of Massachusetts, in which were lost more than 90
vessels, and nearly 200 dismasted, driven ashore and other wise
damaged, and more than 150 lives destroyed, of which full
statistics are given; comprising also a particular relation of the
shipwreck of the following vessels: barque Lloyd, brigs
Pocahontas, Rideout and J. Palmer, and schs. Deposite,
Catharine Nichols and Miller. And also of the dreadful
disasters at Gloucester
Boston, press of J. Howe, No. 39 Merchants Row, 1840 [fourth edi-
tion]
On inside front and back covers, ''Loss of the steamer Lexington.'' There were at
least six editions of this pamphlet.

305C. ANONYMOUS
Loss of the steamboat ''Lexington'' in Long Island Sound on the
night of January 13th, 1840. A full and particular account of
all circumstances attending . . .
Providence, 1840
Barnes Catalogue
See 306C.

306C. ANONYMOUS
Loss of the ship Lexington
Portsmouth Journal, New Hampshire, January 18, 1840
The *Lexington* left New York for Stonington on January 13, 1840, with 33 in the
crew and about 93 passengers. At about 7:00 that evening a fire broke out
aboard and spread so rapidly that nothing could be done to fight it. The
engines could not be stopped, and therefore boats which were hoisted out were
swamped. Only four survived of the 126 on board; they had floated on cotton
bales and wreckage. One account claimed that a sloop could have saved many
of those in the water, but that the captain feared to lose the tide, and made his
home port.

307C. ANONYMOUS
The mariner's library, or voyager's companion, containing narratives of the most popular voyages . . . with accounts of
remarkable shipwrecks . . .
Boston, C. Gaylord, 1840

308C. ANONYMOUS
   A narrative of the loss of H.M.S. Royal George, of 108 guns, sunk
      at Spithead August 29, 1782 . . .
   Portsmouth, 1840
   Cox II, 468

309C. ANONYMOUS
   Perils of the ocean or disasters of the sea
   New York, Murphy, n.d. [1840?]
Bookseller's note: ". . . contains the stories of five ships lost at sea." See 332C.

310C. ANONYMOUS
   Perils of the sea: being authentic narratives of remarkable and af-
      fecting disasters upon the deep
   New York, J. and J. Harper, 1840
Apparently not the same as 321C, also published by Harper's.

311C. ANONYMOUS
   The sea. Narratives of adventures and shipwrecks, tales and
      sketches, illustrations of life on the ocean
   Edinburgh, W. and R. Chambers, 1840. 144 pp.

312C. COMSTOCK, WILLIAM
   The life of Samuel Comstock, the terrible whaleman, containing an
      account of the mutiny and massacre of the officers of the ship
      Globe, of Nantucket . . .
   Boston, J. Fisher, 1840
Another account of the mutiny on the *Globe,* by a brother of the leader and
   murderer. Probably most of the material for this book came from George
   Comstock, another brother, who was a member of the crew of the *Globe* but
   took no share in the mutiny. See 237C and 247C.

313C. HOWLAND, S.A.
   Steamboat disasters and railroad accidents in the United States, to
      which is appended accounts of recent shipwrecks, fires at sea,
      thrilling incidents, &c.
   Worcester, Dorr, Howland & Co., 1840. 12mo, 408 pp., illus.
The following table of contents is taken from an edition published in Worcester by
   Warren Lazell, 1846, "Revised and improved."
   1. Loss of the steam packet *Home,* on her passage from New York
      to Charleston, S.C., October 9, 1837, by which melancholy oc-
      currence ninety-five people perished
   2. Escape of the *Charleston,* on her passage from Philadelphia for
      Charleston, S.C., in which she experienced, and rode out in
      safety, the same gale in which the steam-packet *Home* was lost,
      October 8, 1837
   3. Loss of the steam-packet *Pulaski,* by the explosion of her
      starboard boiler, when off the coast of North Carolina, and on
      her passage from Charleston to Baltimore, June 14, 1838; by
      which disastrous event nearly one hundred persons perished

4. Loss of the steamer *Monmouth,* on the Mississippi River, on her passage from New Orleans for Arkansas River, October 31, 1837; by which melancholy catastrophe upwards of three hundred emigrating Indians were drowned

5. Conflagration of the *Royal Tar,* in Penobscot Bay, while on her passage from St. John, N.B., to Portland, Me., October 25, 1836; by which melancholy event there were thirty-two lives lost, and a menagerie of wild animals destroyed

6. Explosion of the steamboat *Moselle,* at Cincinnati, on the Ohio River; whence she had just started on her passage for Louisville and St. Louis, April 26, 1838; by which awful catastrophe nearly two hundred persons lost their lives

7. Explosion of the *Helen M'Gregor,* while stopping to land passengers at Memphis, Tennessee, February 24, 1830; by which disaster upwards of forty persons lost their lives

8. Destruction of the *Ben Sherod,* by fire and explosion, on the Mississippi River, while on her passage from New Orleans for Louisville, May 8, 1837; by which terrible catastrophe nearly two hundred persons lost their lives

9. Burning of the *Washington,* on Lake Erie, while on her passage from Cleaveland to Detroit, on the morning of June 16, 1838; by which many lives were lost

10. Explosion of the *New England,* on the Connecticut River, October 7, 1833, on her passage from New York to Hartford; by which fatal occurrence many lives were sacrificed

11. Loss of the steamer *New England,* which was run into by a schooner, and sunk, on her passage from Boston to Bath, May 31, 1839

12. Explosion of the steamer Aetna, in New York harbor, while on her way to the City, from Washington, N.J., May 15, 1824; with the loss of several lives

13. Explosion of the *George Collier,* on the Mississippi River, during her passage from New Orleans for Natchez, May 6, 1839; by which upwards of twenty-five lives were lost

14. Loss of the *General Jackson,* a New York steam ferryboat, which was run down in the harbor by the steamboat Boston, August 23, 1836; by which occurrence several persons lost their lives

15. Explosion of the *Chariton,* on the Mississippi River, near St. Louis, July 27, 1837

16. Explosion of the steamer *Oronoko,* on the Mississippi River, near Princeton, Miss., April 21, 1838; by which many lives were lost

17. Loss of the steamer *Tiskilwa,* on Illinois River, April 18, 1837; by which upwards of twenty persons perished

18. The steam-ship *President,* which was probably lost in the storm of March 12, 1841, between Nantucket Shoals and George's Bank; having on board upwards of one hundred human beings

19. Conflagration of the *Lexington,* on Long Island Sound, while

on her passage from New York to Stonington, January 13, 1840; by which terrible catastrophe upwards of one hundred and fifty persons perished; only four escaping of the entire number on board

20. Conflagration of the *Phoenix,* on Lake Champlain, on the night of September 5, 1819; wherein, owing to the coolness and self-possesion of the commander, not a soul was lost

21. Conflagration of the steamer *Erie,* on Lake Erie, while on her passage from Buffalo to Chicago, August 9, 1841; by which awful calamity nearly two hundred persons perished

22. Explosion of the steamer *Persian,* on the Mississippi River, while on her passage from New Orleans to St. Louis, November 7, 1840; by which fatal occurrence upwards of nineteen lives were lost

23. Loss of the *North Carolina,* while on her passage from Wilmington, N.C., to Charleston, S.C., July 25, 1841

24. Explosion on board the *Wilmington,* on the Mississippi River, November 12, 1839

25. Loss of the steamer *Bedford,* on the Missouri River, April 27, 1840

26. Explosion of the *John Hancock,* on her passage from Norwich to New London, in 1817

27. Explosion of the steamer *Greenfield,* on the Connecticut River, May 18, 1840

28. Explosion on board the *Motto,* on the Ohio River, during her first passage from Louisville to Pittsburg, August, 1836

29. Loss of the steamer *Green River,* on Green River, April 22, 1840

30. Accident on board the *Flora,* on the Ohio River, November 17, 1836

31. Loss of the steamer *Mary Express,* at Mobile, April 29, 1840

32. Explosion of the steamer *Franklin,* at Mobile, March 13, 1836

33. Explosion on board the *Union,* a new steam ferry-boat, which had just commenced running at Alexandria, July 12, 1837

34. Accident on board the *Samson,* in New York harbor, July 4, 1839

35. Loss of the *Odd Fellow,* a miniature steamer, November 6, 1841

36. Loss of the *Bunker Hill,* on Long Island Sound, November 15, 1841

37. Recent disasters on the Mississippi River

38. Escape of the steam-ship *Britannia,* from the rocks and breakers off the harbor of Halifax, during a fog, May 19, 1841

39. Loss of the steam-packet *Savannah,* which sprang a leak off Cape Hatteras, during a gale, while on her passage from Savannah to New York, November 28, 1841

40. An abstract of the law, relative to the management of steamboats, passed by the Congress of the United States, July 7, 1838

41. Loss of the steamer *Columbia,* which was wrecked upon Black Ledge, Seal Island, during a fog, July 2, 1843
42. Railroad accidents
43. Wreck of the barque *Mexico,* on Hempstead Beach, Long Island, January 2, 1837,—by which melancholy occurrence, one hundred and eight lives were lost
44. Wreck of the brig *Regulator,* in the outer harbor of Plymouth, February 5, 1836, by which five lives were lost
45. Wreck of the schooner *Isabella,* which foundered at sea, in a gale, November 1, 1837
46. Wreck of the brig *Trio,* on Deer Island, in Boston Harbor, February 20, 1837
47. Wreck of the schooner *Mary,* of Richmond, Va., near New York, September 14, 1837
48. Wreck of the brig *Ellsworth,* on Hull Beach, near Boston Light-house, February 20, 1837
49. Shipwreck of the *Bristol,* on Far Rockaway Beach, near New York, November 21, 1836; in which upwards of sixty lives were lost
50. Wreck of the sch.'r *Pennsylvania,* which was struck by a squall at sea, and foundered, September 16, 1837
51. Wreck of the barque *Lloyd,* of Portland, on Nantasket Beach, Hull, December 23, 1839, with the loss of the whole crew, excepting one person
52. Encounter of the ship *Byron,* and narrow escape from an iceberg, August 3, 1836
53. Conflagration of the *Burlington,* on her passage from New Orleans to Havre, March 17, 1840
54. Conflagration of the *Poland,* on her passage from New York for Havre, May 18, 1840
55. Wreck of the brig *Tariff,* on Cohasset Rocks, March 26, 1840; in which four lives were lost
56. Wreck of the brig *Escambia,* on her passage from Charleston to New York, March 25, 1840, with the loss of all on board, excepting one
57. Encounter of the *Gov. Carver,* and remarkable escape from an iceberg, May 29, 1818
58. Shipwreck of the *Glasgow,* on the Irish coast, Feb. 15, 1837; by which disaster a number of lives were lost
59. Conflagration of the *Harold,* on her passage from Calcutta to Boston, October 26, 1837
60. Miraculous preservation of the crew of the Scotch ship *Scotia,* by the New York packet ship *Roscius,* Dec. 5, 1839
61. Shipwrecks and other disasters, in the vicinity of Boston and Cape Ann, which occurred during the tremendous gale and snow storm of Dec. 15 and 16, 1839
62. Disasters in Boston harbor
63. Disasters in Gloucester harbor, in the gale of December 15, 1839

64. Disasters at other places, on the shores of New England,—at Newburyport, Marblehead, Cohasset, and at Provincetown, in the gale and snow storm of December 15 and 16, 1839
65. Another disastrous gale, in the vicinity of Boston and Cape Ann, December 27, 1839
66. Wreck of the *Catherine Nichols,* on Nahant Rocks, in the gale and snow storm of December 15, 1839
67. Wreck of the schooner *Deposit,* on Lakeman's Beach, Ipswich, in the gale of December 15, 1839
68. Wreck of the brig *Pocahontas,* on Plum Island, December 23, 1839,—with the loss of the whole crew
69. Burning of the packet-ship *Boston,* on her passage from Charleston, S.C., to Liverpool, on the 25th of May, 1830
70. Interesting narrative of the miraculous escape of the United States ship *Peacock* from shipwreck, after striking and grounding on a coral reef, September 21, 1835
71. A thrilling description of the burning of the lighthouse on Cape Florida, by the Seminole Indians, and the miraculous escape of Mr. Thompson, the keeper, July 23, 1836

314C. VAN TYNE, J. P.
Letter from J. P. Van Tyne to the Hon. J. R. Underwood, with a schedule of accidents to American steam vessels since the year 1830, &c.
Dec. 21, 1840 [Washington, 1840]. 8vo, folded, 7 pp.

315C. WAITE, JOSIAH KENDELL
A discourse delivered in the First Parish Church, Gloucester, Sunday, December 22nd, 1839, on the interment of eleven mariners, wrecked on Cape Ann, December 5, 1839
Gloucester, H. Tilden, 1840. 14 pp.

1 8 4 1

316C. ANONYMOUS
Perils and adventures on the deep: a series of interesting narratives of naval adventure and suffering
Edinburgh, 1841. Lge. 12mo, engraved title page

317C. ELLMS, CHARLES [compiler]
The tragedy of the seas . . .
Philadelphia, 1841
Probably another edition of 276C.

318C. SCOTT, JOHN LEE
Narrative of a recent imprisonment in China after the wreck of the Kite
London, W. H. Dalton, Cockspur Street, 1841, 1842. 5 engravings, 129 pp.

Scott sailed from Shields for Bordeaux in the *Kite* on July 8, 1839. From Bordeaux the ship sailed to the Mauritius and then to Madras. There the *Kite* was chartered by the British government to carry stores to the British fleet off the coast of China; the Opium War had broken out. The *Kite* joined the forces off Chusan, and then was sent to aid in a survey of the Yeang-tze-keang River. There the ship ran on a bank in a rapid current and upset, on September 15, 1840. The captain and some other crew members and passengers were drowned, but a majority of those on board were taken off the wreck by Chinese junks. All these survivors were imprisoned for about five months, under somewhat severe conditions, and then were released when the war ended. This narrative gives an interesting picture of Ningpo, where Scott was imprisoned. He reached Spithead on August 10, 1841.

319C. [SLIGHT, JULIAN]

A narrative of the loss of the Royal George, at Spithead, August, 1782; including Tracey's attempt to raise her in 1783, also, Col. Pasley's operations in removing the wreck, by explosions of gunpowder, in 1839–40–41

Portsea, S. Horsey, Jun., 151 Queen Street, printed and published by S. Horsey, Sen., 43 Queen Street; London, Whittaker & Co., 1841; [4th edition] 1843

This edition has a paper label inside the front cover stating that the covers, which are of wood, were made from timbers of the *Royal George.* The *Royal George* was at anchor in the harbor when she was canted for a minor repair. The officer of the day refused to heed a seaman who warned him that the ship was taking in water through the ports. The ship sank as she took in water, and went to the bottom with almost a thousand people on board. Probably about nine hundred people drowned. Cowper's poem made this one of the best known of English disasters.

According to W. H. D. Adams, *Famous Ships of the British Navy,* the *Mary Rose,* sixty guns, five hundred men, sank with all on board at almost exactly the same spot where the *Royal George* went down, on July 18, 1544.

1 8 4 2

320C. ANONYMOUS

Lines composed on the loss of the barque Isadore of Kennebunkport, which went ashore near Bald Head, Wells, November 30, 1842, in a tremendous storm and all her crew perished

n.p., n.d. [1842?]. Broadside

321C. [SARGENT, EPES]

American adventure by land and sea, Volume II

New York, Harper and Bros., 1842. [copyright, 1841]

1. *Nottingham* galley
2. The *St. Lawrence*
3. Captain Norwood's narrative
4. Famine in the *Peggy*
5. Narrative of Mme. Denoyer
6. Narrative of Captain Woodward [Woodard]

7. Narrative of Captain Woodward [Woodard]
8. Loss of the *Commerce,* Captain Riley
9. Loss of the *Commerce,* Captain Riley
10. Loss of the *Commerce,* Captain Riley
11-12. Loss of the *Commerce,* Captain Riley
13. Stranding of the *Mexico*
14-15. Loss of the *Mentor*
16. Loss of the brig *Regulator,* 1837
17. Loss of the *Albion*
18. Narrative of Captain Cazneau
19. Loss of the *Pulaski*
20. Loss of the *Home*
21. Loss of the *Lexington*
22. Loss of the *Scotia*
23. Loss of the *William Brown,* by ice, 1841 [See note]
24. Loss of the *Erie,* by fire, 1841

The loss of the *William Brown* in 1841 supplied one of the most harrowing narratives in the history of maritime disasters. The *William Brown* sailed from Liverpool for Philadelphia March 13, 1841, with sixty-five Scotch and Irish emigrants and seventeen crew. The captain was named Harris, and the first mate, Rhodes. The voyage was a difficult one, with storm after storm, but the ship was sturdy and fought her way westward. On April 19, 1841, in a thick fog, the vessel struck an iceberg and was holed. Crew and some passengers tumbled into the longboat and the jolly boat, but thirty-one passengers were left to drown when the *William Brown* sank. There were nine in the jolly boat, which should have held seven, and forty-two in the longboat, capacity eighteen. Two days later, when the wind rose and waves threatened, sixteen passengers were thrown out of the longboat to lighten it, including two sisters who refused to stay in the boat after their brother was thrown out. Those remaining in the longboat were picked up by the *Crescent,* New York for Le Havre, and those in the jolly boat by a French fisherman. There was considerable protest because all seventeen crewmen survived; only passengers died. The captain and the mates made themselves scarce, and only one miserable crewman named Holmes was ever tried in court. He was convicted of manslaughter and was sentenced to six months in jail and a fine of $20.00. The *William Brown* and the *Mignonette* cases did something to settle responsibilities when disaster struck at sea.

1 8 4 3

322C. STIRLING, MAJOR (late Captain) W.
        Narrative of the loss of the ship Tiger of Liverpool, Captain Edward Searight, on the desert isle of Astova, August 12, 1836 . . .
        Exeter, printed by W. Roberts, 197 High Street, 1843. Map

1 8 4 4

323C. ANONYMOUS
        Accident on steam-ship "Princeton." May 15, 1844 . . .
        [Washington, 1844] *House Report* no. 79. 43 pp.

The steam frigate *Princeton* took a party on an excursion down the Potomac River. An explosion occurred, and the Secretary of State, the Secretary of the Navy, and others of the party were killed.

324C. BOLTON, WILLIAM
A narrative of the last cruise of the United States steam frigate "Missouri" from the day she left Norfolk, until the arrival of her crew in Boston, including a full and circumstantial detail of the general conflagration which took place at Gibraltar . . .
Philadelphia, 1844
Barnes Catalogue

325C. CHAPIN, E. H.
The catastrophe of the Princeton. A discourse . . . March 3, 1844
Boston, 1844. 16 pp.
See 323C.

326C. CUTLER, BENJAMIN C.
Twelve hours on the wreck; or, the stranding of the Sheffield
New York, T. C. Butler, 1844. 1st edition, with original hymns for seamen, 6 full-page plates
The *Sheffield,* Captain Popham, sailed from Liverpool for New York on October 5, 1843. Crew and passengers numbered about 130. The voyage was long, about thirty-seven days, and the weather severe, but the ship sighted Long Island on November 10. The next day a pilot came aboard, and they set out for the harbor. Apparently the storm and perhaps fog led the pilot astray, and the ship struck on the Romer shoal. Fortunately the *Sheffield* had a sturdy hull, and the ship was so close to New York that rockets sent up from the ship were seen. Captain Vanderbilt, of Staten Island, in the *Wave,* came to the rescue and took off most of those on board the *Sheffield*. A little later those left on board—all crew members—were taken off. There were no casualties.

327C. ELLIS, GEORGE W.
A poem on the awful catastrophe on board the U.S. steam frigate "Princeton." Together with a full description of the terrible calamity . . .
Boston, printed by A. J. Wright, 1844. 12mo, 72 pp.
See 323C.

328C. JACOBS, THOMAS MORRELL [Maggs Catalogue says Jacobs, Thomas Jefferson]
Scenes, incidents, and adventures in the Pacific Ocean, or, the islands of the Australasian seas, during the cruise of the clipper Margaret Oakley, under Captain Benjamin Morrell
New York, Harper's, 1844. 372 pp.; plates, one fldg., map
Bookseller's note: "Neither the ship nor its Captain ever returned, the narrative told by a survivor of sometimes hair-raising adventures." The *Margaret Oakley* was lost on the coast of Madagascar, where Captain Morrell died.

329C. LAFOND, GABRIEL
Voyages autour du monde et naufrages célèbres
Paris, Administration de Librairie, 1844. 8 vols., illus., ports., vols. 6–8, naufrages célèbres

330C. PRENTIS, STEPHEN
        The wreck of the Ros-common
        Dinan, Huart, 1844. 8vo, wrappers
These verses commemorate the loss of the *Roscommon* in the Irish Channel.

331C. SMITH, THOMAS W.
        A narrative of the life of Thomas W. Smith
        Boston, 1844
Bookseller's note: "Contains the stories of eighteen voyages, five shipwrecks."

[1 8 4 5]

332C. ANONYMOUS
        Ben Boatswain's yarns or tales of the ocean
        New York, Murphy, 384 Pearl Street. Wraps.
        Contains:
        Loss of the *Betsy*
        Destruction of the *Prince*
A juvenile with materials taken from the same publisher's *Perils of the Ocean or Disasters of the Sea,* New York [1840s] (309C).

1 8 4 5

333C. ANONYMOUS
        The British log book or tales of the ocean, containing a collection of
            well-spun tough yarns. . . . shipwrecks and disasters, . . .
        London, ca. 1845. 14 fortnightly numbers, each with a vignette

334C. ANONYMOUS
        Fate of the steam-ship President, which sailed from New-York,
            March 11th, 1841, bound for Liverpool
        Boston, 1845. 8vo, 34 pp., pictorial wraps.
The *President,* Captain Roberts, sailed from New York for Liverpool on March 11, 1841. She carried a crew of about eighty, and thirty-one passengers, among them Tyrone Power, a well-known British actor. The ship encountered a severe storm soon after sailing, and was last seen by Captain Cole of the *Orpheus,* which had sailed in company with the *President* the day before. Nothing is known of the *President* from that last sighting, but most people apparently believed that she foundered that night somewhere between Nantucket Shoals and George's Bank. Whitman wrote in "Thought":
        Of certain ships, how they sail from port with flying streamers
            and wafted kisses, and that is the last of them,
        Of the solemn and murky mystery about the fate of the President, . . .

335C. ANONYMOUS
        The Friend, a semi-monthly journal devoted to temperance,
            seamen, marine, and general intelligence. 8 pp. an issue
        Honolulu, 1845–1857 [?]
Bookseller's catalogue states: "Includes material on whaling, shipwrecks."

336C. ANONYMOUS
Perils and adventures of the deep
Thomas Nelson, Edinburgh and London, 1845
Probably the same as 316C, 1841.

337C. ANONYMOUS
Piratical and tragical almanac for 1846
Philadelphia, J. B. Perry, 198 Market Street; Zieber and Company,
3 Ledger Bldg. [1845]
Woodcut—loss of the steamer "Swallow."

338C. ANONYMOUS
Tales of shipwrecks and adventures at sea
n.p., n.d. [London, 1840s?] 4to, 912 pp., double columns

339C. DARTNELL, GEORGE R.
A brief narrative of the shipwreck of the transport "Premier," near
the mouth of the river St. Lawrence, 4th November,
1843 . . . having on board the head-quarter wing of the second battalion of the First or Royal Regiment. . . . Illustrated
with several engravings from sketches made on the
spot. . . . The drawings in lithotint by J. A. Hammersley
London, Jeremiah How, 1845. Pp. xv. 37. 6 plates

340C. DARVALL, JOSEPH
The wreck on the Andamans: being a narrative of the very
remarkable preservation, and ultimate deliverance, of the
soldiers and seamen, who formed the ships' companies of the
Runnymede and Briton troop-ships, both wrecked on the
morning of the 12th of November, 1844, upon one of the Andaman Islands, in the Bay of Bengal. Taken from authentic
documents by Joseph Darvall, Esq. At the request of Capt.
Charles Ingram and Capt. Henry John Hall, owners of the
Runnymede
London, Pelham Richardson, 23 Cornhill, 1845. Five plates
The *Runnymede,* 507 tons, Captain Doutty, sailed from Gravesend June 20, 1844,
for Calcutta. She carried a crew of 28; enlisted men and officers of the East India Company forces, 148; and women and children, 26; making a total of 202
on board. The ship touched at Penang, and then was caught in a hurricane on
November 10, 1844, in which the rudder was lost. On November 12 the *Runnymede* struck on rocks off an island east of Great Andaman, and was lodged
solidly there just as the storm was dying out. Another ship was seen ashore
nearby, and she was discovered to be the *Briton,* Sydney for Calcutta, with 404
on board including soldiers and officers of the Eightieth Regiment. The two
groups joined forces, divided provisions, set up defenses against the natives,
and repaired a longboat for a rescue mission. The longboat sailed for Burma
on November 25, and a small ship with provisions reached the castaways on
December 15. Three larger ships arrived on December 29, 1844, took off
everyone, and delivered them to Calcutta. All in all, this narrative tells the
story of one of the best managed of all shipwreck adventures. The people of the

Runnymede and the *Briton* were fortunate that they struck just as the storm was ending, and fortunate also in getting provisions ashore, but they kept discipline and deserved their good fortune.

341C. ISAACS, NICHOLAS PETER
    Twenty years before the mast, or life in the forecastle . . .
    New York, J. P. Beckwith, 1845. 12mo, pp. [2] [xvi] [3] 199
Bookseller's note: "Isaacs . . . was impressed, shipwrecked, and had other adventures as well." Isaacs sailed on a sealer, trading ships, and cod fishermen out of Mystic, Connecticut.

342C. VAN TENAC [editor]
    Histoire générale de la marine, comprenant les naufrages célèbres, les voyages autour du monde, les découvertes et colonisations, l'histoire des pirates, corsaires et négriers, . . .
    Paris, Penaud [1845]. Four vols., 8vo, 10 colored costume plates, 26 engraved plates of shipping, naval engagements, etc.

1 8 4 6

343C. ANONYMOUS
    Naufrages célèbres ou aventures les plus remarquables des marins depuis le 15e siècle jusqu'a nos jours
    Tours, Ad Mame & Cie Editeurs, Imprimeurs-libraires, 1846
      1. Naufrage d'Emmanuel Sosa, 1553
      2. Le *Jacques,* 1558
      3. Le *Saint-Jacques,* 1586
      4. *L'Ascension,* Camboya
      5. La Nouvelle-Hoorn, 1619
      6. Le *Parow* (l'*Epervier*), 1653
      7. Le *Batavia,* 1630
      8. Le *Taureau,* Cap-Vert, 1665
      9. Le *Laosdun,* du Gange, 1672
     10. Frégate Espagnole, mer du Sud, 1678
     11. Naufrage D'Occum Chamnan, 1686
     12. Patache Portugaise, mer des Indes, 1688
     13. Le *Degrave,* 1701
     14. La Comtesse de Bourk, 1719
     15. *Sussex,* 1738
     16. Le *Prince,* 1752
     17. Vaisseau Hollandaises, Cap de Bonne-Esperance, 1773
     18. *L'Union,* 1775
     19. Le *Duras,* Maldives, 1777
     20. Naufrage de M. Saugnier, 1784
     21. Naufrage de M. Brisson, 1785
     22. Aventures de Pierre Viaud
     23. Le *Sydney,* 1806
     24. La *Meduse,* 1816
     25. Naufrage sauve par son chien

344C. ANONYMOUS
Shipwrecks and disasters at sea; narratives of the most remarkable
wrecks, conflagrations, etc.
London, 1846. 420 pp., illus. I. J. Chidley, 123 Aldersgate Street
Ship *Sea Venture*
Ship *New Horn*
French vessel (Sieur de Montauban)
Adventures of Philip Ashton
Byron and the ship *Wager*
Alexander Campbell and the ship *Wager*
Morris and the ship *Wager*
Ship *Peggy*
Ship *Antelope*
Captain Bligh and the *Bounty*
Ship *Pandora*
Ship *Lady Hobart*

345C. DIX, WILLIAM G. [editor? Attributed also to Oliver, James]
Wreck of the Glide; with an account of life and manners at the Fijii
Islands
Boston, William D. Ticknor, 1846. 12mo, 122 pp.
Bookseller's note: "Copyright by William Dix, but evidently by his brother (ac-
cording to a letter once catalogued by another dealer)."
The *Glide* sailed from Salem in 1829. She was called a whaler, but when
she reached the Fijis was apparently after *bêche de mer*. The ship was caught in
a hurricane on March 20, 1831, and was driven ashore, where the natives
treated the crew quite well. Another narrative of the *Glide* was written by
William S. Cary, the only survivor of the whaler *Oeno*, wrecked on Turtle
Island on April 5, 1825. Cary was picked up by the *Glide*, suffered shipwreck
again, and finally reached Nantucket after a nine years' absence. His story was
not published until 1887, in a Nantucket newspaper.

346C. MRS. JONES
Loss of five Wesleyan missionaries in the Maria mail-boat
New York, published by G. Lane and C. B. Tippett for the Sunday
School Union of the Methodist Episcopal Church, J. Collard,
Pr., 1846
See 229C, 1826.

347C. LINDRIDGE, JAMES [editor]
Tales of shipwrecks and adventures at sea, being a collection of
faithful narratives of shipwrecks, mutinies, fires, famines, and
disasters incidental to a sea life . . .
London, William Mark Clark, 17 Warwick Lane, MDCCCXLVI
[1846]. 948 pp., 153 engravings

1 8 4 7

348C. ANONYMOUS
American adventures by land and sea being remarkable instances of
enterprise and fortitude among Americans. Shipwrecks, adven-

tures at home and abroad. Indian captivities, &c. In 2 volumes
New York, Harper and Brothers, Cliff Street, 1847. Family Library
#174

See 321C, 1842.

349C. ANONYMOUS
The loss of the Australia: a narrative of the loss of the brig Australia
by fire, on her voyage from Leith to Sydney
New York, Robert Carter, 1847. 98 pp.

350C. GREIG, ALEXANDER M.
Fate of the Blenden Hall, East Indiaman, bound to Bombay: with
an account of her wreck and the sufferings and privations endured by the survivors, for six months, on the desolate islands
of Inaccessible and Tristan D'Acunha in lat. 37° 29″ South.
Long. 11° 45″ West. By Alexander M. Greig, one of the
passengers, from a journal kept on the islands, and written
with the blood of the penguin
New York, William H. Colyer, 1847

The *Blenden Hall,* 450 tons, Captain Alexander Greig, sailed from the Thames for
India May 6, 1821, with eighty-four passengers and crew. On July 22 the ship
struck a reef off Inaccessible Island in the South Atlantic; she was swept onto
the reef by currents in a foggy calm. Two men were drowned but the others
reached the island. After some months on Inaccessible some of the crewmen
sailed a boat to Tristan da Cunha for help, and the survivors—six crewmen had
been lost in an earlier attempt to reach Tristan—were ferried to that island.
They were finally taken off by the ship *Nerinae.* The author of this narrative
was the son of the captain; he had become a citizen of New York. The story is
well told in J. G. Lockhart's *Blenden Hall,* London, Philip Allan, 1930.
      See 208C and 210C.

351C. HARRIS, W. SNOW
Remarkable instances of the protection of certain ships of Her Majesty's navy, from the destructive effects of lightning, collected
from official and other authenticated documents; to which is
added a list of two hundred and twenty cases of ships of Her
Majesty's navy struck and damaged by lightning, . . .
London, printed for the author, 1847. 8vo, 61, 3 blank, 8 addenda
pp., illus. in text, 2 litho plates

Bookseller's note: "Harris, a Fellow of the Royal Society, was in the business of
manufacturing lightning conductors for ships."

352C. KEY, ASTLEY COOPER
A narrative of the recovery of H.M.S. "Gorgon" stranded in the
Bay of Montevideo, 1844
London, 1847. 18 plates and 23 detailed construction drawings

353C. SAMPSON, ABEL [Edmund Hale Kendall]
The wonderful adventures of Abel Sampson, related by himself;
written by Edmund Hale Kendall, Esq.
Lawrence City, Mass., 1847. 16mo, 88 pp., illus., wrappers

Bookseller's note: "Sampson was born in Turner, Maine, in 1790, and spent much of his life at sea. His adventures include several impressments, a slaving voyage to Africa, privateering in the War of 1812, and shipwreck."

1 8 4 8

354C. ANONYMOUS
> An authentic account of the destruction of the Ocean Monarch, by fire, off the port of Liverpool, and loss of 176 lives, with an engraving
> Liverpool, William McCall, 1848

355C. ANONYMOUS
> Destruction of an emigrant ship, the Ocean Monarch, by fire
> Liverpool, 1848, reprinted from *Liverpool Journal;* available in Liverpool Record Office

356C. CLARK, JOSEPH G.
> Lights and shadows of sailor life, as exemplified in 15 years experiences, including the more thrilling events of the U.S. Exploring Expeditions . . . Life in the "Mountain Wave" . . . the wreck of the "Peacock"
> Boston, 1848. 6 engravings

357C. DEXTER, ELISHA
> Narrative of the loss of the whaling brig William and Joseph, of Martha's Vineyard
> Boston, Mead, 1848

358C. ELLMS, CHARLES [editor?]
> The tragedy of the seas
> Philadelphia, W. A. Leary; Boston, W. J. Reynolds & Co., 1848

Probably the same as 279C. Ellms, like R. Thomas, was a tireless compiler of collections of narratives of disasters and piracies.

359C. GORTON, J. [editor?]
> Mariner's chronicle of shipwrecks, fires, famines and other disasters at sea . . . with an account of whale fishing and Jewitt narrative . . .
> Philadelphia, 1848. 2 vols. in one, 80 narratives, 60 engravings

Probably the same as 365C, the anthology published by Harding in Philadelphia in 1849.

360C. HOWISON, LIEUTENANT NEIL M., USN
> Oregon. Report . . . to the Commander of the Pacific Squadron; being the result of an examination in the year 1846 of the coast, harbors, rivers, soil, productions, climate, and population of the Territory of Oregon. February 29, 1848
> [Washington, D.C., 1848] 30th Congress, 1st session, House, Miscellaneous, 29

Howison's vessel, the *Shark,* was wrecked in the Columbia River; the flag of that ship, taken ashore, was the first United States flag hoisted in the Territory.

361C. LEGG, JAMES HENRY
        The Ocean Monarch, a poetic narrative, with an original and authentic account, in prose, of the loss of this ill-fated vessel . . .
        Liverpool, Deighton and Langton; London, Smith, Elder, 1848

362C. PALMER, AARON H.
        Memoir, geographical
        Congressional 1st session, Senate Miscellaneous Document 80, June 3 [1848]. 8 vo, disbound, 105 + 2 pp., 2 folding maps
Bookseller's note: "2nd. issue with additional appendices, including descriptions of the wreck of the whale ship Lawrence of Poughkeepsie, and several others off the coast of Japan, and the treatment of the crews by the Japanese."

363C. SPENCER, THOMAS
        Narrative of the events attending the massacre of part of the crew belonging to the whaleship 'Triton' of New Bedford, by the natives of Sydenham's Island
        Honolulu, E. A. Rockwell, Sandwich Islands News Press, 1848
This listing is from H. E. Maude's *Of Islands and Men.*

1 8 4 9

364C. ANONYMOUS
        Burning of the ship Ocean Monarch
        New York, 1849

365C. ANONYMOUS
        The mariner's chronicle of shipwrecks, fires, famines, and other disasters at sea . . . together with an account of the whale fishery
        Philadelphia, J. Harding, 1849. 2 vols. in one

366C. ENDICOTT, CHARLES M.
        Narrative of the piracy and plunder of the ship "Friendship" of Salem, on the west coast of Sumatra in Feb. 1831; and the massacre of part of her crew, also, her recapture out of the hands of the Malay pirates
        Salem, printed at the Gazette Office, 1849. Sm. 4to, 20 pp.

1 8 5 0

367C. ANONYMOUS
        Stories about the whale; with an account of the whale fishery, and of the perils attending its prosecution
        Concord, N.H., Rufus Merrill, 1850. 12mo, 24 pp., wraps.
Contains an account of the loss of the *Essex.*

368C. [CROCKER, THOMAS R.]
       Ship Chandler Price, owners and crew of. . . . Mr. Grinnell, from
           the Committee on Commerce, made the following report: . . .
       [Washington, D.C., 1850] U.S. 31st Congress, 1st session, House
           Report 177. 8vo, 8 pp.
Report on the rescue of the crew of a New London whaler, the *Columbia,* by the
   crew of the *Chandler Price.* Contains a description of the loss of the *Columbia*
   by the cooper on that ship, Thomas R. Crocker.

369C. DUNHAM, JACOB
       Journal of voyages: containing an account of the author's being
           twice captured by the English and once by Gibbs the pirate; his
           narrow escape when chased by an English war schooner; as well
           as his being cast away and residing with Indians. To which is
           added some account of the soil, products, laws and customs of
           Chagres, the Musquitto Shore, and St. Blas, at the Isthmus of
           Darien
       New-York, published for the author, and sold by Huestis & Cozans,
           104 and 106 Nassau-street, 1850
Captain Dunham was at sea from 1813 to 1842. He lost two small ships from striking reefs and foundering, but he was close to shore in both cases and there was
   no loss of life. Dunham's twelve voyages were mostly to the Mosquito Coast of
   Central America and to Haiti, and the book is chiefly valuable for its pictures
   of the people and trade of those areas. It most resembles Richard Cleveland's
   Narrative of Voyages and Commercial Enterprises, 1842, and the story of Captain Gorham P. Low in *The Sea Made Men,* 1937. Dunham was captured by
   pirates off Cuba, but there is no evidence presented in the text that the leader of
   the villains was the notorious Gibbs named in the title. This reference must
   have been an attempt to get more attention for the book.

370C. HOWARD, HOSEA
       An account of the shipwreck of Rev. Hosea Howard & family (as
           published by M. B. Anderson, in the New York Recorder,
           1850). By Hosea Howard
       New York [1850]. 24 pp., 12mo

371C. NUNN, JOHN
       Narrative of the wreck of the "Favorite" on the Island of Desola-
           tion; detailing the adventures, sufferings, and privations of
           John Nunn, and historical account of the island and its whale
           and sea fisheries
       London, 1850. Fifty-six engravings, fldg. chart of Kerguelen
Nunn was one of five men left on the island in 1825, on a sealing voyage. They took
   care of themselves very well for two years, and were then taken off by the
   schooner *Sprightly.* This narrative is much like Goodridge's story of being
   stranded on the Crozets (297C).

372C. TWYNING, JOHN P.
       Shipwreck and adventure of John P. Twyning among the South Sea
           Islanders: giving an account of their feasts, massacres, etc.,
           etc. . . .

London, printed for the benefit of the author [1850]. Second edition, enlarged

Twyning, a boatsteerer on the Australian whaler *Minerva,* was wrecked in that ship on a reef near the Tonga Group in September, 1829. The crew reached Vatoa, in the Lau Islands, in boats, and was well treated by the natives there. His narrative is an important anthropological document. For another narrative of the same wreck see 243C. This listing is taken from H. E. Maude's *Of Islands and Men.*

1 8 5 1

373C. ANONYMOUS [Captain Deblois?]
       "Wreck of the Ann Alexander"
       Daily Evening Traveller, Boston, Nov. 3, 1851

The *Ann Alexander* struck a whale, and sank. The incident occurred just as *Moby Dick* was about to be published.

374C. CLARKE, REV. J.
       The wreck of the Orion: a tribute of gratitude from the Reverend J. Clarke, M.A., incumbent of the parochial church of Stretford, near Manchester. . . . N.B.—The entire proceeds of this volume will be given to the "Good Samaritans" to whom they are due
       London, Longman, Brown, Green, and Longmans; Manchester, T. Sowler, St. Anne's Square, 1851 [Second edition]. Pp. ix, 81. 1 pl.

The *Orion,* the largest steamer sailing between Liverpool and Glasgow, sailed from Liverpool on June 17, 1850. Sometime that night the vessel went off course and struck. She sank in fifteen minutes and more than twenty-five people were drowned. The Rev. J. Clarke was so completely wrapped up in his own concerns, and so interested in exploring the reasons for his having been spared, that he told almost nothing about the shipwreck, but one sailor told him it was the result of a faulty compass. This book is a good example of how *not* to write the story of a shipwreck.

375C. GILLY, WILLIAM O. S. [compiler]
       Narratives of shipwrecks of the Royal Navy: between 1793 and 1849. Compiled principally from official documents in the Admiralty. . . . With a preface by William Stephen Gilly, D.D. Vicar of Norham and Canon of Durham
       London, John W. Parker, West Strand, MDCCCLI [1851]. Second edition, revised
       1. The *Sceptre*
       2. The *Queen Charlotte*
       3. The *Invincible*
       4. The *Grappler*
       5. The *Apollo*
       6. The *Hindostan*
       7. The *Romney*
       8. *Venerable*
       9. The *Sheerness*

10. *Athénienne*
11. The *Nautilus*
12. The *Flora*
13. The *Ajax*
14. The *Anson*
15. The *Boreas*
16. The *Hirondelle*
17. *Banterer*
18. The *Crescent*
19. The *Minotaur*
20. The *Pallas* and the *Nymph*
21. *St. George* and *Defence*
22. *Hero*
23. *Saldanha*
24. The *Daedalus*
25. The *Persian*
26. The *Penelope*
27. The *Alceste*
28. The *Drake*
29. *Fury*
30. The *Magpie*
31. The *Thetis*
32. The *Firefly*
33. The *Avenger*
34. List of the shipwrecks of the Royal Navy, between 1793 and 1850

376C. MANBY, GEORGE WILLIAM
A summary of services rendered to the state, in saving the lives of its sailors from shipwreck, . . .
Yarmouth, Chs. Sloman, 1851. With portrait, plates of medals, and illus.

1 8 5 2

377C. ANONYMOUS
The lost steamer: a history of the "Amazon," a newly launched 800 h.p. sidewheel paddle steamer West Indian packet. In 1852 a fire broke out during a gale in the Bay of Biscay
London, 1852. 12mo, cloth
See 380C.

378C. ANONYMOUS
Shipwreck by lightning. Destruction of merchant ships. From the "Nautical Magazine" for Nov. 1852
London, 1852

379C. ANONYMOUS
Wreckage
From the *United Services Magazine.* Reprinted in *Littell's Living Age,* Vol. 35, Oct.–Dec. 1852, pp. 174–178

This article is really a review of a volume of *Lloyd's List,* "A return of all collisions, accidents, and wrecks of vessels, specifying the tonnage of each vessel, and the number of lives lost, since the first day of January, 1847, up to the 31st day of December, 1850." This collection was ordered by the House of Commons, and showed that about 12,400 vessels had suffered in one way or another during the period.

380C. JOHNS, REV. C. A. [editor]
   The loss of the Amazon. Published under the direction of the Committee of General Literature and Education appointed by the Society for Promoting Christian Knowledge
   London, printed for the Society for Promoting Christian Knowledge; sold at the depositories, Great Queen Street, Lincoln's Inn Fields, 4 Royal Exchange, 16 Hanover Street, Hanover Square, and by all booksellers, n.d. [Dedication is dated Feb. 15, 1852.] (8), 116, (4). 1 engraving, 12mo

The *Amazon,* a large steamer-sailing ship, left Southampton for Chagres, Panama, on January 2, 1852. Just after midnight the ship caught on fire in the Bay of Biscay, and was completely destroyed. One hundred four passengers and crew were lost out of 162. The cause of the fire was never exactly determined, but the engine had been stopped twice so that seawater could be poured on overheated bearings, and there seems little doubt that overheating of a new engine somehow started the fire. The flames spread rapidly and there was some panic; many lives were lost because the ship's boats were secured in iron cradles which were new to crew members and this resulted in dumped passengers and swamped boats. The *Amazon* was a wooden ship.

381C. LACON, WILLIAM STIRLING
   The loss of the Orion, the Amazon, and the Birkenhead. A letter to . . . the president of the Board of Trade, on the management of ships' boats
   London, 1852. Second edition. 8vo, 64 pp., illus., wraps.

Bookseller's catalogue: "Much technical data."

   For the loss of the *Orion,* see 374C; for the *Amazon,* 380C. The loss of the *Birkenhead* was one of the best known of nineteenth century wrecks, primarily because of the good conduct of many English soldiers involved. The *Birkenhead,* a troopship, sailed from Cork for South Africa with about 650 on board, more than 500 of them soldiers. The voyage was uneventful until after some of the troops had been discharged at Simon's Bay on February 23, 1852. The ship set out for Algoa Bay to disembark another detachment, and struck a reef near Point Danger at about 2:00 A.M. on February 26. She broke in two and then broke up completely, though a few boats were put off. The troops obeyed orders perfectly and never tried to rush the boats; most of the women and children were taken off. Of the approximately 622 people who were on board only 192 were saved. No account that I have seen explains why the reef was struck. The weather was good and there was no reason for Captain Salmond to take chances. He was lost with his ship.

1 8 5 3

382C. ANONYMOUS
   The book of the ocean and life on the sea, containing thrilling nar-

ratives and adventures of ocean life in all countries from the earliest period to the present time

Auburn, N.Y., Alden, Beardsley & Co.; Rochester, N.Y., Wanzer, Beardsley & Co., 1853; New York, Hurst & Co., n.d. [1860?]. 60 illus., 2 vols. in one

383C. ANONYMOUS
Voyage and venture; or, perils by sea and land. With illustrations by William Harvey
London, George Routledge and Co., Farringdon Street, 1853

Contains:

A shipwreck on the coast of Coromandel, pp. 1-14 [ship not named]

Wreck of the *Drake* schooner, pp. 15-19. H.M.S. *Drake,* Captain Baker, was lost off the coast of Newfoundland in a fog. Captain Baker died in attempting to save all on board. No date is given, but the last paragraph of the narrative states that a memorial to Captain Baker was erected in the chapel of the Royal Dockyard at Portsmouth.

The wreck of the *Meduse,* pp. 20-26

Burning of the *Kent,* pp. 31-33

Pp. 95-121, the whale-fishery and its hazards, describes the loss of the *Essex,* and includes "A Whaler's Inn at New Bedford, in Massachusetts." This last selection is made up from "The Carpet Bag" and "The Spouter-Inn," chapters 2 and 3 in Melville's *Moby Dick,* and must be among the earliest piracies from that book. Melville's name is not mentioned.

384C. ANONYMOUS
Wreck of the Annie Jane
New York *Times,* October 13, 1853

385C. FORBES, R. B.
Shipwreck by lightning. Papers relative to Harris lightning conductors, by R. B. Forbes
Boston, printed by Sleeper and Rogers, 1853

386C. VAN TENAC, CHARLES
Histoire générale de la marine comprenant les naufrages célèbres . . .
Paris, E. et V. Penaud frères, 1853. 4 vols.

1 8 5 4

387C. ANONYMOUS
Emigrant vessels. Return to an address of the Honorable the House of Commons . . . for copies of reports to the colonial office, in the six months ending the 31st day of January 1854, of the loss of vessels carrying emigrants . . .
House of Commons, 1854. Vol. 46

388C. ANONYMOUS
Full account of the loss of S.S. Arctic, with nearly 300 lives
Boston, n.d. [1854]

The *Arctic,* a Collins Line steamer, sailed from Liverpool for New York on
September 20, 1854. The voyage was uneventful until the twenty-seventh at
about noon when the ship collided with the French *Vesta,* a smaller steamer.
The collision took place on the Newfoundland Banks in fog, and the vessels
soon drifted apart.The *Vesta* reached port with only a few casualties, but the
Arctic was badly holed and sank at about 4:45 P.M. Crewmen had rushed the
boats and had kept passengers out of them, and there was a general panic on
board. The ship had sailed with 233 passengers and about 150 crew; over 300
died, and every woman on board was drowned. The story of the loss of the
Arctic has been well told recently by Alexander C. Brown in his *Women and
Children Last: The Loss of the Steamship Arctic,* N.Y., 1961. Whitman wrote
in "Thought,"

> Of the flower of marine science of fifty generations founder'd
>   off the Northeast coast and going down—of the steamship
>   Arctic going down,
> Of the veil'd tableau—women gather'd together on deck, pale,
>   heroic, waiting the moment that draws so close—O the moment!
> A huge sob—a few bubbles—the white foam spurting up—and then
>   the women gone, . . .

389C. ANONYMOUS
        The Shipwrecked Mariner. A quarterly maritime magazine
        London, "Shipwrecked Mariners' Society." Vols. 2–26, January,
            1855–October, 1879
Vol. I was probably published in 1854.

390C. VAN RENSSELAER, CORTLAND, D.D.
        God's way in the deep—a discourse on the occasion of the wreck of
            the Arctic . . . delivered at the Presbyterian Church, Burling-
            ton, N.J., October 25, 1854
        Philadelphia, 1854. 32 pp.
See 388C.

391C. WALTERS, R. C.
        A story of the wreck of the Annie Jane, 1853
        London, Partridge and Oakey, *Ragged School Union Magazine,*
            April, 1854

392C. WEISS, JOHN
        A discourse occasioned by the loss of the Arctic . . .
        New Bedford, 1854
See 388C.

1 8 5 5

393C. [ANONYMOUS]
        Shipwrecks by lightning in the United States
        Nautical Magazine, vol. 2, pp. 527–535, 1855

394C. ANONYMOUS
        Tragedy of the seas; or, the sorrows of the ocean
        Philadelphia, published by Leary and Getz, No. 138 North Second
            Street [1855?]. 12mo, cloth

Perhaps Ellms's anthology of 1841, but Ellms's name is not mentioned in Leary and Getz's advertisement at the end of their *Life of the Notorious Stephen Burroughs.*

395C. BRAYMAN, JAMES O. [editor?]
       Thrilling adventures by land and sea
       Auburn, N.Y., 1855. 12mo, 7th thousand

396C. COOPER, REV. W. H.
       Incidents of shipwreck, or the loss of the *San Francisco*
       Philadelphia, 1855

The *San Francisco,* a new steamer-sailing ship hybrid, left New York on her maiden voyage December 22, 1853. Bound for San Francisco, she had been chartered by the United States government to carry the Third United States Artillery Regiment, about 500 men and officers, to California. The second day out, on the edge of the Gulf Stream, the ship ran into a hurricane which was simply too powerful for her engines to cope with. The *San Francisco* broached to and was struck by an enormous wave which swept away the lifeboats and the after-saloon with its cabins. About 140 enlisted men were lost overboard and drowned. While the ship wallowed helpless she was spoken by the *Napoleon* and the bark *Kilby.* The captain of the *Kilby* stayed in company with the wrecked ship and eventually took off many of the passengers; others were taken off by the ships *Three Bells* and *Antarctic.* About 246 lives were lost of the 712 on board the *San Francisco.*

   Among the Army men on board were Lieutenants W. A. and C. S. Winder, and Asst. Surgeon H. R. Wirtz. Halfway through the Civil War General Winder, in charge of all Union prisoners, recommended Henry Wirtz, or Wirz, to be superintendent of Andersonville Prison. Wirtz was, of course, charged with atrocious cruelties, perhaps unfairly, and was executed. It is ironic that Wirtz may have got to know General Winder through his young relations on board the *San Francisco,* an acquaintanceship that condemned him to a shameful death.

   Whitman read of the loss of the *San Francisco,* and was stirred by the courage of Captain Lowe of the *Kilby:*

I understand the large hearts of heroes,
The courage of present times and all times,
How the skipper saw the crowded and rudderless wreck of the
    steamship, and Death chasing it up and down the storm,
How he knuckled tight and gave not back an inch, and was
    faithful of days and faithful of nights,
And chalked in large letters on a board, *Be of good cheer,*
    we will not desert you;
How he followed with them and tack'd with them three days
    and would not give it up,
How he saved the drifting company at last,
How the lank, loose-gown'd women look'd when boated from
    the side of their prepared graves,
How the silent old-faced infants and the lifted sick, and the
    sharp-lipped unshaved men;
All this I swallow, it tastes good, I like it well, it becomes
    mine,
I am the man, I suffer'd, I was there.
                                        "Song of Myself," Section 33

397C. HOWE, HENRY [editor]
       Life and death on the ocean: a collection of extraordinary adven-

tures in the form of personal narratives; illustrating life on
board of merchant vessels and of ships of war; combined with
thrilling relations of experiences and of suffering. Illustrated
with elegant tinted engravings, from designs by Darley,
M'lenan, Hamilton, etc. By Henry Howe, author of
"Historical Collections of Virgina," "Ohio," and "The Great
West;" "Travels and Adventures of Celebrated Travelers,"
etc.
New York, Geo. F. Tuttle, publisher, No. 100 Nassau Street; Cin-
cinnati, Henry Howe, Publisher, No. 111 Main Street, 1855
[copyright]. Other printings, 1856, 1860. Pp. vii, 624. 12
engravings
The perilous voyage of Captain Norwood . . .
Seven years of a sailor's life, among the savages of the Caroline
Islands . . .
Successful resistance of three sailors against several thousand sav-
ages . . .
Paddock's narrative of bondage among the Arabs . . .
The abandonment of Alexander Selkirk . . .
Ethan Allen's narrative of his captivity . . .
Incidents in the war with Tripoli . . .
The chase of the United States Frigate Constitution . . .
Description, by an English sailor boy, of the battle between . . .
the United States, . . . and the Macedonian . . .
The extraordinary sufferings of Danald Campbell . . .
The captivity of Thomas Andros . . . on board the old Jersey pris-
on-ship . . .
A sailor's story of what he saw and suffered . . . in the Revolu-
tion . . .
The narrative of the mutiny of the Bounty . . .
How they live on board of an American Man-of-War . . .
Narrative of an old English sailor . . .
Destruction of the ocean steamer Arctic . . .
The lost Russian sailors . . . the Russian ship St. Peter . . .
Experiences of a naval officer . . . Captain Basil Hall . . .
Narrative of a sailor among savages . . . John R. Jewett . . .
Adventures of Philip Ashton . . .
Shipwreck of the French frigate Medusa . . .
The story of Robert Drury . . .
Incidents in the life of a Yankee sailor . . . William Nevens . . .
Adventures of a slave-trader . . .
Convict life in Australia . . . in Norfolk Island . . .
The horrors of a fire at sea . . . burning of the Prince . . .
A sailor's life and duties . . .
Scenes on a man-of-war in a hurricane . . .
A man overboard . . .
Narrative of a mutiny on the Somers . . .
Abstract of American nautical laws . . .
Men and things in the Navy of the United States . . . by the Rev.
Charles Rockwell . . .

1 8 5 6

398C. KNELB, DR. PH. H.
>   Perilous incidents in the lives of sailors and travellers. Translated
>   from the German of Dr. Ph. H. Knelb, by a Lady
>   Philadelphia, Willis P. Hazard, 190 Chestnut Street, 1856
>   Adventures. Pirate life
>   Captivity among the Japanese
>   A sea-fight on the Cuban coast
>   A winter in the frozen ocean
>   The shipwreck [ship unnamed]
>   Voyage to the East Indies
>   Home-sickness of a Siberian

399C. LLOYD, JAMES T.
>   Lloyd's steamboat directory and disasters on the western waters.
>   . . . Early scenes and steamboat navigation on the Ohio and
>   Mississippi rivers
>   Cincinnati, 1856. 100 fine engravings and 46 maps
>   Howes, 406

400C. [PAYSON, EDWARD]
>   The new age of gold; or the life and adventures of Robert Dexter
>   Romaine. Written by himself
>   Boston, Phillips, Sampson and Company, 13 Winter Street, 1856

This book is listed in Wright, and properly, as fiction. The author knew little of
ships and shipwrecks, but wanted to write another *Robinson Crusoe* with a
bride and a bear added to the list of characters. Mr. Payson may have been influenced by 248C, *Sir Edward Seaward's Narrative . . .* ; This story of
Robert Romaine resembles that book more than it does any genuine narrative
of shipwrecks and disasters at sea.

401C. SHEA, JOHN GILMARY [editor]
>   Perils of the ocean and wilderness: or, narratives of shipwreck and
>   Indian captivity. Gleaned from early missionary annals. By
>   John Gilmary Shea, author of the "Discovery and Exploration
>   of the Mississippi," "History of the Catholic Missions,"
>   "School History of the United States," etc.
>   Boston, Patrick Donahoe, n.d. [Shea's preface is dated 1856.]
>   1. The shipwreck of Father Charles Lalemant, Philibert Noyrot,
>   and others, off Cape Breton
>   2. Captivity of Father Isaac Jogues among the Mohawks
>   3. Account of the captivity and death of René Goupil. By Father
>   Isaac Jogues
>   4. Death of Father Jogues
>   5. Captivity of Father Francis Joseph Bressani
>   6. Voyages of Rev. Father Emmanuel Crespel, in Canada, and his
>   shipwreck, while returning to France. Published by Sieur Louis
>   Crespel, his brother. Frankfort-on-the-Meyn, 1742

See 13C and 49C.

1 8 5 7

402C. ANONYMOUS

A home on the deep; or, the mariner's trials on the dark blue sea. By
a son of the ocean

Boston, Higgins, Bradley & Dayton, 20 Washington Street, 1857

1. Columbus
2. Magellan
3. Sir Francis Drake
4. The beacon-light
5. The Spanish wreck [Sir William Phips's; treasure hunting]
6. Dampier
7. A man overboard [Captain Hall]
8. Captain Woodes Rogers
9. Story of Alexander Selkirk
10. The ocean [Poem]
11. Scene off Bermuda [Scottish Magazine]
12. Captain John Clipperton
13. Ferocity of the Polar bear
14. Le Maire and Schouten. First voyage around Cape Horn
15. The Florida [Explosion of Armada ship at Mull]
16. Commodore Anson
17. Fishing on the Grand Banks
18. Byron [Admiral John]
19. Nautical philosophy [Poem]
20. A tale of the sea
21. Wallis
22. Voyage from Halifax to Bermuda
23. De Bougainville
24. History of the buccaneers
25. The wreckers [Poem]
26. Voyage of Captain James, for the discovery of a north-west
    passage
27. The pirate's treasure [Fiction]
28. Missionaries in Greenland
29. Dolphins and flying fish
30. The dying dolphin [Poem, Falconer]
31. Henry Hudson
32. Famine on board the French ship Le Jacques
33. The law of arrest. A tale from facts
34. A sea song [Poem]
35. Captain Cook
36. Captain Cook's second voyage
37. Captain Cook's third voyage
38. Narrative of events which occurred subsequently to the death
    of Captain Cook
39. Sufferings of Ephraim How
40. An escape through the cabin-window
41. Lament for Long Tom [Poem, J. G. C. Brainard]

42. The fatal repast
43. Captains Portlock and Dixon
44. Curiosity baffled Sir Brook Watson, [*New England Magazine*]
45. The return of the admiral [Poem, Barry Cornwall]
46. Shipwrecked mariners saved through a dream [Ship *Mary,* 1695]
47. A polite sea-robber
48. The sea-bird's song [Poem, J. G. Brainard]
49. Feelings excited by a long voyage. Visit to a new continent, by Washington Irving
50. Forty-five days' sufferings [Ship *Peggy,* 1769]
51. The Grecian mariner's song. By Thomas Moore, Esq.
52. Monsieur De La Perouse
53. Midshipman's pranks. By Captain Hall
54. The sound of the sea. By Mrs. Memans
55. Account of the loss of His Majesty's ship Phoenix, off Cuba, in the year 1780. By Lieutenant Archer
56. Mutiny on the Bounty
57. The Shetland Isles
58. A sea-ballad [Poem]
59. Dangers of a Nova Scotia fog. By Captain Hall
60. The Eddystone light-house
61. John Paul Jones
62. James Lawrence
63. Address to the ocean
64. Early American heroism
65. Captain G. Vancouver
66. A visit to Rockall. By Captain Hall
67. The subterranean stream. By Mrs. Hemans
68. Captain Inglefield's narrative [Ship *Centaur,* 1782]
69. A monkey trick
70. Captain Kennedy's narrative [Unnamed ship lost off Jamaica, 1818]
71. As fast and far o'er waves we fly [Poem]
72. Tom Cringle's Log [Michael Scott]
73. Nelson
74. Casabianca [Poem]
75. The Cumberland Packet [Off Antigua, 1804]
76. Captain D'Entrecasteaux
77. The mariner's address to his mistress
78. Captain Riley [Brig *Commerce,* 1815]
79. Adventures of Captain Woodward and five seamen in the island of Celebes
80. Shipwreck of the Blindenhall [Blendenhall] on the Inaccessible Island
81. The cliffs of Dover
82. The mariner's hymn

83. An account of the whale-fishery; with anecdotes of the dangers &c. attending it
84. The loss of the Peggy [1785, not the same wreck as 50 above]
85. The Medusa
86. The main-truck, or a leap for life
87. The Harpooner Transport [Near Newfoundland, 1815]
88. Captain Barney. "The old Commodore, the fighting old Commodore he."
89. Cruise of the Wasp
90. Hornet and Penguin
91. Algerine War
92. The American flag
93. Captain Parry's first voyage of discovery
94. Captain Parry's second voyage of discovery
95. Captain Parry's third voyage of discovery
96. Narrative of the loss of the Alceste
97. "Old Ironsides" [O. W. Holmes]
98. Kotzebue
99. Wreck of the Rothsay Castle steamer
100. Narrative of Captain W. L. Cazneau [Brig *Polly*]
101. New York and its environs
102. Narrative of Captain Lincoln [Schooner *Exertion* captured by the pirate schooner *Mexican,* 1821]
103. Greenwich Hospital
104. Loss of the ship Boston [Struck by lightning and burned, six days out from Charleston, n.d.]
105. The loss of the Kent. Communicated by an eye witness
106. Properties of the sea, &c.
107. Classification of clouds

403C. ANONYMOUS

Ocean scenes, or the perils and beauties of the deep; being interesting, instructive, and graphic accounts of the most popular voyages on record, remarkable shipwrecks, hair-breadth escapes, naval adventures, the whale fishery, etc. etc. Illustrated by fine engravings

New York, Leavitt & Allen, No. 379 Broadway, 1857

This book is an exact duplicate of *The Mariner's Trials,* 1857 (402C) except that there are two short added chapters:

108. Literary pursuits of sailors
109. Abstract of American nautical laws

The same plates were used for these two books.

404C. ANONYMOUS

Voyage and venture; or, the pleasures and perils of a sailor's life
Philadelphia, H. C. Peck and T. Bliss, 1857. 300 pp., illus.

1. Ship Mary
2. Sir Francis Drake
3. Ship Medusa

    4. Arctic regions
    5. Ship Kent
    6. Whale fishing
    7. Ship Lexington
    8. Ship Ann
    9. Ship Blendenhall
   10. Ship Papin
   11. Ship Essex and other whalers
   12. Ship Caroline
   13. Ship Pennsylvania
   14. Ship St. Andrew

Note that this book is entirely different from *Voyage and Venture,* 1853 (383C).

405C. ARNOLD, EDWIN
    The wreck of the Northern Belle
    Hastings, G. P. Bacon, 1857

A poem by the author of "The Light of Asia," written to raise funds for relatives of the crew of the lugger *Victory,* which was lost while trying to aid the *Northern Belle,* which also sank.

406C. HOLMES, LEWIS
    The arctic whaleman; or, winter in the Arctic Ocean; being a narrative of the wreck of the whale ship Citizen, of New Bedford, . . . and the subsequent sufferings of her officers and crew during nine months among the natives. Together with a brief history of whaling
    Boston, Wentworth & Co., 1857. 8vo, 296 pp., 15 plates

Bookseller's note: "Holmes tells the story second hand, having gotten it from four of the seamen involved. Much on the Eskimo, and notes of a stop in Hilo on the voyage out."
    The wreck of the *Citizen* occurred on September 25, 1852.

407C. BATES, MRS. D. B.
    Incidents on land and water, or four years on the Pacific Coast
    Boston, 1857. Plates

This book by Mrs. D. B. Bates is chiefly valuable for its material on early life in California, soon after the Gold Rush, but the first few chapters describe a strangely eventful sea voyage. Mrs. Bates was the wife of the captain of the *Nonantum,* which sailed from Baltimore for San Francisco on July 27, 1850, with 1,050 tons of coal. When the ship was about 800 miles from the Falkland Islands it was discovered that the cargo was on fire. Fortunately the *Nonantum* made Port Stanley in the Falklands, where the ship was run ashore and scuttled, a total loss. Everyone on the *Nonantum* was taken on board the *Humayoon,* Captain McKenzie, Dundee for Valparaiso, but just off Cape Horn that ship caught fire and burned. All on board were taken off by the *Symmetry,* Captain Thompson, from which ship they transferred to the *Fanchon,* Captain Lunt, Baltimore for San Francisco, again with coal. The *Fanchon also* caught fire and burned, but was run ashore near Payta, Peru. From there the much-suffering Mrs. Bates reached Panama and at last San Francisco. The last lap of the voyage was made in the steamer *Republic,* which caught fire—but the fire was put out. They reached San Francisco in late April, 1851.

1 8 5 8

408C. MERSHON, STEPHEN L.
> Funeral sermon preached at the burial of the crew of the John
> Milton . . . February 28, 1858, at East Hampton, Long
> Island, N.Y.
> New York, Nesbitt, 1858. 8vo, 24 pp., wraps.

The *John Milton* was a clipper out of New Bedford.

409C. [MOON, H.]
> An account of the wreck of H.M.'s sloop "Osprey," with the en-
> campment of her crew and their march across the island of New
> Zealand . . . by one of her crew
> Landport, 1858

410C. POND, CAPTAIN B. F.
> Narrative of the wreck of the barque Julia Ann, Captain B. F.
> Pond, in the South Pacific Ocean
> New York, 1858. 36 pp.

1 8 5 9

411C. ANONYMOUS
> Total loss of the Royal Charter and 454 lives
> Liverpool *Courier,* October 29, 1859

The *Royal Charter,* an auxiliary steam clipper, sailed from Melbourne, Australia,
for Liverpool in August, 1859. The ship carried £322,000 of gold besides what
the passengers had; it was an extraordinarily rich cargo. The voyage was
uneventful until the ship was close to her destination. Passengers were put off
at Queenstown and the owners were told of the ship's safe arrival. Unfortunately, as the ship moved up the Irish Sea toward the Mersey she encountered one of the worst hurricanes that ever struck the British Isles, a storm
with winds of over 100 miles an hour. The *Royal Charter* was caught just north
of Anglesey and was driven ashore on that island near Moelfre Point, where
she broke up. Of 493 people on board only 39 survived. One hundred thirty-
three ships were sunk around the British Isles in this storm, and more than 800
lives were lost. Most of the gold was recovered from the *Royal Charter.* The
story of this wreck is well told in Alexander McKee's *The Golden Wreck,* London, 1961.

412C. EYRIES, M.
> Histoires des naufrages—incendies de navires et autres disastres de
> mer . . .
> Paris, 1859. 8 steel engravings

Bookseller's note: "40 narratives from Quirini in 1431 to a revolt of negroes on
board the *Regina Coeli* in 1858." See 207C, 1821.

413C. MOSSMAN, S.
> Narrative of the shipwreck of the "Admella" intercolonial steamer
> on the southern coast of Australia: drawn up from authentic
> statements furnished by the rescuers and survivors
> Melbourne, 1859. Map and 2 plates

1 8 6 0

414C. ANONYMOUS
Book of the sea. A nautical repository of perils and pleasures,
adventures, joys, and sufferings on the briny deep . . .
London, n.d. [1860?]

415C. ANONYMOUS
The boys' book of shipwrecks . . .
Philadelphia, 1860. 348 pp., 8vo

416C. ANONYMOUS
Les naufrages épisodes intéressants, instructifs & édifiants recueillis
par l'auteur des souvenirs de jeunesse. Oeuvre de Saint-
Charles N.D.
Lille, Maison Saint-Joseph Grammont (Belgique), Oeuvre de Saint-
Charles, n.d. [1860?]
Les Naufrages Bontekoe
Prenties
Bouset
Heemskerke
De Chaumareys
Boscawen
Epilogue

417C. ANONYMOUS
Report of the Master and Wardens of the Trinity House of Port
Adelaide. . . . Loss of the "Melbourne" at the mouth of the
River Murray
Adelaide, 1860. 10 pp.

418C. ANONYMOUS
Shipwrecks and adventures at sea
[n.p.] Christian Knowledge Society [1860]

419C. ANONYMOUS [preface signed W. and R. C. (Chambers, William
and Robert)]
Shipwrecks and tales of the sea
London and Edinburgh, 1860

420C. ANONYMOUS
The terrors of the sea, as portrayed in accounts of fire and wreck,
and narratives of poor wretches forced to abandon their
floating homes with food or water, thus compelling them to
resort to cannibalism, with its attendant horrors. By an Old
Salt
New York, Hurst & Co., Publishers, 122 Nassau St., n.d.
Same as Vol. I, *Book of the Ocean* (422C).

421C. ANONYMOUS
Thrilling narratives of mutiny, murder, and piracy. . . . Tales of
shipwreck and disaster . . . including the whale fishery and
naval battles of the War of 1812 . . .
New York, n.d. [1860?]. Woodcuts

422C. [BEARDSLEY, JOHN E., editor]
       The book of the ocean and life on the sea: containing thrilling nar-
         ratives and adventures of ocean life in all countries, from the
         earliest period to the present time. With sixty illustrations
       New York, Hurst & Co., Publishers, 122 Nassau Street, n.d. Vol. 1
         [1860?]

Vol. I
Shipwreck of the *Frances Mary*
Loss of the ship *Albion*
Loss of the ship *Logan* by fire
Loss of the ship *Margaret*
Burning of the *Kent* [By an eye witness]
Loss of the ship *Boston*
Loss of the whale ship *Essex*
Narrative of the wreck of the *Isabella,* off Hastings, Eng.
Loss of the United States Steam Frigate *Fulton*
Skeleton of the wreck
Steam Boat *Helen McGregor*
Loss of the ship *Beverly*
Loss of the ship *Hercules,* on the coast of Caffraria
Description of a storm at sea
Wreck of the Brig Commerce, on the western coast of Africa,
    August 28th, 1815, and the slavery and sufferings of the crew
    on the Desert of Zahara. Compiled from the narratives of
    Capt. Riley and Archibald Robbins
The Spanish wreck
The fatal repast
Adventures of Madame Denoyer
Narrative of Captain W. L. Cazneau
The Main-Truck, or a leap for life
Frigate Constitution, commonly called "Old Ironsides"
British ship *Hibernia*
Mutiny of the ship *Bounty*
Narrative of Captain Lincoln, who was taken by the pirates, off
    Cape Cruz, Dec. 17, 1821, and subsequently left, with his crew,
    to perish on a desolate island
Narrative of the sufferings and adventures of John R. Jewett, only
    survivor of the crew of the ship Boston, during a captivity of
    nearly three years among the savages of Nootka Sound
A monkey trick
The Eddystone Light House
A polite Sea-Robber
Forty-five days' sufferings
The pirate's treasure
The *Cumberland* Packet
Loss of the Brig *Sally*
Sufferings of Ephraim How
Voyage from Halifax to Bermuda

Loss of the transport *Harpooner*
A tale of the sea
Loss of the *Lady of the Lake*

Volume II
Adventures of Captain Woodward and five seamen in the island of
    Celebes
An occurrence at sea
Account of the loss of His Majesty's Ship *Phoenix*
An account of the whale fishery with anecdotes of the dangers at-
    tending it
Loss of the Brig *Tyrrel*
The loss of the *Peggy*
Loss of His Majesty's Ship *Litchfield*
Wreck of the *Rothsay Castle* Steamer
Shipwreck of the French ship *Droits De L'Homme*
The loss of His Majesty's Ship, *Queen Charlotte*
A scene in the Atlantic Ocean
Shipwreck of the French Frigate *Medusa,* on the western coast of
    Africa. By Madame Dard, one of the sufferers
The loss of the *Royal George*
Loss of the *Aeneas* Transport
The absent ship
Loss of the *Halsewell*
An account of four Russian sailors, abandoned on the island of
    East Spitzbergen
Loss of the *Amphitrite* Convict Ship
The mutineers—a tale of the sea
Fate of seven sailors, who were left on the island of St. Maurice
Seamen wintering in Spitzbergen
A man overboard
An escape through the cabin-windows
Tom Cringle's log
Loss of the *Nautilus* Sloop of War. On a rock in the Archipelago
Wreck of a slave ship
The wrecked seamen
Adventures of Philip Ashton, who, after escaping from pirates,
    lived sixteen months in solitude on a desolate island
Explosion of His B. Majesty's Ship *Amphion*
Loss of H. B. M. Ship *La Tribune,* off Halifax, Nova Scotia
Burning of the *Prince,* a French East Indiaman
Wreck of the Schooner *Betsey,* on a reef of rocks
Early American heroism
Fingal's Cave
The loss of the *Ramillies* in the Atlantic Ocean
Preservation of nine men, in a small boat, surrounded by islands
    of ice
Captain Ross's expedition
Loss of the *Catharine, Venus* and *Piedmont* transports; and three
    merchant ships

Wreck of the British ship *Sidney*. On a reef of rocks in the South
Sea
Loss of the *Duke William* Transport
Commodore Barney
Naval battles of the United States
Hornet and *Penguin*
Algerine War
Address to the Ocean

423C. BOLTON, JOHN
Account of the loss of the ship Omartal [Imartal?], by the bearer,
one of the crew, John Bolton
n.p., n.d. [1860?]. 8 vo

424C. FROST, JOHN [editor]
Perilous adventures by land and sea, in Europe, Asia, Africa and
America
Chicago, Donohue, Henneberry & Co., 407 to 425 Dearborn St.,
n.d. [1860?]. Illus.
Adventures of Mr. William Mariner
Terrible shipwreck at the Cape of Good Hope
Wreck of the *Francis Spaight,* January 7, 1848, in Table Bay. The ship parted her
anchor cables and struck. Only two out of twenty on board survived, and a
number of rescuers lost their lives as well. Not the same as 287C.
Wreck of the *Forfarshire* Steamboat
Shipwreck at King's Island
The ship *Cataraque,* Captain Findlay, sailed from Liverpool for Australia April 20,
1849, with 423 passengers and crew. On August 3, in a storm, the ship struck a
reef off King's Island in Bass Straits. The *Cataraque* broke up, and only 9 people were saved.
Destruction of an East Indiaman by fire
Loss of the *Blendenhall*

425C. K., A. and J.
Wreck of the Royal Charter
Dublin, 1860
Cited in Alexander McKee's *The Golden Wreck*. See 411C.

426C. PERRY, JAMES C.
A brief treatise on collisions at sea and shipwrecks; being a research
into the cause of these disasters, and an introduction of a
preventive in the use of the patent anti-collision dial and shipwreck preventor . . .
Melbourne, W. Fairfax and Co., 1860. 8 vo, 70 pp., tables and 12
plates
Bookseller's quotation from text: "The following research . . . is due to a con-
templation of the circumstances under which several very calamitous disasters
have befallen ships upon the coast of Victoria, and that of her sister colonies;
and more particularly those which led to the deplorable losses of the steamer
'Champion,' by collision, and the ship 'Dunbar,' by stranding."

INDEX

1/08

ML